in **DETAIL** Work Environments

in **DETAIL**

Work Environments

Spatial concepts
Usage strategies
Communications

Christian Schittich (Ed.)

Edition DETAIL – Institut für internationale
Architektur-Dokumentation GmbH & Co. KG
Munich

Birkhäuser
Basel

Editor: Christian Schittich
Editorial services: Cornelia Hellstern, Sandra Leitte,
Eva Schönbrunner, Cosima Strobl
Editorial assistants: Carola Jacob-Ritz, Michaela Linder

Translation German/English: EUROCAT Translations, Sulzbach
Proofreading: Anna Roos, Bern

Drawings: Ralph Donhauser, Michael Folkmer,Daniel Hajduk, Martin Hämmel,
Nicola Kollmann, Emese M. Köszegi, Elisabeth Krammer, Dejanira Ornelas

DTP: Simone Soesters

A specialist publication from Redaktion DETAIL
This book is a cooperation between
DETAIL – Review of Architecture and
Birkhäuser GmbH

Bibliographic information published by the German National Library
The German National Library lists this publication in the Deutsche
Nationalbibliografie; detailed bibliographic data is available on the Internet at
<http://dnb.d-nb.de>.

This book is also available in a German language edition
(ISBN: 978-3-920034-37-9).

© 2011 Institut für internationale Architektur-Dokumentation GmbH & Co. KG,
P. O. Box 20 10 54, 80010 Munich, Germany
www.detail.de and
Birkhäuser GmbH, P. O. Box 133, 4010 Basel, Switzerland
www.birkhauser.com

Printed on acid-free paper produced from chlorine-free pulp (TCF ∞)

Printed in Spain
Reproduction:
Martin Härtl OHG, Munich

ISBN: 978-3-0346-0724-7

9 8 7 6 5 4 3 2 1

Contents

New work environments

Christian Schittich

With the rapid spread of information and communication technologies and developments within society, both working processes and the locations of work are undergoing far-reaching changes. At the same time, the proportion of office work is constantly increasing in our modern information, knowledge and service-based societies and the boundaries with other forms of work are fluid. For example, today there is hardly an artisan-craftsperson business that does not use computers in its production processes as well as for sales and bookkeeping. Yet workflows are also changing in buildings where there are only offices. Flexibility and space-focused solutions that promote communication between employees are increasingly in demand. The long-dominant, small-scale cellular office is falling out of favour.

In fact, if we look at the predictions of futurologists from the end of the 20th century, then the non-territorial office, the hallmark of which is the end of the fixed allocation of employee to workplace, should now be the norm, or at least the majority of units planned today should be going in this direction. However, the reality remains different in most cases. Although we have had a whole series of structures that function in this way for a long time, where the employee docks on to an available workstation via laptop and stores his or her belongings in a locker overnight – usually in the Internet and telecommunications sector – this is not how most units currently being realised are structured. Furthermore, many companies – and their employees – are unable to separate themselves from the small individual offices, which were pronounced defunct long ago.

The fact that rented offices, in particular, are built as investments with no knowledge of who their users will be is just one of the many reasons for this. However, what is key for investors is economic efficiency, which means that in most cases efficiency in the use of space remains the key planning criterion.

Yet, there is no doubt that a working environment that is fashioned in a logical and attractive way makes an important contribution towards increasing employees' comfort and motivation and thus, the quality of their performance. Having said that, there cannot be a one-size-fits-all formula for achieving these goals that cannot easily be measured. The field of office work alone, which ranges from municipal administration through to insurance companies up to the so-called creative professions, comprises activities and associated requirements that are simply too diverse. Yet, it is noticeable that the creative sector in particular, which also includes architects' offices, alters its furnishings, working

and organisational structures far less than elsewhere. The sector still feels comfortable in inspiring and cost-effective old buildings, whilst at the same time the provisions of workplace regulations are ironically taken less seriously than when they are planning for others.

Alongside a stimulating working environment that promotes productivity, spatial structures that enable social contact, human interactions and flexibility, noise pollution and acoustics, lighting, air quality and room temperature are key parameters for users' comfort. Furthermore, energy efficiency and sustainability play an increasingly important role.

Finally, it should be noted that, for the company itself, the quality and design of its offices or production location make a key contribution to its corporate identity and communicate a lot about its philosophy and corporate culture.

"Working Environments", the title of this publication, is intended to do justice to the changes to working processes discussed here and the associated effects on spatial structures. Corresponding to their significance and their proportion of workplaces; the focus is on office buildings. The examples section deliberately illustrates a broad spectrum of different requirements and solutions.

Furthermore, this volume also presents other forms of use, such as the mixing of office, development and production areas, or different production locations. Institutional buildings occupy a special position in this respect – alongside several projects in the examples section they are analysed in an article dedicated to them. The other contributions tackle the essential criteria for workplaces such as floor-plan arrangement in office buildings, communication, ergonomics, acoustics or lighting.

People spend most of the day at their workplace, mostly in the office. However, today's working locations often look characterless and monotonous. This book seeks to make a contribution to them becoming vibrant and inspiring places to work.

The world of office work in flux – usage strategies and freedom of choice

Martin Kleibrink

Today's working environments have a long historical development. The office as a place of work has existed ever since people settled at a location or assembled to set matters down in writing and negotiate. Starting with early examples such as the Uffizi in Florence, which was originally an administrative building, the concept of an office came to be generally agreed over the centuries. Today this once clear scheme is beginning to dissolve in the face of a wave of new tendencies that are accompanied by a flood of concepts and neologisms for the various office typologies that have sprung up recently. It even appears questionable, in view of the supposedly unlimited possibilities of information and communication technology – "your office is where you are" – whether offices are still required at all: a question which is answered by the many millions of square metres of empty office space. However, the message of this text is that the office as a communicative locus that promotes community, entrepreneurship, contact, exchange and personal synergies will indeed continue to exist in future. Adapted working processes and increasingly intelligent technologies enable "office work" to be decoupled from space and time and demand new working forms and spatial concepts.

The question as to which office concept is the appropriate one usually arises in the context of changes in spatial requirements. These are often necessary when growth, often over decades, has caused extreme overcrowding and shortage of space and assistance is sought by means of extensions, new-build or relocation, or else if a modernisation of the building technology is needed. However, globalisation, competition and the associated pressure on costs require new solutions and call into question established rights and the existing space usage strategies of many companies. Often the focus is on finding a new, more economical and efficient form of building occupancy and usage of space. For companies whose view of the future is not obscured by the often blinkered focus on cost-cutting opportunities, modernisation and relocation provides the chance not only to use their space more efficiently, but at the same time to drive the company's modernisation forward in small or large steps by means of a shift in its use of space. In doing so they are faced with the choice between vastly different office scenarios that can further or hinder the aims of organisational development.

Changing technology – changing work

Ever faster developments in IT infrastructure, which is used extensively by all organisations, are accompanied by a networking of the world that has given rise to new value-creation processes. The integration of tasks and procedures paperless processes, the linking of different locations and organisations, through to the completion of coherent tasks, decoupled in space and time is now a firm feature of many or our working lives. Whilst we might still be fascinated by the latest smartphones, technical evolution has already moved on by many generations. The effects that developments such as augmented identity, context-aware computing or cloud computing will have on our living and working habits can only be speculated about today.

In the light of these developments changes to office activity itself appear less dramatic than expected. Information and knowledge services still require a more limited traditional repertoire of tasks: collation, processing, management and exchange of information. Merely the boundaries between the media and the extent of the use of technology for support and partial automation have shifted.

This affects almost everyone who works in an office environment irrespective of their function and position. In most organisations the overwhelming proportion of written information has been exchanged by e-mail for some time now and meetings and the exchange of information increasingly dominate the spectrum at all levels. The number of hours which "office workers" spend in meetings on a daily basis shows that the exchange of knowledge and collaborative processes are becoming increasingly important.

Formerly predominant routine information processing has largely been automated and replaced by creative forms of information processing – working with people. This increases the proportion of team and project work and communication. Disruption and hindrances ensue if appropriate spaces are not available. Alongside this, some concentrated individual work still requires freedom from interruptions in order to be productive. All activity profiles are increasingly characterised by the rapid shift between these two forms of working, which in turn informs the fundamental, yet contradictory, requirements of office design. Contemporary solutions need to be found for the co-existence of concentration, collaboration and communication that are also flexible enough to cope with unpredictable changes in terms of requirements. Traditional, contemporary and, to-date, less widespread but innovative office concepts fulfil these challenges in various ways.

Cellular office

In the most traditional office form, the cellular office, single and double rooms line corridors that are usually only lit artificially – pure circulationareas that, as escape routes, do not

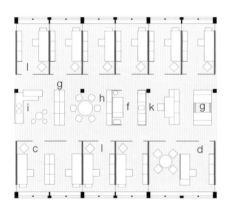

a Group office
b Face-to-face
   double office
c Wall-facing
   double office
d Manager
e Kitchenette
f Printer station
g Archive
h Team meeting
i Espresso
   bar
k Hot desk
l Individual
   office

permit furniture (fig. 2). Infrastructure such as meeting spaces, multi-function devices, post points, floor archives, kitchenettes etc. that mostly do not require daylight have to be arranged between the offices along the facades. They therefore absorb expensive, front-row office space and increase the length of communication channels.

Those working in a typical double room, which is necessary for this office concept to be at all economic, are regularly distracted by their colleagues' telephone calls. Those who occupy a single office can go about their business without distractions, but the concept offers little incentive or scope for informal exchanges with colleagues.

Organisational changes generally result in disruptive and expensive conversions. Shortage of space has caused some double rooms to mutate into three-person rooms in which disruptions increase exponentially and adherence to regulations applicable to computer workstations become difficult to comply with.

The cellular office works in hierarchically-organised companies in which working processes are broken down into many small working steps. This office form is also suited for companies in which the focus is on individuals' work as opposed to communication amongst the employees. The cellular office is the expression of the requirement for one's own room as an evidence of one's status within the company. With the exception of the combi-office, this office type more than any other satisfies the need to withdraw and have one's own territory to work in behind closed doors without distraction.

Open-plan and group office

In the 1970s group rooms and office landscapes with 100 and more people in an artificially lit, expensively air-conditioned room were very common. In Germany, in particular, these have been on the decline since the 1980s. Many of these offices, which were intended to thrive on openness and thus free communication, mutated into partitioned fortresses no sooner than they were fitted out. A thicket of cupboards, partitions and plants was intended to provide separation, usually above eye level. However, open-plan offices remain unloved. Not least, they are rejected due to the air-conditioning being controlled by a third party, permanent artificial lighting and the feeling of being boxed in with no connection to the outside world. This also applies, in part, to the group room (fig. 3).

Open offices for manageable groups, where the department is the unit of measure for sizing the office space, originally arose as a reaction to the problems of the open-plan offices

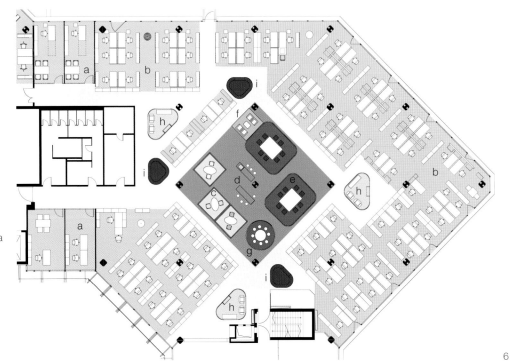

6

and are still implemented today. For routine handling of matters with a high level of information exchange and need for communication, but low requirements in terms of concentration, the open-plan office and the group office are ideal. However, due to a lack of individuality, difficulties in adapting air-conditioning and illumination, and in particular because of the permanent widespread disruptions, they are generally not in keeping with current tendencies and requirements. However, these office forms, in particular the open-plan office, have been experiencing a renaissance for some years. Reasons for this are the cost pressures already mentioned that require higher efficiency of utilisation of floor space, a reduction of fitting-out costs and high flexibility in terms of occupancy. Ongoing development of technical and physical building facilities and the open room structures, resulting in a differentiation of various usage zones, have given the open office typologies a new form and thus secured their raison d'être.

Multi-space concept

In the usage strategy best referred to as the "multi-space concept" the floor space of open-plan and group offices is arranged in open workplace zones and communal zones (fig. 6). In these special spaces, opportunities for communication and retreat, as well as for informal meetings and exchange, complement the workspace zones that are accommodated in manageable room sizes. They create spatial opportunities that are far more in tune with today's working practices and modern communication behaviour than the open structures that are often crammed full of workplaces. In the case of multi-space usage the office spaces are interfused with cosy design elements that generate a quality of ambience previously unknown in open-plan offices and contribute to a new, motivational working and corporate culture. Alongside the workplace zones, key components are team meeting rooms, coffee bars, small lounge areas, think-tanks and other communication opportunities, which include areas for ergonomically beneficial meetings held standing up. The

technology is bundled in decentralised service stations with short communication channels, which reduces disruptive through circulation traffic in the workplace zones. The new room concepts give rise to places with a positive quality for meetings that promote communication, exchange and working processes as well as employee motivation.

Combi-office

The combi-office was developed at the end of the 1970s in Scandinavia. It combines the advantages of the cellular office and open-plan office – hence the name – and at the same time largely avoids their drawbacks. The workplaces are all located directly alongside the facade and are grouped primarily as individual rooms around an indirectly-illuminated inner zone from which they are separated by floor-to-ceiling-high glass walls (fig. 4). Each workplace has a discussion space, a direct view outside and daylight, individual control of the working environment and the freedom to do concentrated work behind closed doors without being isolated from the goings-on in the office or to open the door to the office community.
The individual offices only contain items that are individually assigned to the employees. The communal or central zone houses all functions that are used by multiple employees. The glass walls between the working rooms and the communal area fulfil a dual function: if required they provide a high level of acoustic sound insulation and thus protect against disruptions and create the conditions for focused working or confidential conversations. At the same time they enable visual contact between the individual and the group (see and be seen). They also enhance the natural illumination through the glass walls and the view outside. Functions such as group repository, document centre with multi-function device, library, team meeting spaces and coffee bars are located here. The facilities that are allocated to multiple employees and the quality of the ambience promote (ad hoc) communication, which is widely agreed to be essential for creativity and synergy. The extent to which

7 Floor plan of business club bank concept,
  Zurich (CH) 2011, office planning: congena with
  Greutmann Bolzern Design   Scale 1:750
  a Homebase: standard workplaces in blocks
     of two and four with staff lockers in the open
     team area
  b Quiet area: shielded individual workplaces
     for focused work
  c Business garden: lush green team area with
     double workplaces
  d Project area: workbenches with communication
     and presentation equipment
  e Lounge: different areas for retreat for informal
     communication and relaxation
  f Espresso bar
  g Printer station
  h Group repository
  i Team meeting
  k Standing meeting
  l Think tank
  m Touchdown
  n Single office meeting
8 Desk landscape, Creative Valley, Utrecht (NL)
  2009, Architects: MONK Architecten; Interior
  design: YNNO

central zones are filled with activity depends to a significant extent on the company and its working and communication processes.

Combi-offices perpetuate some conventions (one employee = one workplace), but at the same time they relativise established rights: hierarchical distinctions in terms of room dimensions are largely avoided and all employees work in individual rooms as a rule. By removing a flexible partition, double offices can easily be created for special functions, such as assistants' offices. Thanks to the high level of standardisation and the intelligent use of floor space by locating the infrastructure in the communal zone between the workplaces the company gains a positive meeting quality and flexibility. Furthermore, this can save on rented floor space as compared to conventional cellular offices.

Flexible office/business club

What are termed flexible offices or business clubs progress a clear step further than the combi-office in terms of flexible use of the office space. This office type also originated in the liberal working societies of Scandinavia and the Benelux countries. They were introduced into German-speaking countries in the 1990s. Personally-assigned workplaces give rise to a diversity of scenarios that are adapted to different patterns of activity, as opposed to employees, and can be used on a fixed-term basis as required: areas for retreat and think-tanks, team and project zones, informal meeting spaces, meeting rooms, reading areas and also lounge-style zones for meeting and informal communication (fig. 7). Only a few of these task-based scenarios can, or need to be, reserved: most are freely available on a "first come, first served" basis.

The concept assumes a modernisation of management instruments, organisational concepts and working habits. Agreement of goals and monitoring of results replace roll calls. The information associated with processes is largely paper-free and accessible anywhere. The individual is responsible for selecting his or her working time and place and in doing so is guided predominantly by the requirements of his or her current tasks. The loss of a personal working space is contrasted by the freedom to choose a working location and working time. An inspiring ambience and the quality of the environment generate identification with the concept and forge a bond with the company. This ambience and the spatial opportunities between the workplaces promote desired forms of behaviour and support the processes across departmental boundaries.

Despite high investment costs, business clubs provide economic advantages through considerable saving of floor space of 20 to 40% depending on the "sharing ratio" (proportion of workplaces to employees using them). The infrastructure – diverse in its modular structure and highly standardised – is used to its maximum capacity, in contrast to personally-assigned offices, which are left empty too often. However, the concept only offers the prospect of a "breathing" occupancy capacity if a proportion of staff combine it with work in the home office (one to two days a week). Thus, the demand for sparse working places (e.g. relaxation rooms) regulates itself along the time axis.

Flexible offices or business clubs are the concept of the future as they are best suited to the need of increasingly well-qualified employees for self-determination and the ability to combine career, family and leisure.

Co-working space

The conceptual approach to what are called "co-working spaces", which have increasingly sprung up in recent times, is not really new. The idea of offering offices and conference rooms on demand and for a fixed term, where the occupant individually specifies usage, rental times and the associated services, has been successfully implemented for years by small and large, regional and international companies. Plain functionality through to a refined atmosphere and excellent locations are hallmarks of these business centres. This is reflected in the composition of the users of these offices who need the corresponding financial means to afford the usually high fees for such favourable flexibility.

As a reaction to the shortage of office space and astronomical rents, sharing concepts for offices have been developed in recent years based on the New York model. The model served as the starting point for the initiatives of mainly young people involved in the creative professions who have set up conceptually comparable co-working spaces in recent years. Options such as the global "The Hub" project or the "Beta-haus" in Berlin, as well as countless other offices in nearly all large cities in Europe, confirm the large demand for the availability of such affordable and flexible office space. The spaces are not usually located in classical office buildings, but instead in loft-type buildings and are usually in less prominent locations. The offices are often simply equipped and adhere to non-classical planning principles or layout structures. They mostly still resemble the business club due to their diverse options in terms of rooms. However, a glance at the offices at various international locations gives rise to doubts as to whether the ergonomic and functional prerequisites are in place to support healthy and productive work. However, in this case such criteria appear to be secondary considerations. In the home, office isolation is a threat – in spite of Twitter, Facebook and other networks. Co-working offers the users the option to network physically and in doing so to make contact with kindred spirits or people operating in similar fields, to compare notes and to collaborate. Common activities and events promote community spirit and networking.

As early as the 1990s various companies had launched a comparable initiative that was expressed in what were termed satellite offices. Under the concept of decentralisation and flexibilisation of the workplace, and as a reaction to the new possibilities of telecommunications, local offices arose as branches of large companies in which as a rule whole divisions or larger units were accommodated. This enabled employees to find a new working base close to home and reduced commuting times. This gave rise to the neighbourhood office that was intended to provide working space to a wide range of target groups at the same time: the employees of different companies who used the synergies of the commonly-operated areas, just as the independent self-employed contractor who could not afford the overheads for the infrastructure provided here on his or her own. However, this caused problems in terms of data protection given that employees of different companies were operating in a single network. This circumstance ultimately prevented the breakthrough of this early form of co-working spaces.

Highly flexible and decentralised offices that can be used as a small, adaptable and readily available unit on demand, locally and for a fixed term will have an even higher profile in future. However, an even larger range of quality and services need to be offered if the offices are also to attract the self-employed who expect more than merely the lower end of the spectrum in terms of equipment and functional quality.

Choice of concept

It appears to be increasingly difficult to find an answer to the question of which office concept is the correct one for which organisation. The office will continue to change in future as a result of the dynamic shift in forms of living and working that is accompanied by a shift in society, its demographic composition and its values. However, core tasks will remain untouched by this change, as discussed at the beginning. Thus, in future there will also be companies in which routine information processing predominates and the interaction of individuals and teams has little significance. There cellular offices will continue to be suitable and desirable. Small companies, in particular, are unconcerned by the high space overheads and limited flexibility.

However, irrespective of the tasks, processes or industries, synergies between individual employees and teams, including across departmental boundaries, will become increasingly important. Therefore, the future belongs to those office forms that promote and support such synergies.

Open-plan offices and group offices in their traditional form are generally disliked by users and also counter-productive for highly-skilled employees and their knowledge work. Yet they still appeal to companies due to their high space efficiency, flexibility and support of communicative processes. If it is possible to reduce the universal disruptions and distractions in these rooms, and if additional options for meeting, communication and relaxation can be created in the multi-space concepts as described, these spaces can be attractive and optimally support contemporary working processes.

For organisations with a high proportion of creative information processing in which working with people is more important than classical administrative handling, combi-offices still represent an ideal option. They support processes that are

8

characterised by the constant shift between concentrated individual work and coordination: the focus is on synergies and the intensive use of communal facilities. Furthermore, combi-offices increase the transparency of working processes, the flexibility of the organisation and can also save space. Consequently, they are a good starting point for future developments such as shared workplaces, project work, tele-working, paperless processes etc. However, in recent years the high fitting-out costs and the lower space efficiency as compared to the open structures have forced this office form with all its advantages into the hinterland.

Companies whose working processes permit, and who want to utilise the opportunities of information technology in their spatial organisation, are increasingly opting for business clubs. They thus gain the maximum flexibility that is possible with the current status of information technology, a "breathing" office concept in which they do not need to keep adapting the costly resource of office space in the event of fluctuations in employee numbers. The diverse workplace scenarios thus support individual working processes that vary in accordance with tasks and promote productivity. The higher surface utilisation achieved through the "sharing ratio" also provides for a more efficient running of the building.

Qualities of sustainable offices

Irrespective of the opportunities an organisation uses in the modernisation of its rooms and the office concept it opts for, the employees must ultimately identify and feel comfortable with their task, their work and their location – be it in the company, at home or on the road. If this goal is not achieved dissatisfaction ensues, which in turn impairs productivity. For this reason offices should fulfil the following criteria:

- Flexibility: a standardisation of the workplaces and their layouts has the benefit that occupancy can change without business downtime or workmen, dirt and noise and furnitureless removals are possible. At the same time they should be easily adaptable to personal tasks, habits and individual requirements or provide a varied palette for a spectrum of activities ranging from focused individual work through to communication and to team processes.
- Functionality: the physical conditions (light, air, acoustics) and furnishing of the rooms must comply with the physiological requirements, ergonomic standards and statutory provisions and support the respective activity optimally.
- Positive meeting quality: the use of space should contribute to the transparency of the processes, promote communication and synergy between employees and departments

with different focal points and thus contribute to the quality, speed and flexibility of the processes.
- Corporate culture: the atmosphere of the rooms and their furnishings supports the employees' identification with the company and its products and helps communicate values internally and externally, promoting desired behaviours and hindering undesired ones.

The measure for the quality of working locations remains, and is, in particular, a more flexible, accelerated and technologised economic working environment for people.

Building requirements

The building forms mentioned above demand different structural and technical requirements. The business club has especially high requirements in terms of the infrastructure for information and communication technology and is – still – linked to higher investment costs.

Given the strong tendency in favour of open room concepts, the issue of the correct facade grid plays a secondary role. The few fixed rooms and the functional zones with barely-fixed boundaries require a reduced number of wall connections to the facade. However, small-scale grids are recommended to prevent the individual rooms and meeting rooms becoming too large.

Only a few years ago the discussion surrounding the ideal building grid was still based on the requirements of the cellular office. In its implementation, which is largely dependent on internal floor-space standards or comfort requirements, grids of 1.2 to 1.8 m with a usual building depth of approx. 12 m, were normally realised. Today, the systems of individual office, open-plan office, group- and combi-office and business club sometimes co-exist under one roof. That poses new challenges to developers and planners in the question of the suitable facade grid and the correct building depth. The convertibility of office space to all four office concepts, demanded by investors in particular, makes planning more difficult. For the selection of a suitable grid, however, it is sufficient to limit ourselves to the consideration of cellular and combi-office as the open-plan, group office and the business club can be derived from their rooms.

The following applies to all considerations in this regard: they can only be derived on the basis of the prescribed minimum dimensions of the individual workplace types (single, double, multi-person rooms) as per the legal requirements relating to computer workplaces and workplace regulations. Thus, the minimum width of the cellular office is 2.5 m, derived from the addition of the following dimensions: desk 90 cm (required depth in order to install flat-screens of more than 22 inches with adequate viewing distance), wall distance 5 cm, room for movement/chair clearance 1 m, storage furniture in the rear 45 cm, proportion of dividing screen 10 cm. A width of 4.95 m is derived for a double office. Four-person rooms are wider still, by 2× 60 cm, due to the required clearance behind the front workplaces (in the case of the usual arrangement of workplaces in blocks of four), that is, 6.15 m. The facade grid with which all these measurements can be mapped most economically is 1.25 m. The facade should be planned such that the entire technical building infrastructure (heating, air-conditioning, room sensors, ground tank and where appropriate window vents) does not need to be fitted every 1.25 m. The grid therefore also maps all ancillary and special rooms with a high space efficiency.

9

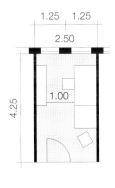
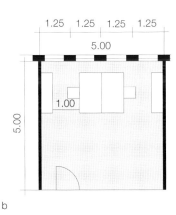
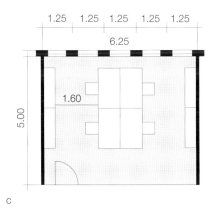

a   b   c   10

The selection of the correct building depth is more significant. It should be measured such that three usage zones can be laid within the depth of the surface.

A room depth typically of 2× 5.0–5.5 m plus 2 m for the central corridor produces a clear building depth of approximately 12–13 m for cellular offices. In the case of the combi-office individual rooms and the central zone become the decisive specifications. For the individual rooms in the combi-office with a room depth of two axes of 1.25 m, a depth of approximately 4.25 to 4.50 m can be set as a comfortable standard that is cost-effective in terms of space. If one adds two corridor widths each of 1.2 m, the two glass walls of the offices each of 10 cm and the central zone with approximately 3.0–3.5 m, then the clear building depth is approximately 14.1–15.1 m. Multi-space concepts and business clubs can also easily be organised around a central zone at these dimensions. This is only possible to a limited extent at the economical depth of 12 to 13 m for cellular offices.

Outlook

The clear trend is towards working methods that are entirely characterised by communication, exchange and the dissemination of knowledge – a development that can no longer be halted. The fascinating innovations in the field of information and communication technology have created the opportunity to decouple workplace and working time from the companies' locations and their core working times. This opens up completely new options and freedom to choose for the employees. Career and family, working time and leisure time can thus be harmonised more easily. The social qualities, and also the requirements in terms of team processes and exchange, render the office indispensable. The freedom of the employees in forward-looking office concepts also stretches to the choice of the correct working environment for the current task. This supports, not only the working processes and their quality, but also increases employees' productivity along with their motivation. Conventional cellular offices with fixed room allocations and generally lower structural economy of space utilisation do little to support the increased flexibility of workplaces and working methods. This also applies to conventional open-plan offices with their one-dimensional provision of space. It is therefore to be expected, today and in future, that office usage strategies prevail that, alongside varied options for different usage zones, also offer the possibility for informal meeting and exchange. The concepts are there, but a strong shift in corporate culture is necessary in order to permit and promote the new working methods adequately.

9   Touchdown, Credit Suisse, Zurich (CH) 2010, Camenzind Evolution
10 Efficient facade grid
    a Individual office with wall-facing workplace (10.2 m²)
    b Two-person office with block cluster arrangement (20.8 m²)
    c Four-person office with block of four and requisite transit areas
       (26.1 m²)
11 Creative communication space, Creative Valley, Utrecht (NL) 2009,
    architects: MONK Architecten; Interior design: YNNO

11

17

Typology of research buildings

Dieter Grömling

Architecture designed for science incorporates a range of diverse building types. This is due to differentiation of research in general, yet linked to the need to operate across disciplines, and is often supported by specific appliances and equipment. Examples are institutes for research in the natural sciences and humanities with labs, libraries, lecture theatres, canteens as well as cosmological observation stations, animal and plant houses or rooms housing large pieces of equipment such as electron microscopes or tomographs. They provide scientists with a framework for experimentation and debate, for observation and research.

Universitates, colleges, palaces

In order to appreciate the principles that are going to shape the future, we should briefly consider typological developments in the past. Modern associations such as flexibility, autonomy and adaptability can be found in descriptions of the forerunners of the western university, the "universitas magistrorum et scholarium" in Bologna and Paris (around 1200). This free association of tutors and scholars was not initially tied to any fixed location: rooms were rented according to their needs.

From the 14th century onwards, the "college" building style developed and gained international currency. Unlike the "universitates", the colleges were founded as institutions from the outset. The most important example is the Collegio di Spagna in Bologna, built between 1365 and 1367. This was the first time that developer and architect collaborated, deploying a space-allocation programme to produce a singularly functional and formal complex on the edge of the city in the style of an elite, exclusive community akin to a monastery – fortress-like, walled-off, introverted. The different functional units were arranged around a central, public courtyard.

After 1550 the architecture of the universities developed – a fusion of "universitates" and colleges – with a tendency towards central and representative holistic structures. In the 17th and 18th centuries palace-like academic buildings testify to increasing power, progress and size as the secular and ecclesiastical powers that supported scholarly life expected representation in the baroque style. The university became an institution dependent on authorities.

At the beginning of the 19th century the spirit of neo-humanism influenced developments, under the leadership of Wilhelm von Humboldt. The aim was liberation from elitist, sclerotic exclusivity and from dependence on the state. The ideal of forming one's character through engagement with

science and learning established itself. This was expressed through the classical architectural style – with reference to the intellectual cosmos of ancient Greek scholarship – paired with the need for representation. In Vienna and Paris colossal structures arose for the whole university – mostly double-height, multi-storey complexes grouped around courtyards. However, this approach ultimately turned out to be flawed: the buildings quickly became too small. The aggregation of all disciplines and functions under one roof was unfeasible both typologically and technically. Lab buildings for scientific experimentation needed to be regrouped and separated.

Demand planning and determination of spatial groupings

Thorough demand planning forms the key to the success of a project. Based on a scientific concept and financial resources for staff and equipment, spatial quantities and qualities are aggregated in a spatial requirements plan. The usage areas are differentiated as follows in functional terms:
- primary area: research (theoretical and experimental);
- secondary area: information, communication (internal and external); administration; provision of energy, material, services; and
- tertiary area: social spaces, living, leisure.

What is important for the design typology is to disentangle the spatial requirements plan and to identify spatial groups that are each subject to different conditions:
- illuminated rooms for concentrated, theoretical work (offices with low level of technical installation);
- illuminated, installable rooms for experimental work (high level of technical installation, labs); and
- non-illuminated, installable rooms for appliances and special uses (high level of technical installation, dark zones).

Alongside the usable areas, the transit areas and functional surfaces are typologically significant and relevant to design. The arrangement of the corridors and open areas determines the communicative quality. Instead of large, obsolete halls, a differentiated gradation of available rooms for ad hoc or scheduled meetings should be considered to achieve an appropriate density of communicative spaces. Adequately dimensioned and easily extendible functional spaces are essential in the basement and inside the roof space for the technological control rooms and are also needed on lab floors to house distribution chambers and shafts. The dimen-

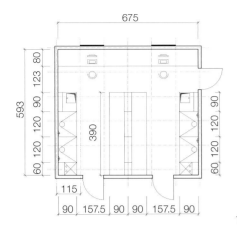
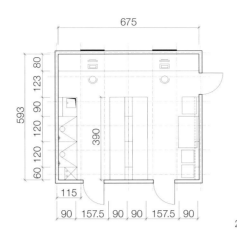
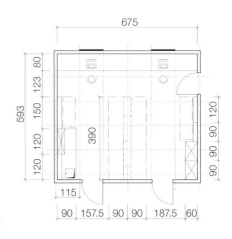

1   2   3

sions are often underestimated or ignored, which can cause considerable functional and economic disadvantages in operational terms. Alongside town planning, or other considerations determined by the location or the function, the sum of all spatial requirements influences the appropriate design of the building typology in terms of loading and number of storeys.

Basic lab building block for chemistry / biology / physics

The most important room type for a scientific research building is the laboratory, the working room for scientific experiments. Essentially comparable with a well-equipped fitted kitchen, the lab structured in the way we know today has existed for around 100 years with a usable surface of around 40 m². There has been a tendency towards larger spatial units for around the last ten years.

The spatial requirements derive from the scientists' activities and associated demands.

Scientists collect, analyse, interpret and condense information. They take notes, talk, discuss, argue – with a few colleagues or in larger groups. For efficient team work, rooms with a minimum density of people and working processes are required. In order to be able to plan them, the following information is needed:

- type and frequency of working processes;
- length and composition of workbench rows;
- required media;
- number of people working in the lab;
- special appliances;
- requirements for lighting and ventilation conditions;
- use of hazardous substances, requirements for vents / extractors;
- required writing or evaluation desks, workstation computers; and
- routing and provision of general supply of media.
- risk assessment

A distinction is drawn between the following lab types:
- chemical lab: for wet preparations or dry, high number of 2–6 fume cupboards (extractors) per 40 m², relatively high requirement for cupboards for hazardous substances,

fridges and freezers, high exchange of room air (fig. 1);
- biology lab (biochemical, molecular-biological): for wet preparations or dry, 1–2 fume cupboards per 40 m², lab cupboards, surfaces for apparatus (fig. 2); and
- physics lab: "workshop character", fewer or no fume cupboards, low levels of lab furnishing, surfaces for experimental apparatus and/or technical appliances required (fig. 3).

Zoning and stacking

Due to the specialist and costly technical building services in research buildings, which constitute some 40% to 60% of the total construction costs, it is especially important to combine rooms with comparable requirements. There are different requirement profiles in terms of surface area needed, furnishing, type of usage, structural supporting capacity and technical supply and waste disposal. The most common room types, which consequently have the strongest impact on design, are labs and offices. Alongside this there are specific "core facilities" (e.g. special labs), social rooms and the like. A randomly-mixed allocation of room types based purely on organisational criteria would be extremely uneconomic. For this reason, room types with comparable requirements in terms of their function and technical building installation density should be grouped by means of zoning or stacking in room groups and functional units.

Zoning means the cohesive arrangement of the same room types, for example along a corridor. The dimensions result from legal building specifications such as fire safety and escape routes (depending on the specific building regulation used) and the economical routing of technical building

1 Schematic floor plan of a chemistry laboratory
2 Schematic floor plan of a molecular biology laboratory
3 Schematic floor plan of a physics laboratory
4 Max Planck Institute for Molecular Biomedicine, Münster (GE) 2006, Kresing Architekten
   The lab zone, primarily north-facing, is largely open.

4

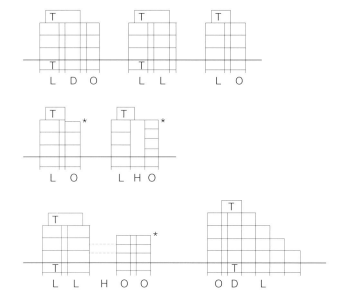

Single bays

Central bays
(outside accordingly central)

Mixed central
and single bays

5

6

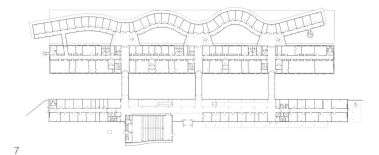

7

services: the gradient of sanitary installations and the diameter of ventilation channels are determined by the length of the corridor.

Stacking refers to arranging rooms next to one another identically on all floors on various levels. Town-planning considerations play a part here, above all the technical shaft development concept.

Structural units of around 25–30 m in length and up to three to four lab storeys high, plus basement and under-roof technical control room, have proved to be an economical size.

Structure – shafts, dimensioning, grid

Today's research buildings are usually executed as three- to four-storey steel-concrete skeleton buildings with flat slabs without joists. The separation of load-bearing and dividing roles enables modularity and flexibility as well as transparency of external appearance. Drawbacks are the low thermal mass and the relatively low vibrational stability.

The choice and dimensioning of the shaft concept (the "main arteries" of a research building) influence installation routes, storey heights, the fire safety concept as well as the building volume. A distinction is drawn between:

- central shafts: low number of fire dampers and small under-roof technical control rooms, but long conduit paths and higher storey heights; and
- individual shafts: advantage of minimising storey height, short conduit paths and individual service provision, but greater use of surfaces, more fire dampers, ceiling voids and under-roof control room required.

A combination of central and individual shafts with differentiated design for fresh air, extracted air and media has proven to be successful. If the storey heights are to be limited, for example for reasons pertaining to building regulations, individual shafts are recommended. On the other hand, high quantities of air such as are needed in chemical labs with many fume cupboards, require central shafts.

Below the concrete ceiling, which is visible and can be used as thermal mass, it is beneficial to plan the horizontal routing or conduits with no suspension. This is legal (except in safety areas) but does require a well-coordinated plan of the conduits. Operating benefits are good ability to upgrade, maintenance, hygiene (no hidden cavities) and cleaning. Functional conditions determine the width dimensions and the lab furniture determines the depth. The established interior grid for lab zones has a standard width of 1.15 m (range 1.05–1.30 m; Euro grid 1.20 m) and a constructive dimension

8

between centre lines of 6.9 m. This optimises the distance between the lab workbenches. Less distance would no longer comply with the lab guidelines and greater distances would produce surface areas which would be difficult to monitor. The depth of the lab room of usually around 6.00–7.20 m is determined by the standard lab furniture of 0.60 × 1.20 m. Reasonable storey heights for labs are between 3.80 and 4.10 m; for offices, between 2.90 and 3.40 m.

A storey height of 4.00 m is basically sufficient and will satisfy requirements in the long term. In the case of individual shafts and a lower number of fume cupboards, the room height can be reduced to 3.80 m.

The potential distance between labs and offices, which should be agreed with the scientists before the planning stage, has a considerable influence on the typology of the design. As a rule, short routes between the two are required and desired. This results in structures with relatively high office storeys, the dimensions of which are dictated by the arrangement of the labs. In some cases acoustic and visual measures may be required in the offices. Greater distances enable a separation of buildings into lab building and office building, each optimised in terms of the building structure. It is also possible to differentiate the storey heights, for example with a split-level type around an open area.

Technical building services – ventilation and air conditioning, media, electrical

Buildings for research and teaching frequently have a high level of technical installation and are therefore expensive to build and operate. It is thus essential to be "technology-friendly" right from the first planning concept. This does not mean that technical requirements determine design, but that only a design-planning process that integrates technology on a conceptual level will yield successful and economic buildings. Intelligently designed technology that is not installed on spec that can be upgraded and operated flexibly opens up the opportunity to build economically, which in turn creates scope for internal and external room quality.

The guiding principle of technology concepts is disentangling, that is, crossover-free vertical and horizontal routing of installation paths on separate levels. The overall appearance of research buildings is determined by large-scale technical equipment, delivery zones, supply and disposal concepts that are in part comparable with commercial industrial buildings.

- Ventilation and air conditioning: the arrangement of the fresh-air and extracted-air stations, the shaft and routing concept and the intake and exhaust openings influence the structure and external appearance. The differentiation between rooms that are ventilated mechanically and naturally plays a vital role. The proportion of rooms requiring mechanical ventilation depends on the thermal loading and/ or legal requirements. This applies to all labs, interior rooms and any rooms with a high density of appliances or staff. The prescribed room-air exchange (e.g. eightfold or fourfold in the labs) should be optimised in consultation with users and authorities.
- Cooling: recooling plants (usually on the roof) and refrigerating machines (usually in the basement or on the roof) are relevant visually, acoustically and in terms of vibration technology. A distinction is drawn between cooling for air-conditioning systems and process cooling for experiments.

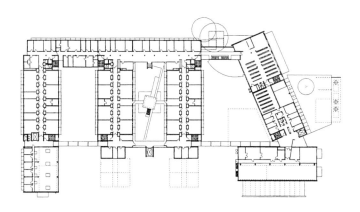

9

5 Possible building structure
Lab (L); office (O); dark room zone (D); technical control room (T); hall or exterior room (H); Office storey height not adapted to lab height (*)
6 Possible shaft arrangements
7–8 Research centre "caesar", Bonn (GE) 2003, BMBW Architekten + Partner
Zoning in three structures arranged in a linear fashion linked by piers: entrance structure with multifunctional interior room, lecture theatre, canteen, administration and open areas; double-loaded cubic lab construction with lab and dark zone as well as single-loaded, wave-shaped office building.
9 Max Planck Institute for Chemical Physics of Solids, Dresden (GE) 2000, PPS-Planungsbüro Prof. Peter Schuck
10–11 Max Planck Institute for Ornithology, Seewiesen (GE) 2008, Adam Architekten
Central new-build lab as the new centre of the institute as well as bundling of the extensively equipped lab areas. It has a single- and double-loaded construction and is open on one side.

10

11

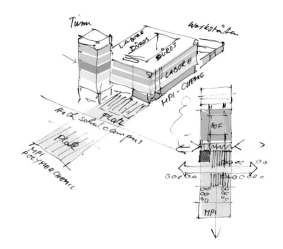

12

13

The requirement for cooling is constantly increasing, one reason for which being the greater density of appliances used.

- Water/wastewater: usually wastewater and lab wastewater are installed as two separate systems. Reservoirs of water for use by the fire service and seepage systems for rainwater influence the layout of the external facilities.
- Heating: this is a service that is not critical in terms of planning typology: ventilation and cooling technology have more of an influence on research buildings.
- Gases and media: relatively subordinate typological influence in terms of routing and spatial requirements. The nitrogen supply should be resolved at an early stage as the voluminous tank with filling and safety devices has an effect on the external facilities and the loading bay.
- Electrical: increasing data volumes, dense use of appliances in the lab and the digitisation of working processes require that electrical routings are planned at an early stage. Double floors are only used in special cases. Usually one or two routes are required to supply the room.

Precision labs

Research buildings of a physical-technical character with pioneering working methods and generation of appliances measurable in the nano zone (millionths of a millimetre) place new, extreme requirements in terms of temperature constancy and vibrational stability that often cannot be satisfied in traditional structures. This has fundamental typological consequences. In the case of new-builds, the principles of zoning and stacking become subordinate. Labs are ideally arranged on one level, directly linked to the ground, located close to the technology control rooms, with no requirement for natural lighting which would be detrimental due to its influence on temperature. Office areas can be located above. At existing sites this results in the relocation of certain areas to certain special buildings that are designed in compliance with the user-specific and technical requirements.

Floor-plan organisation

Alongside the public main entrance with a distribution function close to the common facilities such as the seminar spaces, library and cafeteria area, a research building also requires a technical entrance with all supply and waste-removal functions. In terms of this, it is also necessary to take account of traffic-routing and operational requirements and issues of material transport in the basic planning phase.

Internally, the relationship between labs with a high level of technical installation and less comprehensively installed offices is key and should be considered at the beginning of the planning phase. Scientists often prefer short routes or even a mixture of lab and office. Planners point to the economic and technical advantages of a functional separation – in the ideal case of pure lab buildings and office buildings. Double- or triple-loaded complexes are often appropriate with labs and offices facing each other and, if required, a middle zone for dark rooms (fig. 14). If the focus is biology then the requirement for refrigerated, freezer and appliance rooms usually suggests triple-loading. If the focus is on chemistry and above all physics, fewer dark rooms are needed and double-loading is more commonly encountered.

Based on the space-allocation programme, the plot shape, town-planning requirements, other specific functional units (such as large appliances, lecture theatre, workshop, library, animal or plant house) and the level of openness of the lab zones, a wide range of floor-plan typologies are possible. Future developments will be influenced by:

- limited budgets;
- increasing speed of all processes;
- interdisciplinarity;
- international cooperation, transparency, benchmarking; and
- significance of energy efficiency and sustainability;

The international world of science will increasingly demand the "interdisciplinary, scientific experimental research institute" to be built. Now more than ever, the most important core competence for architects, engineers, operators and developers confronted with these challenges are the topics of building typology and building technology.

An analysis of international projects of the last two decades provides four fundamentally different approaches in respect of the chosen design concept:

- Context: impacts the design as a determining parameter through town-planning conditions, strong link to the topography or a very specific location if the project is part of a research campus or connects old buildings with new ones.
- Zoning: architectural-typological approach, conceptually derived from functional principles of spatial allocation and zoning of specific spatial groups.
- Communication: the design reflects an overall atmosphere that facilitates and promotes scheduled and ad hoc communication.

22

- Form: individual interpretation of the location, the task, the research topic. Function and technology are subordinate to this principle.

It is not possible to produce a generally valid typological categorisation for research buildings in view of the different tasks and the diversity of the potential solutions. However, the categories may be differentiated into simplified yet illustrative overriding typological concepts (fig. 15):
- linear systems;
- comb systems; and
- core systems.

These typify a range of different variants whose basic principles are always derived from a typological system. More complex facilities are derived from multiple types. Framework conditions such as the guiding principle of the research institution, plot, building laws, space-allocation programme, working environment, ease of installation, budget, sustainability etc. influence the choice of the floor-plan and development concept.
For forward-looking research projects, the approach of zoning is likely to establish itself as the most important conceptual and typological guiding principle. By optimising technology and building typology, it enables good spatial quality to be achieved whilst remaining within budget. Both scientific considerations, such as promoting sustainability and energy efficiency in investment and operation, and reasons for interdisciplinary communication mean that there is an increasing tendency towards compact core systems.

Interdisciplinarity and acceleration of information processes

Research locations are not only required to be technically up-to-the-date, they also need to motivate and promote communication. Starting with the schools from ancient times through the medieval colleges up to the universities in the 19th and 20th century, communication has always been an important factor on the path to acquiring knowledge. In the past two decades the speed of information flows and the need for interdisciplinary exchange has increased enormously. Specialisation within the academic disciplines and the complexity of research increasingly demands team-orientated, interdisciplinary cooperation. Buildings and parts of buildings – right up to lab and office zones of small teams of scientists – that promote conversations and meetings will therefore become ever more significant in future. As a part of the networked world, institutes are also entering into a communicative exchange with an increasingly virtual environment. What spatial anchor points they will require

12 Max Planck Institute of Molecular Cell Biology and Genetics, Dresden (GE) 2001, Heikkinen-Komonen Architects with Henn Architekten
Institutional new-build consisting of two four-storey lab structures with open group labs (with integrated lab and writing points), in between building-high entrance structure with open and public areas. The spatial and organisational conditions are intended to motivate frequent communication.
13 Max Planck Institute for Chemistry, Mainz (GE) 2011, Fritsch + Tschaidse Architekten
Office tower as the link between the two campus parts. The lab building is arranged around a courtyard on three levels (double-loaded), with chemistry labs and offices facing each other.
14 Loadings
Lab (L); office (O); dark room zone (D); hall or exterior room (H)
15 Typological systems

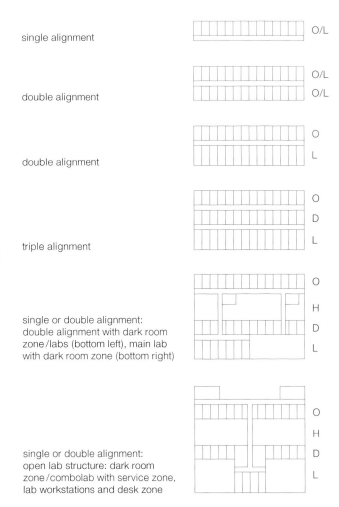

single alignment — O/L

double alignment — O/L, O/L

double alignment — O, L

triple alignment — O, D, L

single or double alignment: double alignment with dark room zone/labs (bottom left), main lab with dark room zone (bottom right) — O, H, D, L

single or double alignment: open lab structure: dark room zone/combolab with service zone, lab workstations and desk zone — O, H, D, L

14

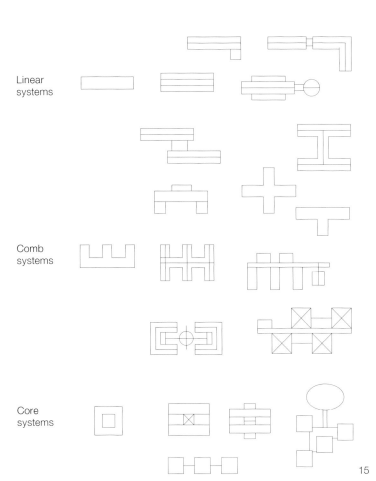

Linear systems

Comb systems

Core systems

15

23

16

17

18

in future, and how these will be expressed architecturally, remains to be seen. From the perspective of spatial topography, the desire to promote scheduled and ad hoc exchanges lies somewhere between an over-sized entrance hall and pure functionally optimised thoroughfares.

Opening up of the lab structures

For the past decade there has been a clear trend for larger, open lab spaces, in particular in terms of new-builds and conversions – especially with buildings from the 1970s.

In terms of an academic field, this applies to buildings for molecular-biological and biochemical research.

There are many reasons for this change. It can be explained by means of the interdisciplinary understanding in the training of biologists, chemists and physicists to use convergent working methods and measuring techniques and also from the fact that innovation is predominantly generated through interdisciplinary cooperation. The way that future generations of scientists communicate and also the organisation of their work into flexible, relatively autonomous group structures with flat hierarchies plays a part, as does of course the economic pressure to plan, build and operate as efficiently as possible and to use appliances and surfaces interactively.

In the case of larger lab structures – as with combined office zones – the aspects of safety, acoustics, potential hazards, communication, spatial impression and furnishing should be taken into account.

Typologically this results in greater spatial depths, the integration of writing desks and thus, to a reduction of the need for office and transit space.

However, the trend is fairly controversial and cannot be said to be constant. Modifications and, in some cases, divergent concepts are to be anticipated.

Specialists see the following drawbacks:

- Acoustics: dependent on subjective perception, but very frequently the higher noise level caused by people and appliances is considered adverse. Sound-attenuating measures are possible; however, their effect is limited.
- Safety: those responsible for health and safety at work cite the potential hazard posed by working processes and the lack of protection afforded for example by internal walls in smaller lab units as a problem. Here it is necessary to devise operational resolutions.

The following aspects are considered to be benefits:

- simplification of the building structure and cost savings: this affects fire safety (routings, fire dampers, enclosures) and the detachable elements (walls, doors);
- increase in surface area and intensification of usage by integrating transit routes as an indirect consequence of conversions or as an optimisation of planning data for new-builds;
- flexibility of the allocation of area and workspaces, lab spaces and writing desks;
- promotion of communication and working processes, simple and short routes; and
- synergy effects through the common usage of appliances and service places, thermal mass and supply and disposal facilities.

Overall, the benefits of open, combined lab structures outweigh those of the standardised lab of 20 or 40 m². The conflict between the short routes expected by science on the one hand and the attempted optimisation of installation from a construction perspective on the other, is resolved in view of the benefits set out here. However, there are upper limits on the size of the lab structures due to requirements in terms of health and safety, spatial atmosphere or noise levels. Developments are moving towards intelligently-combined room structures with integrated but acoustically shielded writing zones for purposes of documentation and evaluation, with an atmosphere that suggests not the "large room", but the combined or group lab. This is achieved by way of a series of rooms that alternate between open zones and closed room units (such as special labs) and their manageable room sizes do not exceed 80–100 m².

Sustainability and energy efficiency

The buzz words "sustainability" and "energy efficiency" denote a very wide ranging discussion at the present time. Apart from the fact that a professional demand planning concept that utilises synergies offers the greatest sustainability potential, buildings in future will tend to become more compact and more solid in terms of the materials selected. Differentiated structures with a high proportion of glass facades may be a thing of the past. The proven typology should be linked to a method of construction which, with a glazing proportion of under 50 %, reduces the external heat input and also that benefits from high thermal masses of supporting and non-supporting components that improve the air quality in the rooms and reduce energy consumption. Current initiatives for sustainable construction, bundling of typology criteria, creating a benchmarking catalogue and for influencing the development of an appropriate system of standards (such as BNB, DGNB, EGNATON), coordinated at European level, will accelerate the speed of these trends and strengthen the excellent level of European research building culture. The principles of sustainability and future-orientation can be seen consistently in the decision-making and the typological outcomes in current competition results of the Max Planck Society (fig. 16–22). The designs, which are economic to build and to run, set the course for architecture, have a high interior spatial quality and are optimised for installation. It is impossible not to draw an analogy to the first building type in the history of research buildings, the college, in some of the contemporary designs. The successful symbiosis of the complex requirements could give this design typology – a compact core with a simple building structure – significance similar to that attained by the college building type from the 14th century onwards.

16　Max Planck Institute for Solar System Research, Göttingen (GE), 1. Competition, Carpus + Partner
　　Above a compact pedestal with highly-equipped functional units (labs, clean rooms), a projecting office building marks the entrance.
17–18　Max Planck Institute for Biology of Ageing, Cologne (GE) 2012, hammeskrause Architekten
　　An internal transparent, communicative structure stands counter to the closed exterior. Around the atrium there are open combined labs and ancillary rooms. The offices are located along the facades.
19–20　Max Planck Institute for the Science of Light, Erlangen (GE), 1. Competition, Fritsch + Tschaidse Architekten
　　The strictly zoned, square floor plan (optical labs that can be darkened on the inner yard, offices on the outer sides) permits a small, but spatially ambitious internal communication space.
21–22　Max Planck Institute for Software Systems, Kaiserslautern (GE) 2012, Weinbrenner Single Arabzadeh Architekten
　　The working rooms are arranged orthogonally around the inner hall with single-loading.

19

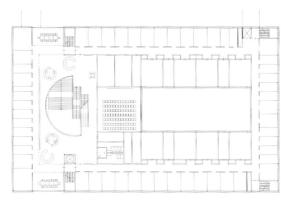

20

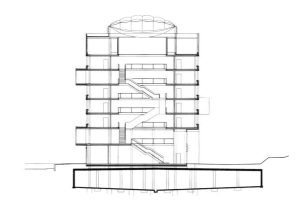

21

22

Office design and knowledge economy

Burkhard Remmers

Globalisation and the rapid development of information and communication technology have led to a fundamental change in office work, in terms of tools and possible work locations, as well as in its growing importance for all types of business. Increasingly, economic value is generated in the creative, administrative and logistical business sectors. It is no longer the product alone that determines success, but its development, marketing, customer service, support and business logistics. Whereas, due to the already highly advanced automation in this field, productivity increases in manufacturing can now only be achieved to a minor extent and with a disproportionate amount of effort, the greatest potential for improvements and increased competitive edge can now be found in the office. Office work should therefore no longer be seen as a necessary overhead cost, but as an opportunity for enhancing profit and growth. If the results of a study by the Fraunhofer Institute for Industrial Engineering (Fraunhofer IAO) are anything to go by, knowledge, creativity and education have long become the real drivers of the global economy.

Digitalisation, Internet, Intranet and the miniaturisation of technology mean that office work can now take place almost anywhere and even while on the move. The only prerequisites are power supply and Internet access, a desk, somewhere to sit, and an environment that allows for a reasonable level of concentration.

At the same time, teamwork, ongoing professional development and knowledge management have become key aspects of office work. Change is no longer the exception, but has become the norm in our complex and highly connected world. Project-based work and working in teams has become commonplace, even in administrative sectors. In parallel with the internationalisation of companies and their business relationships, staff are increasingly working in distributed, virtual teams, based in different locations around the world. Norbert Streitz, one of the world's pioneers in collaborative virtual environments, predicted as early as 1999 that the role of office buildings would change significantly in the future. They would no longer primarily serve as individual work spaces, single offices or cubicles, since working on your own would, in principle, be possible anywhere [1]. But this does not mean that office buildings would become redundant, since the "office building of the future will above all offer a place for communication and collaborative team work. It provides space for pre-arranged meetings, but also – and just as importantly – for casual and spontaneous communication." [2] Indeed, this kind of infor-

mal, opportunist and peripheral communication is becoming increasingly important.

The limits of virtualisation

During the 1990s many people predicted the end of the office as an actual physical space. They believed that in the future we would all be linked up via high-speed Internet access, equipped with 3D glasses and meet only in virtual spaces. The reality, however, seems to suggest the opposite, as no technological innovation, however sophisticated, can really match the quality of real, face-to-face contact in laying the foundations for effective collaboration: trust, empathy, team spirit as well as creativity, commitment and dependability. And above all, as instinctively territorial beings, we rely on physical space as a frame of reference for our social interactions. It is no accident that virtual businesses are generally temporary in nature. Either they become established – literally – by setting up a physical office space, or they disband once the project that brought them together has come to fruition. The time when the primary concern of architects is the design of virtual spaces is therefore still some way off. Instead they will be looking for ways to augment and enhance the physical space with the virtual, in order to connect and amplify the opportunities inherent in both.

At the heart of office design: promoting human interaction

Highly focused solitary work is generally easier to do away from the office, i.e. somewhere less prone to interruptions. The communal and team-oriented aspects of work are therefore becoming a much more central theme in office design: the office as a space that promotes social interaction and a sense of identity, a place where people come together to generate and share knowledge and new ideas, a place for collaboration and cooperation, where processes of change are initiated and new requirements implemented as fast as possible. Managers already spend 80 % of their working day in meetings, other office staff around 20 % – and these figures are set to continue to rise.

Digitalisation has reduced the need for storage space for archives; desk space can shrink as a result of technological miniaturisation and flatscreen monitors, but instead more space is needed for the whole range of communal spaces – from tea kitchens to informal meeting areas and lounge corners to project, seminar, meeting and conference rooms. Correspondingly, the proportion of ancillary space in office design has risen from an average of 15 % in the past to

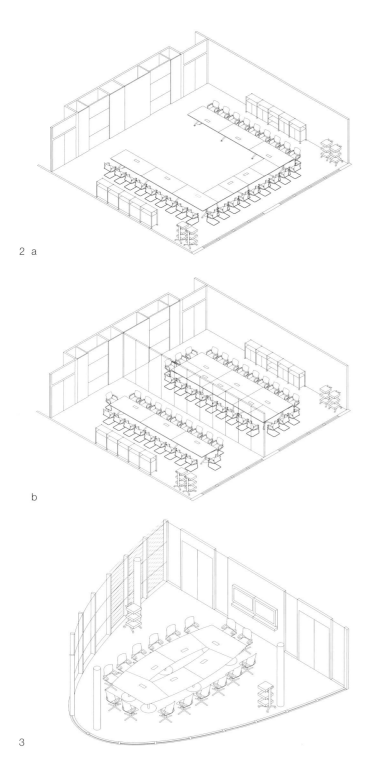

2 a

b

3

4

almost 40 % in modern offices, and is still rising. How efficient and effective the communication really is, however, is determined to a great degree by the design and equipment of the space and whether it has been designed to be truly conducive to communication. The purpose that is implicitly attached to a space is as important here as the user profile, the number of people, the communication methods used and the equipment provided. Maintaining, asserting or familiarising, for example, requires a completely different spatial and methodological context than questioning, innovation and change processes.

Traditional meeting rooms as a reflection of an organisation

There have always been symbolic places and gatherings, reflecting the hierarchies within a community. The traditional meeting format probably forms part of our social make-up. Officially, the objective is to convey information and to help with decision-making. The other – often subconscious – objective, meanwhile, is to assert identity and preserve the current social structure. Rituals, seating arrangement and methodology all follow the company's internal code of conduct. Invitations, agenda, procedures and minute-taking are formalised accordingly. The chairman chairs the meeting, often from a raised or otherwise prominent position. The places next to him or her reflect the importance or familiarity of other dignitaries and denote their role within the system. The quality of equipment and overall comfort of the meeting room matches the level within the company hierarchy of its intended users. Furniture and interior design therefore serve representation purposes – internally as well as externally.

Some people feel that traditional forms of meetings and conferences are no longer appropriate for our time. But this disregards the fact that their location, symbolism und protocol provides a sense of continuity and stability for staff and management. They represent the culture and inherent systems of an organisation. Especially now, as everyday work experience is dominated by constant change, familiar company rituals are increasing in relevance as a fixture and orientation point.

Equally though, the design of meeting and conference rooms holds a highly important key when it comes to communicating new values such as transparency, openness and participation. The shape and design of tables not only determines the number of participants but also the potential scope for interactivity. This ranges from long, rectangular boardroom tables, with a prominent seat for the chairman and a limited level of possible interaction, to round tables without any indication of hierarchy and allowing equal interaction for all participants. Even subtle aspects such as table-top segmentation, cut-outs or the location of table legs can have a direct influence on communication, behaviour and interaction.

In addition to these most basic aspects, the technological equipment plays an increasingly important role and needs to be integrated in the design concept from the outset. The greatest limitation is often the height of the room, which determines the size of the projection and therefore the maximum distance from the screen and the appropriate depth of the room.

Globally networked corporate headquarters now also need to consider video conferencing options in the design of their office. Depending on tne frequency of usage, it may be worth having a dedicated room with the necessary equipment set up or to allow for a flexible and easily adjustable table configuration. The v-shaped conference table can be used as a large oval boardroom table for general meetings, but also opens up into a v-shape, allowing all participants to view the projection screen during a video conference, as well as giving participants on the other side an unobstructed view of everyone at the table. Modern lighting control technology can automatically modify lighting to match the display technology in use – from low lighting during Powerpoint presentations to highlighting participants' faces during video conferences.

On account of both space-efficiency and environmental concerns, frequency of use needs to be considered in the design of conference and meeting rooms. Divisible rooms, using the latest sound-proofing partition walls, allow varying room sizes, which offers greater flexibility in the utilisation of each room. To be able to modify table sizes and seating arrangements accordingly, flexible table systems are recommended. Even so, the effort involved in rearranging tables, as well as storage space requirements for unused furniture, also needs to be taken into account – for example by choosing stackable chairs. Alternatively, divisible conference rooms can be equipped with a combination of movable or folding and static tables, which minimise the time and effort involved in rearranging the room, while still providing high-quality equipment. In this case it would make sense to incorporate power points and Internet sockets within the tabletops rather than in the floor. These days simple socket systems can provide easy and flexible access to the most up-to-date media technology for up to 40 delegates, including power points, USB, network sockets, audio, VGA and interactive button, allowing individual participants to access the current presentation on their own laptop. The key here is to ensure that these concepts are integrated at the design stage. If the table is seen as an installation level in itself then power points set within the floor can be reduced, thereby avoiding a complex floor construction and maximising room height to benefit projection sizes. It also means that the technology is easier to access for updates, and in the event of relocation the entire technological infrastructure can be taken along. For the refurbishment or conversion of old – or even listed – buildings this also offers a suitably intelligent solution.

Rooms for education and training

In years gone by, the end of one's training meant that learning was complete. These days, the accepted wisdom is that learning only really begins with the start of one's professional career. The ever-increasing amount of information to take in and knowledge to accumulate in a rapidly changing marketplace has dramatically shortened the life expectancy of what we thought we had learned for life. Instead, the concept of life-long learning denotes the dynamic change of the world of work and is also reflected in organisations' training budgets.

The demographic transition and its resulting decline in working-age population will require more effective staff retention strategies. In addition, as sufficiently qualified staff are becoming increasingly hard to find, company-internal training and qualifications are gaining in significance. Another category of office space for formal communication is therefore

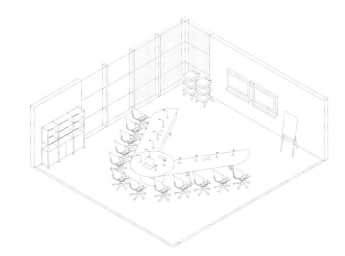

5

1 Communication space, architecture office in Geneva (CH), 2010, group8
2 Divisible meeting room with two static rows of tables and mobile folding tables; multimedia access points are integrated in the table top and easy to access.
  a In a U-shaped layout.
  b As two separate rooms with partition wall in place.
3 Desk configuration dependent on the kind of space, with integrated media connections for medium levels of interaction and defined seating layout
4 Traditional boardroom layout with high-quality design and aesthetic appeal.
5 V-shaped conference table, shown open for use in video conferencing (or closed as oval boardroom table).
6 Integrated technology ranging from "plug & play" table sockets to retractable display screens, enabling delegates to view presentations at the back of the room.
7 Instantly adaptable: mobile, folding or flip-top conference and seminar tables.

6

7

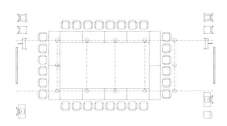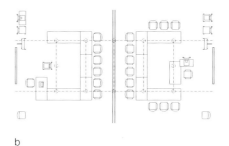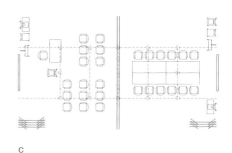

8 a   b   c

the seminar and training room. The primary objective in the design of this space is to be conducive to learning.

In order to create the best possible learning environment, a neutral design and easy adaptability of the space itself, as well as its equipment and furniture are key. Even more than in the case of conference and meeting rooms, table arrangement, room size and technical equipment need to support the respective training objective.

Storage space requirements, room reconfiguration time and the need for extra staff should be assessed and compared from a budgetary perspective, as they can quickly exceed the capital costs of equipment. This is true in particular for media technology, which requires qualified personnel for its installation and again for any alterations necessary to suit different training concepts. As described above, solutions are now available that offer fully equipped individual tables – either as stackable tables with detachable or foldable legs or as mobile tables with swivel table tops. These may initially be more expensive to purchase, but faster and easier set-up will offset the additional cost. Robust surfaces and frames are essential to avoid damage from frequent room reconfigurations. The room design needs to take account of the different permutations of table arrangements – for individual tables, rows, closed or open layouts – to arrive at a workable pattern for the floor boxes.

The symbolic importance of seminar room design is often overlooked: room ambience and quality of equipment will influence the value that is subconsciously attached to the training session by participants. Whether taking part in a training seminar is seen as a tedious chore or as a valued opportunity is largely determined by the social prestige associated with training, and this is also expressed in the room design and set-up. To scrimp here seems absurd in the context of the high importance attributed to training, the size of the training budget overall and the costs associated with sending staff on training seminars in the first place.

Innovate, develop, change

A third category of dedicated communication space are project and workshop rooms for initiating and developing organisational change processes, improvements and innovation. Working with facilitators, methodologies such as mindmapping, written discussion and other processes to encourage creativity, all involve working collaboratively across hierarchies and disciplines, and engaging with stakeholders who will be affected by any planned changes. In addition to the psychological benefits of enabling staff to "own" the process,

it is now also becoming more widely recognised that it is wise to tap into the knowledge, experience and expertise of those who are involved in the implementation of organisational change or innovation.

The equipment needs to provide the right setting and tools to actively engage participants, both physically and mentally. It makes an enormous difference whether the meeting starts with a predetermined set-up or whether the methodology is developed collaboratively and in parallel with the room layout. While jointly rearranging the room, team spirit and a positive group dynamic is generated from the outset, without the need for contrived "warm-up" exercises. Furthermore, no additional staff are needed to set up the room beforehand. The concept can be compared to an actual workshop from which the group can take the tools it requires for the task at hand: chairs, desks, display walls, flipcharts, AV equipment, mobile, foldable or swivel tables. Here too, the impact the aesthetic and functional quality of these tools can have on the proceedings and their results should not be underestimated. Dynamic conference tables are therefore also increasingly used, in suitably high quality, in traditional meeting and conference situations – as they allow for cost-effective and efficient use of expensive office space.

Promoting social interaction as a central task of knowledge management

One of the greatest challenges for most organisations is how to document, share and develop the combined knowledge of its teams, beyond formal training sessions. A common misconception here is that knowledge management is mainly a question of data management. Of course, documentation and availability of information is the basis for explaining and clarifying processes and procedures. However, company databases and Intranets store information – not knowledge. The knowledge itself remains inside people's heads. In its true complexity and depth of experience it can only ever be stored as information in rudimentary form.

Sharing knowledge therefore means, above all communicating knowledge, and this is still always achieved most effectively in direct, face-to-face conversation. Change processes that do not also become part of everyday conversation within an organisation have little chance of being implemented. Indeed, research into innovation processes shows that more than 80 % of ideas are generated as part of direct interaction between people. Important insights are often the result of a chance encounter in the staff canteen, in the car park or while waiting for the lift.

8 Different layout permutations for a divisible, multifunctional conference
   and seminar space:
   a Plenary layout
   b Presentation and discussion layout
   c Seminar and meeting layout
9 The aesthetic and functional quality of the tools and spaces used is an
   important factor in the value attached to the process result.
10 Workshop space with storage area to enable a fluid and participatory
   approach in the design of change and innovation processes:
   a Brainstorming and ideas generation
   b Plenary and individual working groups
   c Presentation of results
   d Discussion

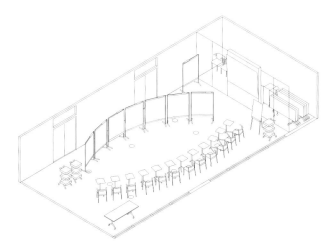

a

Designing office buildings like cities

The key questions for knowledge management are therefore:
where and how can, and should, people meet within the
building – whether by arrangement or by chance? Who
should ideally bump into whom more frequently? How should
office spaces be designed to facilitate chance encounters
and the exchange of ideas and knowledge? Where, within
the building, should these informal meeting places be, and
what kind of quality do they need to have to encourage staff
to use them? How do they need to be designed to encourage
people to spend time there? Knowledge and innovation management therefore has specific requirements regarding the
design of access points and circulation spaces, both outside
and within the building. Since the focus is both on the individual person as well as the collective – the social interactions
between team members – the key here are semi-public
spaces: everything that lies between individual workstation
and seminar or meeting room.

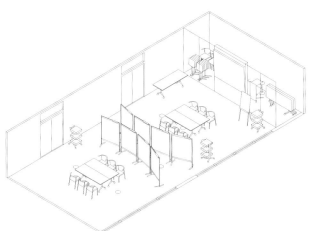

b

It is no surprise that these concepts of semi-public and public space within an office building often use terminology bor-
rowed from an urban design context. Terms such as "node",
"office landscape" or "breakout zone" refer to the social qualities of these "in-between" spaces. While in the past these
spaces were seen as a necessary evil, they are now taking
centre stage in a bid to encourage social interaction among
staff, thereby facilitating the development of new ideas.
Entrances, informal catering areas, kitchens and bistros,
library corners, lounge and recreation zones and company
cafés or restaurants – all these are spaces that promote exchange and interaction. Their range of designs and functions
– from sofa lounge to multimedia table – and their connection

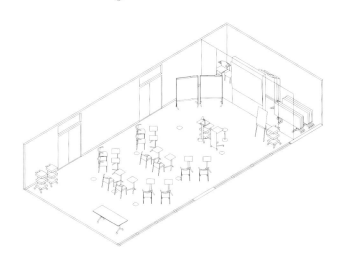

c

9

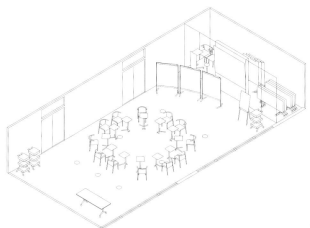

d

10

with basic human needs such as eating and drinking, not only serve the well-being of employees but also fulfil a core function in the internal knowledge exchange network. The building, thereby becomes a "space of potential" [3], which can promote social interaction, allow it – or suppress it. For organisations, these social qualities of office design are becoming an increasingly important consideration, on a par with location. Ultimately, they affect the economic capacity and future performance of the business itself.

Asset and bottleneck: the human factor

"The human being is at the centre" has been the maxim for advocates of high-quality office design for decades – "... and therefore always in the way", its critics counter predictably. But where knowledge workers are concerned, whose full engagement and creativity are paramount, taking account of staff well-being and internal motivation is indeed becoming ever more important. There is growing evidence that the employees of an organisation are an increasingly significant factor in its overall market performance. IT systems, plant and machinery, even management procedures are easily copied and replicated. The competence of one's team members, however, their commitment and motivation, are one's organisation's true USP. The human factor therefore becomes indeed the greatest asset – and at the same time the major bottleneck – of an organisation's economic power. It is no accident that pioneering businesses such as Google have also become pioneers in an approach to office design that considers the psychological and social needs of its staff above all, as the real drivers of productivity and growth.

These businesses have recognised the importance of office design in creating a sense of identity and community within the organisation. The office design attracts and retains "High Potentials" and ensures effective processes for innovation. The uniqueness and variety of informal meeting spaces, beyond the usual standardised workstations and formalised meeting rooms, encourages creativity and curiosity.

Traditional industries are now catching up too: the new Unilever headquarters in Hamburg, for example, also places the social qualities of the building at the centre of its design (see pp. 86). Recent studies by the Fraunhofer IAO and other research institutions have demonstrated impressively the connection between quality of office space, well-being, motivation and staff engagement on the one hand and the economic viability of an organisation on the other. Equipment and machinery are no longer the most important means of production, but architecture and space design.

The shift towards stimulus-rich office environments

Office spaces are becoming increasingly modern; ergonomic considerations ever more sophisticated and almost every aspect is regulated by rules and standards that are designed to serve users' well-being – and increase their productivity. Yet, ergonomics mainly looks at the individual as an object, reducing walking distances and reaching movements in a one-dimensional bid to enhance productivity, guided by the mechanist world view of the 19th century and its understanding of work and health. The justified objective of reducing one-sided and extreme physical strain has led to a situation where office work is now characterised by a complete lack of

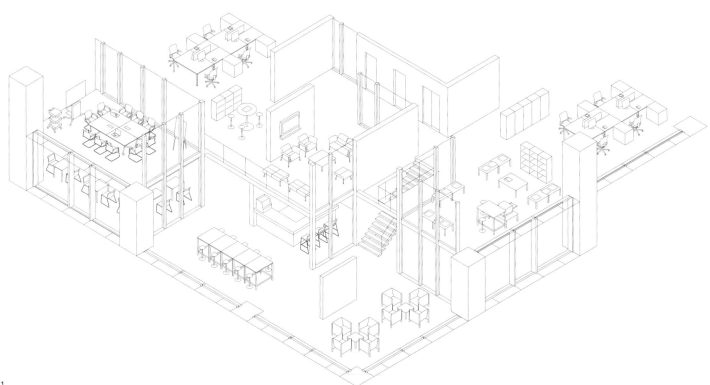

11

physical activity while mental demands and stress have increased disproportionately. With physical demands now reduced to not much more than operating keyboard and mouse, the body lacks important stimuli that are essential for the entire metabolic system.

Some improvements are offered, for example, by flexible office chairs that move in three directions, as well as dynamic office layouts that encourage physical movement. In this context, the design of communication spaces gains an important physical dimension: meeting places are also movement places. The design of the connecting spaces is also just as important as that of the meeting points themselves. A room layout that can be adapted by the users as they see fit, not only allows for mental engagement but also contributes to much needed physical activity. Holding meetings standing upright is not just more efficient but also healthier. A look at innovation research shows to what extent physical movement, mental agility and creativity are interconnected: it has been proven that people show the highest willingness to ask questions, to break away from accustomed patterns and roles and to develop new ideas and trust when taking a walk together.

In order to promote a holistic understanding of the human being as a living and dynamic organism, the "Living Ergonomics" initiative has been set up. Its key audience are occupational health experts and ergonomics specialists as well as product designers, designers of work processes and architects. Living Ergonomics sees human beings as individuals with diverse needs and dispositions. The initiative seeks to establish criteria for a new standard in human-centred and healthy work environments. This requires a multidisciplinary and creative approach. Not least in order to initiate the final, most difficult paradigm shift: a new social and emotional image of work itself. One that is no longer tainted by concepts of work dating back to the industrial revolution. Is work really just a necessary evil? Do we work only to make a living and finance our leisure activities? Does the workplace really have to be a dismal place of toil and misery? Does the perception of wages as compensation payment for inflicted agony on the one side, and inconvenient cost factor on the other still represent the new context of work? Is time spent at the office still an adequate measure of determining pay? And, conversely, are break times, as unremunerated time, really still "work-free"?

A glimpse into the future
No matter which sector of construction you look at, in future, the human being as individual will be at the centre of design, and human well-being will be seen as an important productivity factor. This kind of fundamental shift in approach is likely to have a profound impact on building design, from lighting and services to colour, acoustics and the relationship between internal and external spaces.

In the design and equipment of office buildings thereby lies a significant key to changing social conventions and value systems as a whole.

Future-oriented concepts will see office environments as stimulating and varied settings that serve to support workers as best as possible in their respective tasks and individual needs. They need to offer space for concentrated work and privacy as well as for communication and collaboration in all its different shapes and forms. The main quantifiable benchmark in office desig will become not the traditional

12

11 The office building as a place for a wide range of communication and collaboration processes: from separate rooms for formal meetings to different types of semi-public lounge spaces and meeting points to library corners and coffee bars with high tables. The circulation spaces are deliberately complex to promote physical exercise and chance encounters.
12 Multifunctional foyer and recreational space with flexible high stools, use of walls as digital presentation and information spaces.
13 Standing table with integrated display and multi-touch technology to allow collaborative work on digital documents, also for distributed teams.
14 Informal meeting table with network connection to access and save documents.
15 Interactive display integrated in table.
16 Promoting social interaction and communication through openness and generous circulation space, Middelfart Sparekasse, Middelfart (DK) 2010, 3XN studio.

13

14

15

office floorspace and number of workstations, but optional spaces for retreat, communal and circulation spaces, as well as their technical equipment.

In the sense of a "collaborative building", which both cooperates with its users and promotes collaboration between them, integration of the latest information and communication technologies also plays a crucial role. This also goes far beyond the latest building services technology. Instead, it is a matter of enhancing the reality of the physical space with digital information spaces. Research into "invisible computing" and "ubiquitous computing" has delivered solid foundations for this. "Invisible computing" means the technology itself fades into the background, leaving only the actual user interface visible; "ubiquitous computing" looks at options for providing access to one's digital data anywhere and at any time. Translating these concepts into physical space can range from Internet and server access in canteen and recreational areas, to utilising walls and other elements of the room itself as a communal interface. The iPhone and iPad are a useful start in introducing multi-touch displays, intuitive user interfaces and playful designs into a work context. But most importantly: health and well-being of the user are becoming a significant factor in office design, for which architects will have to find suitable design solutions. Designing buildings with human beings in mind – can there be a more worthwhile challenge?

References:
[1] Norbert Streitz et al., "Kooperative Gebäude und Roomware für die Arbeitswelten der Zukunft", in: Norbert Streitz et al. (ed.), Arbeitswelten im Wandel. Fit für die Zukunft? (Stuttgart 1999), 21ff.
[2] Ibid.
[3] Gunter Henn, "Geleitwort", in: Silke Claus, Kommunikationsorientierte Gebäudegestaltung (Erlangen 2003).

Further reading:
Christopher Alexander, A Pattern Language (New York 1977)
congena (ed.), Die neue Welt der Arbeit (Frankfurt/M. 2000)
Johann Eisele, Bettina Staniek (eds.), Der Bürobau Atlas (Munich 2006)
Guido Englich, Burkhard Remmers, Planungshandbuch für Konferenz- und Kommunikationsräume (Basel, Boston, Berlin 2008)
Fraunhofer IAO (ed.), The Innovation Potential of Diversity. Practical Examples for the Innovation Management (Stuttgart 2010)
Fraunhofer IAO (ed.), Studie Green Office (Stuttgart 2010)
Norbert Streitz et al., Cooperative Buildings. Integrating Information, Organizations and Architecture (Berlin, Heidelberg, New York 1999)
Stephan Zinser (ed.), Flexible Arbeitswelten (Zurich 2004)

Web references:
www.foresee.biz
www.iafob.de
www.iao.fhg.de
www.iw.web-erhebung.de
www.office-score.de

16

"Success factor office" – myth or key to sustainable business success?

Claudia Hamm Bastow

Almost every day we read about the challenges posed by the ever-more rapidly changing world of work, technological progress, extreme fluctuations in economic cycles, increasing globalisation, rising costs and the blurring boundaries between work and personal life. These are developments that every responsible employer needs to face. Commercial viability has become a highly complex maze of key success factors: innovation, agility, the appeal of the organisation as an employer, staff retention, sustainability and corporate social responsibility are just some of the "soft" factors that play an increasingly important role.

Bearing in mind that staff and rea-estate tend to represent the two most significant cost factors for any organisation, it is clear that getting these two aspects in balance is crucial for business success. An organisation that can combine enhanced real-estate performance with an increase in staff effectiveness will have a clear advantage over the competition. To achieve this, a comprehensive, tailor-made strategy is needed that includes attractive design and high-quality architecture. A new, cutting-edge office design, aligned with the organisation's strategic vision and with a focus on supporting optimised processes and good communication, has enormous potential as an authentic expression of organisational culture.

Involving the workforce in the concept development and its implementation is paramount. Change processes inevitably cause anxiety and resistance, which, if not sufficiently acknowledged and understood, will demotivate staff and jeopardise the overall success of the business. The key aspects for a successful office redesign are fully integrated consultation, transparent communication, technological support and, of course, a high-quality, contemporary design. The office, thus becomes a hub of ideas and knowledge sharing, and an authentic expression of the organisation's culture and values – the most important asset and the secret behind every successful business. It thereby represents a true "home" for the organisation's workforce and a place they can identify with.

Promoting innovation and growth
For over three decades, the strategic business consultancy, DEGW, has been committed to creating a balanced relationship between people, place and technology. The company takes a multi-level, multi-dimensional approach and goes a long way beyond the mere development of spatial design concepts. A new workplace strategy, whether for a single building or for a global organisation, is a development process, a quality cycle, which continually integrates new insights and experiences, constantly revealing opportunities for further optimisation. Only by working collaboratively with multi-disciplinary teams of experienced business analysts, economists, organisational development experts, psychologists and, of course, architects and interior designers, can this complex process be successfully steered towards the best solution. The rapid technological development opens up completely new opportunities for flexible working. As work is no longer dependent on a specific location, physical space will have entirely new roles to fulfil, which also leads to a change in its quality.

The key question is, therefore, no longer simply how much physical space a business needs in order to be successful in the marketplace, but also increasingly what kind of space best supports today's knowledgeable workers, how the rise in virtual teams and electronically networked individual workers can be integrated in the design concepts and which aspects of human resource planning and information technology need to be developed simultaneously to reinforce creativity and innovation.

Working collaboratively with the client, the consultant manages this process of change and communication, creating a work environment that not only steers the organisation towards economic success, but which also positively affects the aforementioned "soft" success factors. This requires a profound transformation of the existing status quo, completely revolutionising the way the organisation works. The objective is to facilitate sustainable organisational growth and to create a stimulating environment of collaboration, innovation and communication, helping the organisation to attract and retain the best talent.

Process and strategy
A thorough workplace analysis provides deeper insights into the interactions between people, their environment and technology and explores how these factors affect the value creation of a business. The approach consists of several phases encompassing the entire value chain – from organisational analysis and data gathering to collation and assessment of the data collected, the development of a workplace strategy and design concept, to drawing up overarching workplace design guidelines and navigating the organisation through the implementation process.

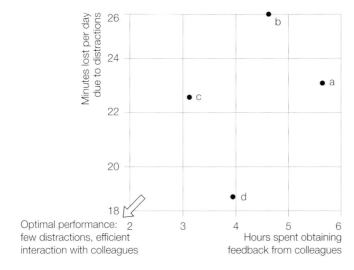

Input

Organizational goals

Workplace performance survey

Development focus groups

Validation focus groups

Start

Concept development phase

Recommendations

Strategy development

Observations

Interviews

Input

1

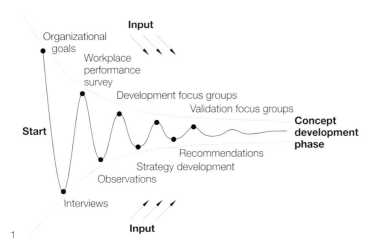

Minutes lost per day due to distractions

26   b

24   a

22   c

20

18

Optimal performance: few distractions, efficient interaction with colleagues

2   3   4   5   6

Hours spent obtaining feedback from colleagues

d

a   closed workspaces: > 30% individual offices
b   mixed workspaces: 5–30% individual offices
c   very open work environment: < 5% individual offices
2   d   flexible workspaces: > 30% of staff have no dedicated desk space

3

Comprehensive change and transition management accompanies every project and includes informing, engaging and coaching all relevant stakeholders to develop the skills needed to ensure that future challenges can be addressed confidently from within the organisation and the change process is taken forward following completion of the workspace project.

Inception phase
In the early stages, the inception phase of the project, the focus is on creating an understanding of the reasons for the change and its aims and objectives. Space offers enormous opportunities for change. By looking at possible strategies and visions together with the client, these opportunities and the overall direction of the design concept can be identified. Buy-in at board level is crucial at this stage, as the process can only be successfully cascaded down the organisational levels with pro-active support from the top and leadership by example.

Organisational analysis
A detailed organisational analysis across all levels of the company hierarchy forms the basis for all further steps. This research phase assesses the status quo of the organisation and collates the data required to develop a bespoke workplace strategy and specific design concept for the organisation (fig. 1). The research has several dimensions, using interviews, staff focus groups and workshops to identify ways in which the organisation's strategic objectives can be supported through the design and use of its workspace. Online surveys and observation studies reveal work and space utilisation patterns, staff perceptions and specifics of the business operation. These survey methods, developed and refined over the years, deliver valuable insights and information about the relevance of different spaces and provide the consultants with a comprehensive picture of the current use of space. The discrepancies between survey responses and actual observation highlight the differences between perception and reality. This paves the way for a discussion about completely new approaches and helps to identify the potential for change.

Concept development phase
The analysis phase, backed up by years of experience, translates the data collected into valuable information that can be used as the basis for future decisions. A degree of flexibility is important, as work should not be dependent on location, but task-oriented. The concepts need to take into account the wide variety of different tasks and activities that members of staff perform every day, to arrive at a creative and innovative environment that provides each and every member of staff with sufficient space to carry out their work.

A new office space also offers an opportunity to express organisational culture and values in the physical design of the rooms. The underlying philosophy of the design concept is therefore developed in close liaison with the client. Existing corporate design guidelines are integrated in the process and a design code is developed defining colours, materials, furniture, lighting and other details. The finished workplace design should reflect the organisation's culture and brand. A tangible, physical change of the work environment and the involvement in something that is visibly new also helps to effect the change in people's minds.

Change and transition management
A critical success factor in introducing a new workplace strategy is managing the transition process involved. Where their own workspace is concerned, employees are often reluctant to accept and embrace change. Change management therefore forms an integral part in this whole process. The core objective here is always to support the client through this transition phase and to introduce teams, individual members of staff and the entire organisation to the new way of working. Adopting new concepts such as desk sharing and flexible work patterns, as well as adapting to a completely new work environment is a learning process. It is important to develop an understanding of how people work and interact with each other and with their work environment. Only if staff have been involved and kept in the loop from the outset, helping them to fully understand and embrace the process of change, will they accept the changes in the long run.

A post-occupancy evaluation at the end of the process, measuring the success of the new concept in use, can put a value against the project, identify scope for further improvements and offer recommendations for the implementation of related projects.

Conclusion
The office space of the future will be increasingly subjected to the conflicting needs of communication, concentration, individualisation and mobility. Somewhere between cellular and open-plan lies the ideal workplace strategy for every organisation. Critical for the success of any workplace change are thorough qualitative and quantitative research and analysis, a professional change management programme and, of course, a design that ensures the new beginning is a positive experience for everyone involved.

4

1 Diagram showing the organisational analysis process and research phase
2 Productivity in relation to workplace design (based on 44,300 survey responses analysed by DEGW between 2006 and 2009). Lost time and time to obtain feedback are based on individual responses. Distractions include both interruptions and noise disturbance.
3 Flexible workspace concept consisting of a landscape of different types of office space. It supports knowledge sharing, improves communication and collaboration and, by using space more efficiently, contributes to enhanced profitability.
4 A modern office design promotes creativity, facilitates teamwork and communicates organisational culture and values.
5 Benefits of the new workspace design.
6 Innovative workspace design for a Sydney-based international real-estate company. Alongside commercial aspects the design considered factors such as environmental performance, teamwork and staff well-being.

Criteria	Result	Objective
Costs	• Improved real-estate portfolio performance • Reduction in real-estate operating costs	-15–50%[1] costs
Performance	• Increased productivity of individuals and teams • Environment supports knowledge sharing and innovation	+5–40%[1] output
Employee satisfaction	• Organisation becomes an "Employer of Choice" • Reflection of organisational culture and values in the workspace design	+10–40%[1] employee satisfaction
Sustainability	• Reduction of CO_2 emissions • Corporate Social Responsibility	-15–50%[1] CO_2 emissions

5   [1] Data provided by DEGW

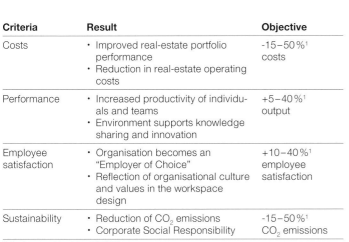

6

Ergonomic workplace design

Sylke Neumann

Ergonomics is the science concerned with designing to fit the human body most efficiently. In designing and equipping workplaces and work processes, the consideration of ergonomic principles is expected of the architect, interior designer, acoustic and lighting designers, as well as of the employer. But what exactly does that mean – designing to fit the human body? How can one guarantee that the workplace and processes fit the human body and human needs?

In 1943 the American psychologist, Abraham Maslow, published his book, "Hierarchy of Needs" [1], which lists human needs in a pyramid structure where one builds on another. Only when the needs of the lower level are met will a person become conscious of the latent, higher-level needs and strive to fulfil them. In this model, the basic physical human needs, such as food, shelter, sleep, health, movement and sexuality, form the base of the pyramid. Above this comes the need for safety and security, social interactions and relationships and the need for self-esteem and recognition. Right at the top of the pyramid, Maslow's model lists self-actualisation, individuality, creativity and beliefs.

The Hierarchy of Needs model can be adapted for the design of workplaces (fig. 2, p. 40) [2]. Here, first of all, the work itself has to be feasible. This may sound obvious, but it can be quite a problem, when, for example, a call centre's acoustic design is insufficient, thereby making it impossible for staff to have a telephone conversation. Equally, it must be possible to perform the task safely, without the risk of accidents or injury. The aim of ergonomic design is to enable workers to carry out their tasks without jeopardising health or well-being – e.g. without developing back pain or being exposed to glare from the sun or computer screen, or suffer stress due to extreme noise levels etc. The prerequisite for this are having the right tools for the job, an optimal workplace set-up and sensible organisation of the work itself. Only once the basic need of being able to perform a task safely and without discomfort has been addressed, is it possible to work creatively on solutions and improvements, develop your own ideas and identify with the organisation you work for, its objectives and philosophy.

Of course, it is still possible for someone to work productively and creatively under adverse conditions for a few months, or perhaps even years, "because the job requires it". But not in the long run as is evident in the rising number of work-related musculo-skeletal and psychological disorders. Given the demographic situation in industrialised countries, their economy will increasingly rely on an older workforce.

Good ergonomic design of workplaces is therefore crucial for ensuring and maintaining a physically and mentally healthy workforce.

Guidelines and quality benchmarks

Every designer knows the relevant rules and regulations, standards and guidelines and uses them as starting point, quality benchmark and reference. Occasionally these rules may also feel like bureaucratic red tape that stifle creativity. Rules that apply to the design of workplaces and offices include work safety regulations and technical factsheets, health and safety guidelines for VDU work, standards and guidelines regarding computer screens and keyboards, desks, swivel chairs, lighting, indoor climate and acoustics. There are rules and recommendations for the height of ceilings and banisters, the width of corridors and the depth of stairs. From the minimum number of toilets and urinals to the recommended colours to be used on walls and floors, these documents contain almost everything the designer needs to know – and perhaps also enough to inhibit his or her imagination and creative flow. Furthermore, there are also economic and environmental factors to consider.

Only regulations are legally binding. However, they usually only point towards general objectives, such as allowing "sufficient" room to change position and for different movements, "adequate" artificial lighting, "acceptable" noise levels, depending on the type of workplace. This kind of phrasing leaves plenty of room for interpretation and is therefore often supplemented with more detailed rules, provided by government or industry guidelines. The so-called "presumption of conformity" (or "presumption of compliance") applies to government regulations. It means that, where the design and construction was based on these regulations, the presumption is that the regulation has been complied with. Rules allow some scope for discretion, provided that the same level of health and safety is maintained. In this case, the responsible party – i.e. the employer – will need to check and approve variations in the design that deviate from the rules.

Standards and recommendations by industry bodies or institutions are generally referred to as "best practice" and can also be used as the agreed basis for designs, in the same way as government regulations. They save the designer a lot of research and individual design decisions while offering all the necessary data to ensure health and safety standards are adhered to in the design. Here, too, there is some room for discretion, as long as this does not compromise the health and safety of future users.

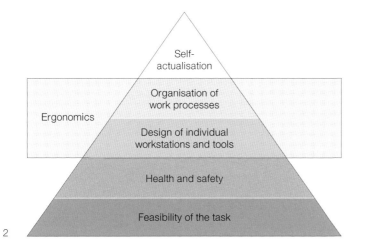

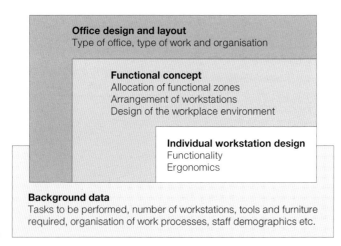

1 The latest in office chair design aims to promote frequent change of position.
2 Abraham Maslow's "Hierarchy of Needs" adapted for workplace design
3 Design aspects within a systematic approach to office design
4 Minimum work surface dimensions
  a single desk
  b split desk
5 Workstation space requirements
6 Minimum space required for user
  a Seated desk work requires a minimum floorspace depth of 1000 mm for the user.
  b For standing tasks using furniture with drawers or pull-out surfaces, the minimum depth required for the office space is derived from the length of the drawer or pull-out surface plus a minimum safety distance of 500 mm.
7 Height-adjustable sit-stand desk

Industry standards and guidelines provide the designer with a framework within which to work, safe in the knowledge that legal compliance is ensured, while still leaving sufficient scope for creative and individual solutions. They give designs a solid foundation.

Rules, regulations and standards, however, cannot prescribe how other human needs, those that go beyond ergonomics and health and safety, might be met. For example, the need for an aesthetically appealing work environment, identification with your place of work and your surroundings or for self-expression and creativity. Here, designers can contribute their own ideas and concepts of a pleasant and stimulating work environment and it is up to them to determine to what extent a workplace merely fulfils the basic quality requirements or goes some way beyond that. In order to arrive at a high-quality design a systematic and holistic approach is needed.

A systematic approach to office design
The office runs like clockwork. Staff are able to complete their tasks efficiently and to a high standard. They are highly motivated and contented. Everyone involved in the design process can contribute to this vision. A systematic approach is supported by identifying the different aspects involved in office design (fig. 3) [3]:
· Assembling all relevant background data
· Individual workstation design – ergonomics and functionality
· Overall functional concept – allocation of different functional zones, arrangement of workstations and design of their immediate environment
· Office design and layout – choice of office type depending on work processes and tasks.

There is no magic formula or set approach for working through these different aspects of office design. Rather, it depends on the individual brief and whether it is a redesign of an existing office, an office relocation or a newbuild project.

Background data
At the beginning of every design project there is background research. In order to achieve a high-quality design it is important that this is performed thoroughly and involves all stakeholders. In terms of ergonomics the following information needs to be obtained:
· tasks to be performed
· number of workstations
· tools and furniture needed in order to perform the tasks
· organisation of work processes
· staff demographics (i.e. gender and age distribution, need for accessibility)

Individual workstation design
The workstation design concept sets out how individual workstations should be arranged to ensure functionality and enable staff to perform their tasks effectively. Starting with each individual member of staff and the tasks they need to perform, the required desk size, storage space, both in the immediate vicinity of the desk (desk caddy, sideboards) and within a short distance (cupboards, filing cabinets, shelves – possibly shared with colleagues), need to be established. The tools and materials (computer screen, keyboard,

paperwork) required to perform the task determine the size and shape of the desk. The minimum desk size should be 1600 mm width and 800 mm depth (fig. 4). For workplaces requiring few tools and materials, for example call centres, the width can be reduced to 1200 mm. The minimum depth remains unchanged, despite the now widespread use of flatscreen monitors.

The more documentation and information is made available in electronic format the less storage space is needed. Space for meetings or client consultation needs to be accommodated too, either by way of extended desk space for face-to-face meetings at the desk, in separate meeting rooms or extended spaces for smaller team meetings, or with fully fledged conference suites and workshop rooms for all staff. European standards for office furniture such as EN 527-1 and EN 1335-1 give minimum dimensions for office tables and desks and detailed specifications for their adjustability, which are based on the physical measurements of the human body. These are derived from anthropometric principles and the so-called 5th and 95th percentile, which means that the ergonomic furniture does not fit the measurements of the shortest 5 % and the tallest 5 % of people. It may also be unsuitable for disabled employees, who may therefore require customised solutions. Beyond these minimum requirements, the DGUV test certificate and the "Quality Office" symbol serve to guarantee ergonomic quality.

The workspace in front of the desk needs to be at least 1000 mm deep (fig. 6). The total depth required for an office workstation is therefore 1800 mm. Where storage space is needed, this is usually provided through a 450-mm-deep cupboard at the back of the workspace.

Sit-stand workstations can help prevent musculo-skeletal problems. It is recommended to change position at least four times per hour: from sitting to standing to walking. This can be achieved in two ways:

- Height-adjustable desks allow work to be carried out both seated or standing at the correct level suited to the individual's own height (fig. 7). Disadvantages of this option include a random, untidy appearance of the desks at different levels in larger offices, and the risk of staff using the facility incorrectly or not at all.
- Staff are provided with desks to work on in a seated position, and caddies, standing desks or tall meeting tables for standing work. The overall appearance of the office can therefore be planned accordingly, but desk heights may not always be optimal for every employee.

The choice of materials, surfaces, shapes and colours of desks and cupboards contributes to the aesthetic appeal of the room and provides a coherent identity. Floor and wall colours and lighting design complete the design concept.

Functional concept
The functional concept identifies the different functional areas and zones within the building (office spaces, communication zones, storage, server room, building services, washrooms and toilets) and within the office areas (e.g. arrangement of workstations). Here, the office workers' various needs – being able to work without disruption, privacy, sufficient space and the ability to communicate with colleagues – must all be taken into account. A successful office design will also provide good orientation, both within the room and towards the outside world.

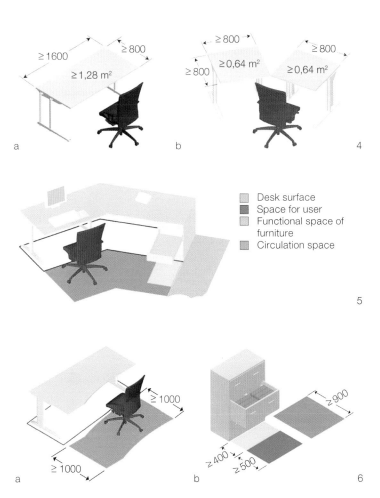

Desk surface
Space for user
Functional space of furniture
Circulation space

41

Depending on the requirements of the specific tasks to be performed, different concepts are developed for each room. The functional concept determines the arrangement of workstations in relation to one another and within the room and thereby also influences how staff members are able to work together and communicate with one another, while, at the same time, minimising unwanted disruption. A certain amount of privacy ought to be maintained. For example, having to work with your back to a door or with colleagues directly overlooking your computer screen can be disconcerting. Sufficient access to daylight and a view of the outside world are also important factors contributing to overall well-being at work. Workstations should be near a window but oriented parallel to it so as to avoid glare or reflections on the computer screen.

Meeting spaces, just as the workstations themselves, will need to accommodate room for cupboards or shelves etc. and circulation spaces at sufficient width must be provided to connect the different zones. Work safety regulations give minimum dimensions for circulation spaces and other defined areas.

Open meeting zones and extended areas, either within an open-plan office or – to avoid disruption – outside the main office space, promote chance encounters and the exchange of thoughts and ideas, which benefits social coherence in the office (fig. 9).

Design factors such as acoustics, lighting, choice of colours and indoor climate, all need to be considered as part of the functional concept. Environmental factors like these define a room's auditory, visual and haptic impression and thereby affect its overall character and atmosphere. Interactions between these different factors can also play an important role. For example, a room is perceived as warm, not only by its actual temperature, but also by using a warm shade of light and choosing warm, yellow, red and brown colours and wood veneers for the furniture. Even acoustic design can contribute to the perception of temperature, as a room with low reverberation can feel warmer than an echoing room.

Acoustics

Especially in office spaces, loud, monotonous and information-rich sounds will be perceived as noise disturbance, even if they are well below the noise levels that are damaging to health. Noise disturbance causes reactions within the human body, such as raised pulse and blood pressure, muscle tension and release of stress hormones. This, in turn, leads to mistakes and adversely affects work performance.

Good office acoustics, therefore, should be considered as part of the original office design process – not as an afterthought when staff are complaining. This is even more important in offices with large areas of glass or concrete. Acoustic design is not merely a matter of reducing noise levels: optimising reverberation times and speech intelligibility is equally important. To achieve this, the room must be equipped with sufficient sound-absorbing surfaces, for example ceiling elements (fig. 12, p. 44), acoustic furniture, partition walls and carpets (see Acoustic design in open-plan offices, pp. 45). Where noise disturbance is likely to come from the outside, windows and walls need to be sufficiently soundproof.

Lighting

The lighting design needs to do more than just provide sufficient light for staff to carry out their work. Light also has a profound effect on the human body. As a result of human evolutionary development in the context of daily and yearly patterns of daylight, the colour, mood and intensity of light can have a stimulating or calming effect. Workstations should, therefore have sufficient access to daylight. It is a natural human need to have different light situations at different times – even if this is provided by artificial light – and to be able to adjust the lighting accordingly (see Planning of integrated daylight and artificial lighting for the work environment, pp. 50).

Section A3.4 of workplace regulations (ASR) in Germany defines the minimum requirements for lighting. An office workstation requires a minimum illumination of 500 lux. If there is little, or no, access to natural daylight, stronger artificial lighting is recommended. Using groups of different luminaires that can be operated and dimmed independently, different lighting scenarios can be created depending on the time of day and requirements of the task. Light bulbs in warm and cool colours can be programmed to create different light intensity and tones – so-called "Dynamic Lighting". The idea here is for the artificial light to mimic the dynamics of natural daylight. For example, warmer and less bright in the morning and at the end of the day, brighter and cooler during the day.

In large office spaces with a flexible workstation arrangement, or in investment properties where the arrangement of desks is not yet known, it is advisable to implement a basic lighting provision of 300 lux to which, for example, floor lamps can then be added to achieve the 500 lux requirement. Using lights with movement and daylight sensors will help save energy. However, staff will also appreciate a desk

8

9

lamp or dimmer switches allowing them to control their own lighting individually (fig. 11).

Colour design
Colour design adds personality to a room (fig. 10). Simply through choice of colour a room can appear professional, straight-laced, elegant, fresh, youthful or funky. Colour choices and combinations can express corporate identity and company culture. Colour psychology is also an important factor to consider here. Lighting and colour design concepts should always be developed hand in hand. The right choice of matching luminaires and light tones supports the desired effect and contributes to an aesthetically appealing and distinctive look.

Indoor climate
ASR A 3.5 on indoor temperature specifies the minimum and maximum temperature in workplaces and the required air quality. For offices, the temperature range should be between 20 and 26 °C, but may be higher on days when the outdoor temperature is above 26 °C, as long as adequate shading is provided. Temperatures above 35 °C are not permitted.
What temperature is perceived as comfortable very much depends on individual preference and is influenced by factors such as gender, physical condition, current mood and the clothes worn. This explains why it is so difficult in larger open-plan offices to achieve an indoor climate that all staff are contented with. The easiest way to "climatise" offices is via a conventional heating system and windows that can be opened. Studies have shown that staff working in rooms with natural ventilation are less likely to suffer from health complaints or "Sick Building Syndrome" [4].
During the summer months, external sun screens can help reduce overheating. In regions where prolonged heatwaves are common, the use of ceiling or floor cooling systems should be considered. In locations where noise could be an issue or where the outdoor air quality is poor, artificial ventilation and air conditioning may be the best option. Air humidifiers for health reasons are not necessary. Recent studies have shown that the human body can obtain the moisture it requires through drinking sufficient water – even in centrally heated rooms in winter [5].
Following a move from smaller to larger offices, staff often complain about health problems, which they attribute to the indoor climate in these larger rooms. The real causes, however, may range from ergonomically inadequate workstations, noise disturbance, poor computer screen resolution or glare, to psychological factors such as personality clashes, problems with line managers or general staff morale issues. This is especially true if staff were not involved in the design of the new offices or had no say in the office move.

Office design and layout
The office design determines the spatial concept best suited to the organisation's work processes. The respective requirements for communication and/or concentration, space for project work or customer consultation, the degree of flexibility required, organisational structures and hierarchies are all factors that influence the design. According to these different needs, various types and formats of office are suitable, ranging from individual offices, team offices for smaller

10

8 Combination of workstations and meeting areas allowing staff to alternate between seated and standing positions.
9 Open extended spaces and canteen areas promote chance meetings and the exchange of ideas.
10 Colour design concept
11 Office lighting concept with floor and desk lamps
12 Open-plan office space with suspended acoustic ceiling elements

11

43

groups, open-plan or newer office concepts known as "Open Space" or "Combi" offices. There are no quality standards or guidelines for the choice of office layout. Here it is a matter of choosing the most suitable format and minimising any disadvantages of the chosen option. (see The world of office work in flux, pp. 11).

Conclusion

Rules, regulations, guidelines and standards provide a frame of reference for ergonomic quality at work. Mere compliance with the rules, however, does not necessarily guarantee quality. To achieve truly high quality standards the interrelationships between the different design aspects need to be considered from the outset. Individual elements that are perfect in themselves, from height-adjustable desks, ergonomic desk chairs and good lighting to ample acoustic surfaces, well-thought-out ventilation and imaginative colour schemes, are still no guarantee for a pleasant office environment. What matters is that all these different elements are looked at holistically and combined into one integrated whole. For every building there are individual solutions which accommodate the need for a comfortable indoor climate, minimum noise disturbance and ideal reverberation levels as well as good lighting and combine all this within an agreeable and ergonomic work environment. This is not something that can be prescribed solely by a guideline or standard. It relies on the knowledge and creativity of the designer.

References:
[1] Abraham Maslow, "A Theory of Human Motivation", Psychological Review, 50 (1943).
[2] Sylke Neumann, "Arbeit & Gesundheit Basics. Ergonomie", Deutsche Gesetzliche Unfallversicherung (ed.) (Wiesbaden 2011)
[3] BGI 5050 Büroraumplanung – Hilfen für das systematische Planen und Gestalten von Büros (June 2009).
[4] Wolfgang Bischof, Gerhard Andreas Wiesmüller, "Das Sick Building Syndrome (SBS) und die Ergebnisse der ProKlimA-Studie", Umwelt-medizin in Forschung und Praxis, 01 (2007), pp. 23–42.
[5] Nadja von Hahn, "'Trockene Luft' und ihre Auswirkungen auf die Gesundheit. Ergebnisse einer Literaturstudie", Gefahrstoffe – Reinhaltung der Luft, 03 (2007), pp. 103–107.

Guidelines, rules and regulations, standards and other information on office and workstation design:
• General
Health & safety guidelines for VDU work (German guideline: BildscharbV).
Work safety regulations (German guideline: ArbStättV).
BGI 650 VDU and office workstations (2007-09) (guidance provided by the Employers Liability Insurance and the Federal Institute for Occupational Health and Safety).
European Directive on Visual Display Units (Directive 90/270 EEC).
DIN 33402-2 Human body dimensions – Part 2: Values (December 2005).

• Office furniture
EN 527-1 Office Furniture – Work Tables and Desks – Part 1: Dimensions (January 2009).
EN 1335-1 Office Furniture – Office Work Chair – Part 1: Dimensions – Determination of Dimensions (August 2002).

• Circulation spaces
German workplace regulation ASR A2.3 Escape routes, emergency exits, escape and emergency plans (August 2007).
DIN 4543-1 Office work place – Part 1: Space for the arrangement and use of office furniture; safety requirements, testing (September 1994).
BGI 5050 Office planning – Assistance for the systematic planning and interior design of offices (June 2009).

• Acoustics
DIN 18041 Acoustic quality in small to medium-sized rooms (May 2004).
VDI 2569 Sound protection and acoustic design in offices (January 1990).
BGI 5141 Office acoustics – Guidance for the acoustic design of offices (July 2011).

• Lighting
German workplace regulation ASR A3.4 Lighting (June 2011).
BGR 131 Natural and artificial lighting in workplaces – Part 1 and 2 (October 2008).
BGI 856 Lighting in Offices – Guidance for the design of artificial lighting in offices (October 2008).
EN 12464-1 Light and Lighting. Lighting of workplaces. Part 1: Indoor workplaces (September 2009).
DIN 5034-1 Daylight in Interior Spaces – Part 1: General requirements (September 2010).
DIN 5035-7 Artificial Lighting – Part 7: Lighting of interior spaces with VDU workstations (August 2004).

• Indoor climate
German workplace regulation ASR A3.5 Indoor Temperature (June 2010).
BGI 827 Solar protection in the office. Assistance in selecting suitable shading and thermal insulation devices at VDU and office workstations (March 2006).

12

Acoustic design in open-plan offices

Rainer Machner

The noisy work environment is one of the most-cited problems when it comes to user acceptance of open-plan offices. A study by the University of Lucerne reveals that spaces where more than only seven people work in the same room are rated as satisfactory by fewer than 30 % of users, while more than 60 % complain about an inability to concentrate in open-plan offices [1].

However, acoustic optimisation measures can achieve a considerable improvement in acceptance, concludes the study "Sound Design of Open Plan Offices" [2], published in 2010, which focused specifically on the problems of acoustics and noise levels in open-plan offices. The study took its starting point in the widely accepted premise that telephone conversations and conversations between other colleagues cause the most distraction for those not involved in them.

Reverberation time, a commonly used term in acoustic design, changes in accordance with its distance from the source of the sound. It also refers mainly to simple orthogonal room shapes with a regular sound field. The researchers therefore based their work on the theory that a larger room needs different criteria to assess its acoustic quality. The aim of the study was to show which other acoustic parameters, such as sound intensity, speech intelligibility, spatial decay etc., are most relevant for creating a well-accepted open-plan office environment that supports effective performance at work. A detailed analysis of the privacy radius between adjacent workstations was not part of the research.

Improved acceptance after acoustic optimisation measures

The study was conducted among employees of five major Scandinavian companies who had volunteered their open-plan offices for the purposes of the study.

A user survey, developed by Stockholm University, was conducted alongside the measurement of acoustic parameters, which was carried out by specialist Swedish acoustic consultants. The initial surveys showed a relatively low level of user satisfaction. The acoustic quality of the work environment, and its impact on work performance, was an especially frequent complaint. The tasks of the office workers surveyed were centred around telecommunication, alternating with phases requiring concentration: typically conflict-prone requirements. Once the current noise levels had been taken and the current situation assessed and analysed, optimising measures were carried out in one open-plan office per organisation.

By way of example, the measures and their results are detailed for a participating electricity supplier as follows: a Helpdesk office of 18 × 11 metres houses around 20 members of staff, mostly working in groups of four. At the start of the study, opposite desks were screened off from each other with 1.16-metre-high sound-absorbing panels. The floor finish was vinyl, with needle felt used for the central corridor. Above the workstations was a suspended sound-absorbing grid ceiling; no sound-absorbing material was installed on the ceiling above the central corridor.

As part of the acoustic improvement measures, sound-absorbing elements were fitted on the ceiling above the corridor. Each cluster of four workstations had a ceiling canopy installed at a height of 2.1 metres. In addition to their acoustic benefits, these canopies also help to break up the room visually thereby enhancing its spatial quality. The existing screens between desks were replaced with double-sided highly sound-absorbing partition walls. To allow visual contact between colleagues, the upper section of the 1.2-metre-high panels were made of glass. As an additional element, a sound-absorbing panel doubling up as a pinboard was added to one wall.

Before the acoustic optimisation measures, 60 % of the employees surveyed had rated the acoustic environment in their offices as poor or very poor. Following the interventions, only 10 % still ranked the acoustic conditions as poor. Overall acceptance of the open-plan offices increased to 60 % in the professionally soundproofed environments. Especially for tasks requiring a high level of concentration, the study showed a marked increase in user satisfaction.

Transparency instead of "cocooning"

What tends to happen in open-plan offices is a gradual "cocooning" of workstations, which is counterproductive and defies the whole concept of open-plan working. Against this background, the study's findings regarding the partition panels are particularly interesting. In the initial survey, 73 % of those surveyed had rated the performance of the existing screening elements as poor or very poor, especially when colleagues on the opposite side were talking on the telephone. The new elements using a combination of sound-proofing and glass, on the other hand, were rated as poor by only 20 % and no longer received any 'very poor' ratings. When it came to screening out noise from conversations between other colleagues, the new elements were rated as poor by only 30 %, as opposed to 79 % 'poor' or 'very poor' ratings before the optimisation measures.

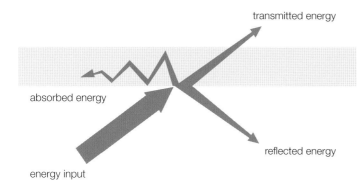

$$\text{absorption coefficient } \alpha = \frac{\text{absorbed energy} + \text{transmitted energy}}{\text{energy input}}$$

This result supports the call for transparency in open-plan offices. People are more prepared to accept noise if they can see its source. High partition walls without visual contact create a simulated private space where noise from an invisible source, such as telephone conversations in the adjacent space, is more likely to be perceived as a nuisance. If, in addition to the noise level itself, the content of the conversation can be overheard, the disturbance is amplified, especially when trying to perform cognitive tasks.

Spatial decay as a key quality criterion

Among the location-specific criteria that measure sound selectively rather than for the whole room (such as reverberation time), the spatial decay showed a notable link with the improved subjective evaluation by employees. It describes how the sound pressure level decreases in line with its distance from the source of the sound and therefore allows for location-specific conclusions to be drawn. The study concluded that the "spatial decay" was therefore a more suitable term than "reverberation time".

From the spatial decay, the so-called "radius of distraction" can be derived, the point at which the sound pressure has decreased to a level that is no longer perceived as distracting. Based on this, recommendations can be made about the ideal distance between workspaces with conflicting demands. Thanks to the study, the spatial decay descriptor originally used in the design of industrial workplaces is being adopted in the revised Part 3 of ISO 3382, which describes the parameters of room acoustics in open-plan spaces. In open-plan spaces, the acoustic qualities of the ceiling decisively influence sound propagation and therefore sound level reduction. Highly sound-absorbing materials, distributed evenly across the ceiling, can help reduce overall noise levels significantly. In order to achieve a reduction of visual, as well as acoustic distractions over short distances, it is imperative that workstations which, due to their mix of different types of tasks are likely to cause disruption to one other, are screened using sound-absorbing partitions that still enable visual contact.

Equivalent absorption area in open-plan offices

The general rule of thumb is: the larger the equivalent absorption area, the less noisy the room. The German standard for acoustic quality in small to medium-sized rooms, DIN 18041, gives guideline figures for the absorption areas needed to fulfil basic acoustic requirements for different room types. An open-plan office space, for example, requires an equivalent absorption area of 90–100 % in relation to its floorspace.

The equivalent absorption area can be derived from the absorption coefficient of the materials used. In principle, every material responds in one of three possible ways when hit by sound waves (fig. 1): it absorbs the sound and converts it into a different energy form (absorption), it lets the sound waves pass through (transmission), or it reflects them back into the room (reflection). In order to objectively describe the acoustic qualities of a material it is necessary to look at the behaviour of the material in terms of these three vectors, in relation to the respective sound frequency and construction used.

The result is the absorption coefficient α, also known as attenuation coefficient, which has a value between 0 and 1, whereby $\alpha = 0$ corresponds to 100 % reflection and $\alpha = 1.0$

2

means 100 % absorption. An overview of the classification of different materials and their sound absorption can be found in EN ISO 11654. It assesses the absorption coefficients for different frequencies and categorises them in Sound Absorption Classes ranging from Class A to Class E. For example, a material that is highly absorbing at the frequency of human speech is categorised as Class A. Using porous materials such as glass wool on the ceiling has a much better sound-absorbing effect than plasterboard ceiling panels.

Individual design of good room acoustics

As the Scandinavian study has shown, the measurement of reverberation time on its own is not sufficient for a design concept that is to be successful in the long term. Spatial decay is the more important measure; this also means that a highly sound-absorbing acoustic ceiling is imperative Another result of the study is the recognition that the type of work to be performed strongly influences the individual and subjective assessment of acoustic comfort. Comparing the initial, pre-optimisation survey results from the Helpdesk office and the finance department, two identical open-plan offices with very similar acoustic measurements, the subjective evaluation by staff working in these offices arrived at very different results. Although, for example, all colleagues at the finance department and 40 % of the Helpdesk staff regarded that the existing partition panels as being inadequate in terms of screening noise from conversations, not one person in the finance department felt that the noise had a negative impact on their performance. In the Helpdesk office, on the other hand, the initial survey showed that 66 % of staff members felt the noise was affecting their concentration. After the optimisation measures this figure dropped to 30 %. The conductors of the study concluded that the reason for this discrepancy is due to in the different types of work. Whereas the finance department is characterised mainly by quiet individual work, the Helpdesk work involves regular telephone conversations – one of the major sources of noise disruption in open-plan offices.

Matching acoustic measures to the primary type of work performed

In planning acoustic design measures for open-plan offices it is important not to rely on physical measurements alone. Rather, the different types of tasks to be carried out in the office need to be taken into account. Technical considerations and their architectural solutions need to be a secondary issue. First of all, the different communication processes taking place in each room and the needs of staff members concerned must be established. This approach, however, requires a thorough understanding of internal processes within the organisation. Staff movements and tasks performed give important clues as to the different zones that need to be created within the office. Finding a right balance will have a significant impact on overall acceptance of the

3

Room type and usage	• Call centres and offices with high levels of communication			
	• Reading rooms and libraries			
	• Workshops			
	• Retail spaces			
Sound Absorption Class	A	B	C	D
Absorption performance of material used	extremely absorbing $\alpha_w =$ 1.00–0.90	extremely absorbing $\alpha_w =$ 0.85–0.80	highly absorbing $\alpha_w =$ 0.75–0.60	absorbing $\alpha_w =$ 0.55–0.3[1]
Area to be equipped with sound-absorbing surface[2]	90–100 %	110 %	120–150 %	160–200 %

[1] Materials with an absorption coefficient of $\alpha_w < 0.45$ are not suitable for this purpose.
[2] These values are calculated on the basis of standard floor heights. Space occupied by other surfaces, e.g. lights, ventilation outlets etc., should not be included in the calculations.

Room type and usage	• Open-plan or group offices with electronic office equipment (printers, faxes etc.)			
	• Banks, ticket offices, etc.			
	• Public buildings (citizens advice, council offices)			
Sound Absorption Class	A	B	C	D
Absorption performance of material used	extremely absorbing $\alpha_w =$ 1.00–0.90	extremely absorbing $\alpha_w =$ 0.85–0.80	highly absorbing $\alpha_w =$ 0.75–0.60	absorbing $\alpha_w =$ 0.55–0.3[1]
Area to be equipped with sound-absorbing surface[2]	70–80 %	80–90 %	90–120 %	130–200 %

[1] Materials with an absorption coefficient of $\alpha_w < 0.35$ are not suitable for this purpose.
[2] These values are calculated on the basis of standard floor heights. Space occupied by other surfaces, e.g. lights, ventilation outlets etc., should not be included in the calculations

1 The three different responses to sound energy
2 Acoustic quality and contemporary design are not mutually exclusive, as this example using highly sound-absorbing free hanging units shows.
3 Thermally activated concrete ceilings cannot be covered up with sound-absorbing material. Instead, well-positioned, highly sound-absorbing free hanging units can be used for acoustic optimisation.
4 In corridors measures should be taken to prevent noise affecting adjacent offices, for example by fitting an acoustic ceiling (according to DIN 18041).

4

 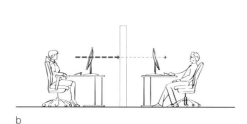 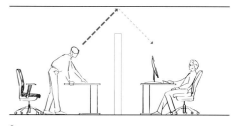

5 a   b   c

6

work environment. Where should the coffee lounge be located? Where are the printer and fax machine? How should individual workstations be arranged? All these questions need to be explored and answered in order to minimise noise disruption.

In the modern-day business world, open-plan offices are becoming the accepted standard due to their proven positive effects on work processes in general. Staff, too, cite the improved opportunities for communicating with colleagues, and the resulting exchange of information and knowledge, as an advantage of the open-plan layout. A general dislike of open-plan offices per se doesn't seem to exist. Criticism is mainly focused around the conflict between communication and concentration, which is typical for larger rooms and appears to increase with the size of the room. Getting the acoustic design right is therefore a key challenge for architects dealing with open-plan offices.

Acoustic comfort in any type of building

It may not always be possible to achieve acoustic comfort in an open-plan office by installing a highly sound-absorbing acoustic ceiling across the entire length and width of the room. Nevertheless, buildings with concrete core cooling, for example, where the ceiling cannot be covered up for thermal reasons, can still benefit from acoustic optimisation. Depending on the type of ventilation system, such buildings can be equipped with acoustic ceiling canopies, slats or baffles to reduce noise levels. The sound-absorbing properties of baffles depend on a variety of factors, including their spacing. Their effectiveness can be further enhanced by suspending them from the ceiling. Ceiling canopies, however, have a notably better sound absorption compared to baffles or slats.

In buildings without thermo-active components, technical elements such as lights, ventilation outlets and fire alarms can be easily integrated into an acoustic ceiling using a standard raster ceiling. Linearly arranged acoustic ceiling systems allow the incorporation of technical components in a systematic way, thereby preserving a homogenous appearance of the room.

Due to the different organisational and architectural starting points there is no standard solution for the acoustic design of open-plan offices. Every office is different in terms of built structure and room layout. Tasks and activities of users, too, vary enormously. The individual requirements for creating a pleasant working environment therefore have to be arrived at on a case-by-case basis.

7

8

9

References:
[1] Lucerne University of Applied Sciences and Arts – Department of Technology & Architecture (and others), SBiB-Studie – Schweizerische Befragung in Büros (Lucerne 2010).
[2] Nordic Innovation Center, Sound Design of Open Plan Offices (Oslo 2010).

Collaboration: Petra Lasar

5   Three key elements in acoustic design:
     a Provision of sufficient sound-absorbing materials, for example on the ceiling. Adequate sound-attenuation is the basic starting point in acoustic design.
     b Zoning according to defined work areas with quiet spaces and individual rooms, supported by soundproof screens to separate individual workstations.
     c Control of sound propagation: sound propagation is primarily determined by the physical boundaries of the room – in particular the ceiling and partition walls.
6   For thermo-active building systems, acoustic baffles or slats offer a suitable solution.
7   To allow flexibility for future reorganisation of the office, ceiling canopies above individual workstations were used instead of a fixed acoustic ceiling.
8–9 Even open-plan spaces can offer a quiet working environment. An acoustic ceiling, using an Absorption Class A material and covering the entire length and width of the ceiling area, ensures sufficient sound attenuation. In addition, furniture and transparent acoustic screens help interrupt the sound waves and reduce noise distraction. Separate rooms and areas for quiet work were introduced to provide a space for cognitive work requiring complete concentration.
10   In corridors measures should be taken to prevent noise affecting adjacent offices, for example by fitting an acoustic ceiling.

10

Planning of integrated daylight and artificial lighting for the work environment

Katja Schölzig

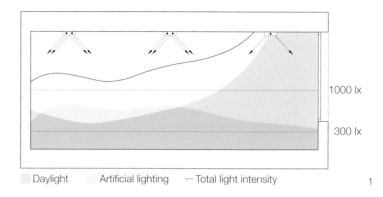

Daylight   Artificial lighting   — Total light intensity

A good lighting concept should be established at an early stage in the planning phase. The spatial geometry, the size, shape, orientation and type of windows, the materials and colours and the surrounding structures are all factors in determining how much natural light can penetrate into a room. As daylight is always the best light, it should be exploited to the full before artificial lighting concepts are considered. It is therefore vital to include a lighting planner as early as possible in the design process.

Any lighting concept should centre around the user. A long-term lighting plan should therefore take into account the users' well-being and comfort.

Use of daylight

Daylight is the most energy-efficient way of lighting a room. Our vision, the way our body functions and our behaviour are adapted and react to natural light. Its constantly changing quality stimulates the organism, increases well-being and fosters creativity. A sensitive approach to daylight and artificial lighting is very important in terms of the performance and health of users of buildings.

The quality of daylight in a room is assessed objectively by dividing it into diffuse and direct components. While diffuse light is essential for lighting a room, the direct component, sunlight, is useful for creating the right kind of atmosphere. In offices with computer workstations direct sunlight and high light density are disruptive. Strong contrasts are tiring for the eyes as they have to accommodate continually, particularly with reflective surfaces such as monitors. The aim of daylight planning for offices should therefore be to exploit diffuse light as much as possible while avoiding direct sunlight. This can be done, for example, with the appropriate solar protection. At the International Coffee Plaza in Hamburg a system was developed whereby the slats on the facade open and close depending on the position of the sun. Thanks to the semi-transparent construction, daylight can enter the building even when the slats are closed. The view of the harbour and city remains unobstructed and the occupants can relax their eyes during their breaks as they look out into the distance. The sophisticated combination of daylight and solar protection enables the building to be lit almost exclusively by natural light during working hours (fig. 3).

Deflection of daylight

There are situations, however, in which diffuse light cannot penetrate sufficiently into the room even with a large number of windows. This is usually because of the obstruction of surrounding buildings. Before considering artificial lighting, the possibility of deflecting the daylight should be studied. This can be achieved with deflecting mirrors and prisms or the less conventional light tubes or optical fibres, which transport the sunlight to the desired area of the building.

An example of mirror deflection can be seen in a six-storey office building in Hamburg which was designed with an inner courtyard to ensure that as many offices as possible would have access to natural light (fig. 4). However, due to building constraints, the courtyard opening was too small. The precisely computed mirror system at the bottom of the courtyard deflects the diffuse daylight so that the offices in the lower storeys receive sufficient natural light. The asymmetrical pyramid structure distributes the light where it is needed. Most of the light is reflected into the bottom floor to achieve the minimum daylight quota specified by the DIN standard.

For the atmospheric component, a heliostat system is to be installed. This set of mirrors on the roof tracks the sun continuously, reflecting some of the sunlight onto a wall in the inner courtyard that has no workstations behind it but can be seen from the offices on the opposite side. In this way the stimulating and constantly changing sunlight is transmitted inside the building.

Model testing

Diffuse and direct light are equally important in the creation of an atmosphere in which users feel comfortable. Crucial to this remains in what amounts the two light components are used. The comfort level of a room cannot be determined through calculations and visualisations alone and the atmosphere can be judged only through the direct and subjective effect of the light on the users. It is therefore useful to build a scale model in order to study concepts for daylight and/or artificial lighting. This is best done with a model that encloses the observer's entire head. Materials and spatial geometry must be accurately reproduced. A study using models with an artificial sky and different daylight simulations will enable the client to have a feeling of familiarity when it comes to the finished building.

Combination of daylight and artificial lighting

An analysis of the daylight situation provides a basis for the planning of artificial lighting and the drafting of specifications. Precise daylight calculations permit artificial light operating times and the corresponding switching circuits, control systems and types of lighting to be determined. This enables the lighting in areas with little daylight to be improved.

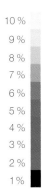
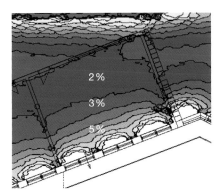

10 %
9 %
8 %
7 %
6 %
5 %
4 %
3 %
2 %
1 %

2 %

3 %

5 %

2

The compensation principle, originally designed for schools, is a very good example of a daylight-dependent artificial lighting concept in which the available daylight is supplemented by the correct amount of artificial light. This enables the lighting in rooms with less daylight to be brought up to the level of naturally lit areas. As mentioned earlier, light has a great impact on the human organism. Certain factors such as the amount of light, the blue light component and the dynamics of changing light have a revitalising and invigorating effect. Together these properties combine to produce bioeffective light and should be taken into account in the overall lighting concept.

In order to foster concentration at work, for example, according to circadian light technology, a light intensity of over 1000 lx is required at a colour temperature of at least 4000 K.

Ideally this is achieved with daylight, and supplementary artificial lighting should be used only if this is not possible. In order to offer all employees a similar quality of environment in differently shaped rooms with varying daylight incidence, the rooms are divided into daylight categories. Artificial light is added as a function of the amount of diffuse daylight available to achieve a combined intensity of 1000 lx. Rooms with bioeffective light from daylight on its own can be equipped with a minimum of artificial light for use only when it is dark outside. This avoids superfluous artificial lighting. It is also useful to install a daylight-dependent light control system to minimise energy consumption and exploit the combination of natural and artificial light to the full. This should provide a total light intensity of 1000 lx for at least one or two hours in the morning (fig. 1).

Planning artificial light

The compensation principle is a lighting arrangement dictated solely by the spatial geometry without taking into account the location of workstations, which are frequently lit by fixed, usually pendant, lighting. The lights are distributed evenly or as a function of the amount of daylight to produce relatively uniform and primarily diffuse lighting for the entire room.

If the room needs to be divided into zones of different brightness, the lighting can be oriented more towards the workstations. In many cases, particularly in open-plan offices, the workstation positions can change and the lighting system ought to be flexible enough to adapt to these alterations, often through the use of standard lamps. These can then be installed directly at the workstation and the light concentrated in that area. The lights should be spaced appropriately, however, so that intermediate zones do not appear too dark.

Even with complicated ceiling constructions it might still be possible to use standard lamps. It must be borne in mind, however, that these normally use compact fluorescent lamps. Linear T16 fluorescent lamps such as those in pendant lamps and compact fluorescent lighting both contain mercury, but only the linear lamps are recyclable. The most energy-saving and environmentally-friendly solution should be sought. In many cases the choice of lighting system also depends on the architect's design criteria.

For artificial office lighting it is usually advisable to select a combination of direct and indirect light with a higher indirect component. This type of light, reflected back from the ceiling, creates diffuse and relatively evenly dispersed, glare-

3

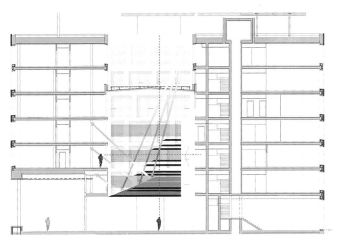

4

5

6

free basic lighting. The direct lighting component focuses on the work area. It helps to achieve the desired lighting intensity and an optimum brightness ratio of 3:1 compared with the surrounding area. This guideline is based on a white ceiling with high reflection. The principle no longer works with a dark ceiling where a different ratio of direct to indirect light has to be considered.

Luminance

Materials, colours and surfaces all have to be taken into account in both artificial and natural light concepts. The human eye is not capable of seeing and assessing luminance directly; it can be perceived only when the light is reflected on a material. Artificial lighting concepts must therefore start by studying the levels of luminance or brightness in a room. When light with a defined intensity, E strikes a matt surface with reflection, ρ, the luminance, L becomes visible and measurable for the eye. The higher the reflection, the more light that is reflected and the brighter the surface appears. When planning the lighting it must ensured that all levels of luminance perceived by the eye are coordinated to achieve stable perception conditions. This means that the work surface should have more luminance than the surrounding area. By categorising luminance in terms of brighter or darker areas, perception priorities and focuses of attention can be defined. Too much contrast is disruptive and dazzling, but too little is lacklustre and unfocused. The different zones in a given situation need to be defined and the most appropriate levels of luminance achieved.

When evaluating and categorising levels of luminance vertical surfaces should also be taken into account. As they are in the viewer's direct field of vision and are usually large, they can often appear brighter than horizontal surfaces with the same luminance but which seem smaller in perspective. The DIN standards generally provide specifications for horizontal luminance. This is a sensible approach when it comes to the workplace itself, but if the overall impression is being considered, all surfaces need to be taken into account. In the case of facades with a large amount of glass, illuminated back walls have the advantage that they make the building appear transparent, bright and inviting during periods of the day when there is less light.

Choice of light source

Only after the luminance distribution and zone priorities have been determined should the question of light sources be considered. Energy consumption, colour temperature, colour rendering, service life and recyclability should be taken into account along with glare, light characteristics and efficiency. The choice is ultimately dependent on the area in which the light is to be installed. Apart from diffuse general room and workplace lighting, for example, additional workplace lighting with a halogen lamp is recommended. This enables the light to be adapted to the individual person's vision. Halogen lamps offer the best possible colour rendering in a light spectrum similar to daylight combined with a warm light and sharp shadow definition. Together with the general room lighting they illuminate objects, shapes and colours in a natural fashion. As the lamps are usually switched on in the evening and used only in defined workplaces areas, the higher energy consumption compared with fluorescent lamps and the shorter service life are acceptable trade-offs for the better colour rendering and agreeable character of the lighting.

There has been great progress in LED technology in the last few years making this technology also a viable alternative. Apart from the light yield, the developments have also focused on colour rendering, and LEDs now achieve Ra colour rendering values of 95. The technology is developing extremely rapidly, and LEDs have the advantage of being recyclable and not containing mercury.

A blue LED in front of which colour-changing luminescent materials are installed initially generates white light in all colour temperatures. The blue receptor in the human eye, which influences the day-night rhythm and the hormone metabolism, reacts to the blue colour. LED lamps are also dimmed by pulse width modulation (PMW), in other words rapid switching on and off in a frequency that is not visible to the human eye. Since the effects of LED technology on the human physiology have not been sufficiently studied to date, LED lamps should be included in lighting concepts only as additional components in combination with other lighting systems or for illuminating workplaces that are occupied only for a short time.

An example of an LED-based lighting concept is the plenary chamber of the North Rhine Westphalia state parliament, where most of the workplaces are used only intermittently. A constant current process is used for dimming to avoid flicker during TV recording and to achieve an ideally tolerated lighting situation for the human eye. The LED light is generated by conversion at a warm white colour temperature. In combination with reflector systems it produces a light atmosphere similar to a downlight system with halogen lamps but with far lower energy consumption. The users were able to test the effect of the lighting in advance on a simulation model and are highly satisfied with the impression of space that the concept creates in the finished building (figs. 8 and 9).

Conclusion

To create a light atmosphere in which building occupants feel comfortable it is important to take account of functional aspects throughout the entire planning phase: atmospheric effects and also the biological influences of natural and artificial light on the human organism and to verify these factors if necessary through studies. The optimum exploitation of daylight, combined with artificial light used merely as a supplement, is not only the most energy-efficient but also the healthiest solution for humans. New technology and research findings help to generate sustainable lighting concepts but need to be examined critically.

5 Office building, Mainzer Landstrasse, Frankfurt (GE) 2003, BRT Architekten
  The use of pendant lamps permits flexible, yet integrated lighting arrangements adapted to the office layout.
6 Office building, Mainzer Landstrasse, Frankfurt (GE) 2003, BRT Architekten
  The distinctive inner courtyard atmosphere is achieved through the interaction of the outer appearance of the office areas and the illumination of the conservatory gardens, which is adapted to the vegetation planted in them.
7 Conference room, Radio Bremen (GE) 2008, Böge Lindner K2 Architekten
  The lamp clusters – one diffuse and two directed lights – are flush-mounted in the dark compartmentalised metal ceiling structure.
8 Scale model of the plenary chamber, North Rhine Westphalia state parliament, Düsseldorf (GE) 2004, Eller + Eller Architekten
  Authentic materials and miniaturised LED lamps provide a realistic impression of the atmosphere.
9 Plenary chamber, North Rhine Westphalia state parliament, Düsseldorf (GE) 2004, Eller + Eller Architekten
  Although the plenary chamber is fully lit by LED lamps, it has the pleasant atmosphere of a room illuminated by halogen lamps.

7

8

9

User satisfaction as a measure of workplace quality in the office

Andreas Wagner, Karin Schakib-Ekbatan

User satisfaction – an (un)fathomable term?

User satisfaction and comfort as concepts have a strong link with the planning, design and use of interior spaces. Yet, although most people have a general idea of what they stand for, possibly even some criteria for defining them, summarising these two terms in a clear and concise definition remains elusive. When it comes to describing the effects of the built environment on people – depending on the professional context or the focus of a particular study – in addition to satisfaction, factors such as well-being, comfort, health or stress levels tend to be examined. (fig. 2). To aid clarity in the discussion below, some definitions of terminology are listed below.

In psychological models about subjective well-being, satisfaction tends to be defined as a "cognitive component". In the context of workplace quality, this may be understood as a process of balanced evaluation, where aspects such as expectations and experience (e.g. from previous employment) can influence the positive and negative assessment of the work environment.

The term comfort is usually associated with sensory perception, including the physical reaction to environmental stimuli such as temperature, light intensity or noise levels. Since these stimuli are always processed with some subjective interpretation – which will vary from one person to another – the assessment of comfort levels is subject to individual evaluation processes. Equally, satisfaction and sense of comfort do not necessarily have to correspond. For example, someone may be dissatisfied with the level or quality of lighting, or would prefer it to be different, but would nevertheless still perceive it to be within the acceptable range.

By comparing the sensory perception of users with threshold levels generated under scientific conditions, the definition of comfort with all its different aspects – thermal, olfactory, visual, auditory – can be narrowed down more easily than the broader term of "user satisfaction"; although the latter can also be delineated to some extent through aspects such as satisfaction with the thermal comfort level. Thermal comfort is also the best researched aspect, as it is mainly influenced by the four measurable dimensions of air temperature, surface temperature of the surrounding walls and surfaces, air velocity and humidity. With this information, together with information about clothing and activity of the users studied, an average comfort rating can be predicted [1]. This is likely to match the subjective user rating relatively well, at least in fully climatised buildings [2].

Interestingly, this does not apply during the summer months in buildings without air conditioning, where users are able to influence the indoor climate themselves, e.g. by opening the window. Instead there appears to be a correlation between the temperature perceived as comfortable by the users and the average outdoor temperature. This suggests that a number of adaptation processes take place (choice of clothing, fluid intake, interaction with the building, etc.) in order to adjust to both the external temperature and that within the building. At this point, the domain of measurable parameters is exhausted and it becomes clear that an understanding of thermal comfort is not limited to physical factors alone. This is referred to as the "adaptive thermal comfort model". The same is true for olfactory, visual and acoustic comfort. The question is therefore, how broad the scope of data to be gathered needs to be in order to obtain sufficient insight into the level of user satisfaction with their workplace environment.

Which factors influence user satisfaction?

The physical work environment comprises built elements, adjustable aspects such as lighting, temperature, air quality, acoustics/noise levels, as well as ergonomic and design aspects. The relationships between physical and subjective factors, i.e. between the individual and his/her environment, are extremely complex and not at all clear-cut. Satisfaction with, and acceptance of, the work environment are, for example, influenced by the extent of control individuals have over their immediate surroundings, e.g. by adjusting the temperature.

A study on user satisfaction in offices also revealed that it is often not the temperature itself, but the feedback received

1

when changes to the indoor climate were sought that had the most profound impact on users' satisfaction with thermal conditions (fig. 3) [3].

Furthermore, the characteristics of the individual work environment, spacial design, organisational, psychological and social conditions of the workplace itself were also found to be relevant. The subjective assessment of workplace satisfaction is therefore influenced by multilayered and complex factors, which go beyond the actual workplace and also include architectural qualities of the building.

How can user satisfaction be measured?

In the design of buildings, methods of measurement exist for all the aforementioned aspects of comfort, together with recommendations and guidelines for minimum and maximum thresholds. Naturally, these can only be based on physical parameters. Beyond that, there are also a number of complex calculations and simulations that can be used to further examine individual aspects. Questions about comfort can therefore be addressed on the basis of the quality of the design data. However, psychological aspects, e.g. user actions that are triggered by certain environmental conditions, are not taken into account by these tools. An exception to this is the Adaptive Comfort Model [4], although, here too, it is not yet possible to use models to describe individual adaptation mechanisms.

In order to gain a better understanding of the factors influencing comfort and be able to assess the workplace from a user perspective, methods are being developed and tested that measure the general level of user satisfaction at work and communicate this in simple and easily comparable figures. On the one hand, this will enable improvements to planning instruments to be made, while on the other hand providing tools for optimising existing work environments that are already in use. For this, the various comfort parameters of the workplace and building in their entirety are subjected to statistical analysis and correlated to the architectural design concepts. The following describes, by way of example, a methodology used by the Karlsruhe Institute of Technology (KIT), which also takes insights from architectural psychology into account [5].

The methodology involves a survey of a representative number of employees in each building. In practice this is a random sample of between 30 and 100 people, depending on the size of the organisation. Age and gender distribution should reflect that of the organisation as accurately as possible. The survey itself was carried out using a standardised questionnaire, based on an existing survey questionnaire compiled by the Center for the Built Environment (CBE) at the University of California Berkeley, which was adapted to match the situation in offices in Germany.

Users were given the option of completing the questionnaire on paper or electronically using their computer at work. In addition to individual questions about relevant comfort parameters, a summarising question at the end of each section asked about the overall satisfaction with this particular parameter (fig. 4). The survey was carried out twice per building surveyed, once in summer and once in winter, in order to capture the climatic extremes.

On the basis of the data gathered it was possible, using multivariate statistical methods, to arrive at firm conclusions about perceived comfort levels and satisfaction with the workplace environment, and to identify relationships between

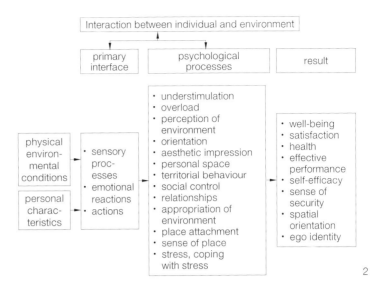

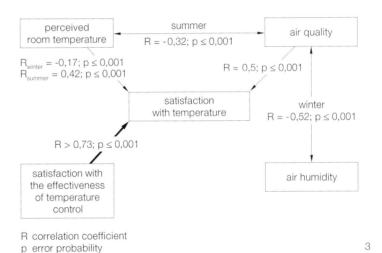

R correlation coefficient
p error probability

1 The indoor climate, ergonomic and design aspects all influence user satisfaction.
2 Basic model of the interactions between individual and environment
3 Interrelationships between different aspects of indoor climate and overall satisfaction with room temperature
4 Sample page from the KIT user satisfaction survey

F Indoor climate at your workplace

Temperature

How do you perceive the **temperature** at your workplace **at this moment?**

cold ⃝ ⃝ ⃝ ⃝ ⃝ ⃝ ⃝ hot

If you had a choice, how would you **prefer** the temperature to be?

much cooler ⃝ ⃝ ⃝ ⃝ ⃝ much warmer

Overall, how satisfied/dissatisfied are you
with the **temperature** at your workplace **at this time of year?**

very dissatisfied 👎 ⃝ ⃝ ⃝ ⃝ ⃝ 👍 very satisfied

4

55

the different influencing factors. The methodology has so far been used to assess more than 40 buildings (around 4,000 sets of data), of varying age and energy-efficiency standards.

Insights gained from user assessment data and their application in planning

Users consider environmental parameters, such as air quality, light, temperature and acoustics or noise levels, as important or even very important for their well-being at work. However, in the everyday running of a building it often seems difficult to achieve high user satisfaction with these parameters, especially during the hotter months. This is partly due to individual differences in temperature preference, but reasons for a negative score here can also clearly be found in specific features of the building itself. These include: inadequate or non-existent protection against glare and sunlight, which affects thermal and visual comfort, fully glazed facades that increase the risk of overheating, windows that cannot be opened, therefore not allowing individual control of ventilation, and offices that open towards an inner courtyard or atrium and therefore lack access to natural daylight – especially on the lower floors of a building. All of these are well-known issues, yet are still often ignored in the design of office buildings, or at least not given sufficient attention. As a result users are forced to come up with improvised solutions, such as sticking paper on the window panes to screen out the glare.

Another aspect is automated control of lighting, air quality and temperature. While on the one hand an important prerequisite for a work environment that is free from distractions, too much technology or technology with functional deficien-

cies can often do more harm than good. Examples include badly configured lighting control systems, poorly adjusted ventilation that dries out the air in winter, or automated external blinds that open and close randomly because of oversensitive wind guards. Some level of manual control can significantly improve acceptance here.

A particularly sensitive subject is acoustics, especially levels of noise – an area where options for individual control are relatively limited. Insufficient sound protection against neighbouring offices is perceived as especially irritating and having a negative impact on concentration.

There is a clear correlation between dissatisfaction with different comfort parameters and office layout and design. There are two discernable groups in this: accommodating between one and four people offices versus open-plan offices (fig. 5). In the latter case, lack of privacy and quiet spaces to work are important factors in the assessment of workplace satisfaction. Glass walls between office and corridors are also often perceived negatively, both in terms of the distraction they cause and the sense of "being watched". What may sound attractive when packaged as "efficient use of space" and "transparency", can turn out to be rather disruptive and adversely affect employee efficiency. The latest user-orientated approaches, known as "combi-office", use flexible allocation of space to cater for different workplace and communication requirements.

In the light of all these different aspects and parameters, how can staff satisfaction of their workplace environment be improved? Field studies have shown that satisfaction is best achieved, or even enhanced, when user needs, requirements of the task (e.g. ability to concentrate, teamwork), organisational aspects and, not least, company culture are brought into harmony with one another [6]. To achieve this, ideally, and where possible, future users should be involved in the planning and briefing process. A more interdisciplinary approach involving planners, designers and psychologists is also desirable. This should involve consideration of the before and after, i.e. planning parameters and the evaluation of both the completed building and the individual workplace experience, with the end user in mind.

User surveys in facilities management

User surveys could play an important role in optimising building maintenance, for example by way of a "building signature" providing a quick overview of the building's strengths and weaknesses in terms of its thermal, visual and acoustic work environment, air quality and workspace design (fig. 6). A matrix showing priorities for action would assist the building manager in creating the best possible environment for the workforce, by indicating both the overarching satisfaction parameters and their relevance for overall workplace satisfaction [7]. Prioritising ongoing and future improvement measures would thereby be possible at a glance (fig. 7).

From the perspective of owners of property portfolios, the comparative assessment of different buildings with similar uses is also valuable. To this end, it was studied to what extent it may be possible to assess a building using only one single user satisfaction indicator, which was then set in the context of the overall portfolio [8]. The results showed – for a sample of 23 buildings of different ages and energy efficiency standards – that a comparison is possible on the basis of an unweighted aggregate index, i.e. its mean aver-

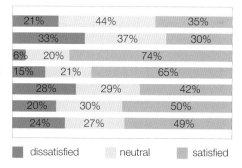

open plan office > 15 people (N = 158)
group office 5–15 people (N = 341)
small group office 2–4 people (N = 1163)
individual office (N = 2048)

Conditions in general
Access to daylight
Room temperature
Air quality
Acoustics/noise levels
Office layout/design

very dissatisfied — very satisfied

5

	dissatisfied	neutral	satisfied
User-friendliness of the building	21%	44%	35%
Furniture	33%	37%	30%
Office layout/design	6%	20%	74%
Acoustics/noise levels	15%	21%	65%
Air quality	28%	29%	42%
Temperature	20%	30%	50%
Lighting	24%	27%	49%

■ dissatisfied ■ neutral ■ satisfied

6

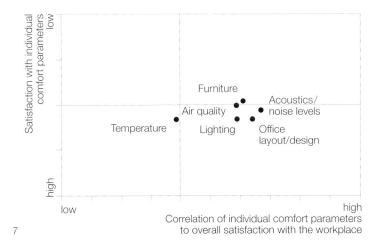

7

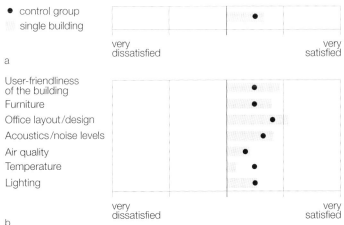

8

age (fig. 8). This provides the real estate industry with a tool that allows the assessment of workplace quality on the basis of user surveys in a larger-scale context.

User satisfaction and sustainability assessment of buildings

Due to their demands on natural resources (space, energy, raw materials), office buildings are increasingly scrutinised as to their sustainability credentials. In addition to internationally recognised sustainability rating systems for buildings, such as LEED and BREEAM, the German Federal Ministry for Transport, Construction and Urban Development (BMVBS) and the German Sustainable Building Council (DGNB) are developing a certification system for offices and administrative buildings. Alongside the assessment of economic, environmental and technical criteria, the assessment scheme for sustainable government buildings (BNB) and the DGNB certificate also assess the socio-cultural quality of a building, using a combination of architectural documentation, building standards and site visits.

For the assessment of environmental and economic aspects, established methodologies and benchmark data exist and are widely adopted throughout the construction industry. To assess the social aspects of sustainability, on the other hand, planning and design stage information is only of limited reliability. For example, the assessment of thermal comfort uses a set of climatic criteria as its basis, which in reality may be perceived very differently depending on the actual use of the building and individual user behaviour. Furthermore, as mentioned above, subjective perceptions of the building itself and the degree of control users have over their working environment can have a significant impact on user satisfaction scores.

Compared to other commodities, buildings tend to have a much longer life expectancy. They are also often subject to numerous changes in use, in maintenance and management and even in their physical appearance (extensions, refurbishment). It is therefore desirable – and this is currently the subject of a number of research projects [9] – to offer sustainability certification and reporting as a continuous process throughout the entire lifecycle of a building, including assessment from the perspective of its users. Only this can provide the evidence to verify that the building's (sustainability) concept matches the reality of its operation, and that calculated benchmark values and projected user satisfaction data bears out in reality.

References:
[1] Povl Ole Fanger, Thermal Comfort. Analysis and Applications in Environmental Engineering (New York 1970).
[2] Richard de Dear, Gail Brager, Donna Cooper, Developing an Adaptive Model of Thermal Comfort and Preference. Final Report ASHRAE RP-884 (1997).
[3] Elke Gossauer, Andreas Wagner, "Nutzerzufriedenheit und Komfort am Arbeitsplatz. Ergebnisse einer Feldstudie in Bürogebäuden", in: Bauphysik, 06/2008, p. 445–452; Elke Gossauer, Nutzerzufriedenheit in Bürogebäuden, dissertation (Universität Karlsruhe 2008).
[4] see note 2
[5] Antje Flade, Architektur – psychologisch betrachtet (Bern 2008); Rotraut Walden, Architekturpsychologie. Schule, Hochschule und Bürogebäude der Zukunft (Lengerich 2008).
[6] Roman Muschiol, Begegnungsqualität in Bürogebäuden (Aachen 2007).
[7] Wolfgang Bischof et al., Expositionen und gesundheitliche Beeinträchtigungen in Bürogebäuden. Ergebnisse des ProklimA-Projektes (Stuttgart 2003).
[8] Andreas Wagner, Karin Schakib-Ekbatan, Nutzerzufriedenheit als ein Indikator für die Beschreibung und Beurteilung der sozialen Dimension der Nachhaltigkeit. Abschlussbericht (Stuttgart 2010).
[9] Research project "Bewertung von Aspekten der sozio-kulturellen Nachhaltigkeit im laufenden Gebäudebetrieb im Gebäudebestand auf Basis von Nutzerbefragungen", carried out by the fbta of the Karlsruhe Institute for Technology (KIT), funded by the Federal Ministry for Transport, Construction and Urban Development (August 2010 to October 2011).

5 Assessment of comfort parameters and overall evaluation of workplace conditions depending on type of office, based on a study of 36 buildings
6 "Building signature" with mean averages and spread of responses to the summary questions for each user satisfaction category (N = 115)
7 Action Priority Matrix: potential for building optimisation on the basis of a user survey (N = 115). It shows satisfaction with the different comfort parameters (e.g. temperature, lighting etc.) and – by way of weighting their respective relevance – their correlation to overall satisfaction with workplace conditions.
8 Results from a user satisfaction survey (single building, N = 112) and a control group sample (15 buildings, N = 915)
  a Index of building overall
  b "Building signature": user satisfaction with individual comfort parameters

Projects

Office building of Claus en Kaan Architecten in Amsterdam

Architects: Claus en Kaan Architecten

In designing their own office premises, the architects set themselves high standards regarding the quality and aesthetics of the rooms.

The slender six-storey office building stands on a corner in the new city district of Ijburg on the artificial peninsula of Haveneiland in Amsterdam. Claus en Kaan Architecten were responsible for designing the urban development master plan. Subsequently they relocated their Amsterdam office to a prominent site directly at the seaside in this growing urban district.

The simple, rhythmic facade with its deep window reveals presents a bold face to the world while creating a variety of different interior qualities. The facade's 55 cm thick supporting reinforced concrete frames provide a base for the ceilings consisting of hollow-core slabs. The intermediate floors have been positioned at an offset to this framework, resulting in a 4.5 m high support-free room on the ground floor which is used as a café. The office levels above have a room height of around 4 m and do not have the customary suspended ceilings, allowing the grey concrete surfaces to shape the character of the interior, too. Doors, partitions and other barriers to communication have been minimised to create an open, well-proportioned room structure. Large panoramic windows frame the views of the Ijmeer. The 3 m high attic storey accommodates the offices' own library with adjoining roof terrace.

This office building demonstrates in impressive fashion how less is often more.

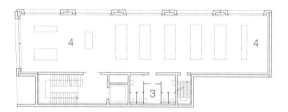

Fifth floor

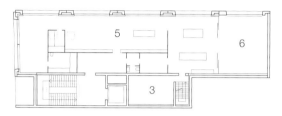

Third floor

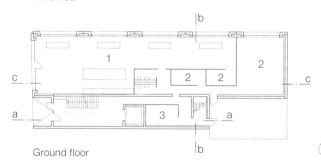

Ground floor

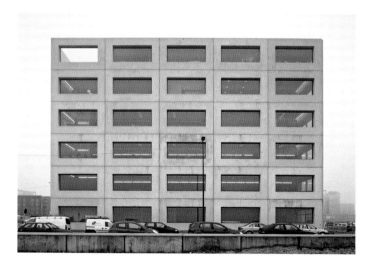

Project data:

Function:	Office
Structure:	Reinforced concrete
Dimensions:	36.0 × 13.4 m
Clear room height:	4.0–4.5 m
Gross volume:	10,600 m³
Gross floor area:	2500 m²
Construction costs:	€ 2.5 million (gross)
Year of construction:	2007
Construction period:	10 months

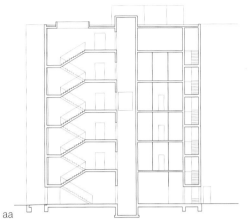

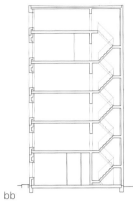

aa

bb

Floor plans · Sections
Scale 1:500

1 Café
2 Storage
3 Service/
  engineering room
4 Open-plan office
5 Library
6 Roof terrace

Section
Scale 1:500
Vertical section
Horizontal section
Scale 1:20

1 Roof structure:
Gravel surface, 60 mm
Bitumen roof waterproof sheeting
Insulation, 2× 70 mm
Hollow-core slab, 200 mm
2 Staircase skylight
Laminated glazing comprising:
10 mm tempered glass + 15 mm gap +
10 mm tempered glass
3 Wall structure:
Prefabricated concrete frame, 550 mm
Insulation, 2× 60 mm
Gypsum plaster board, 12.5 mm
Vapour barrier
Gypsum plaster board, 12.5 mm
4 Thermopane glazing, 10 mm float +
15 mm gap + 15 mm tempered glass
5 Wood fibreboard, painted grey, 18 mm
6 Steel profile, powder-coated, 60/40 mm
7 Floor structure:
Cement screed, 60 mm
Pressure distribution plate,
heated screed, 60 mm
Prestressed hollow-core slab, 200 mm
8 Prefabricated concrete edge
9 Firewall
Prefabricated reinforced concrete unit, 300 mm

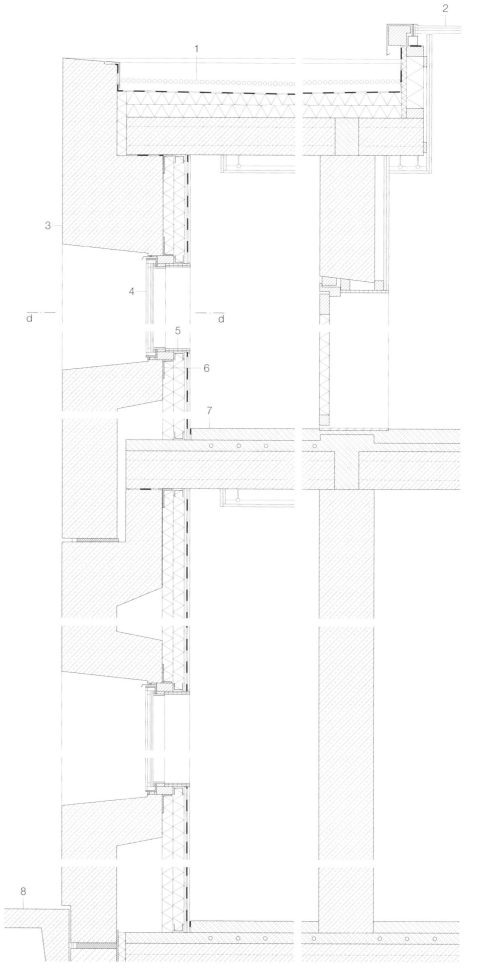

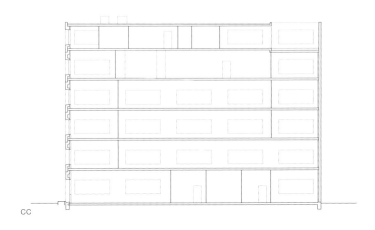

cc

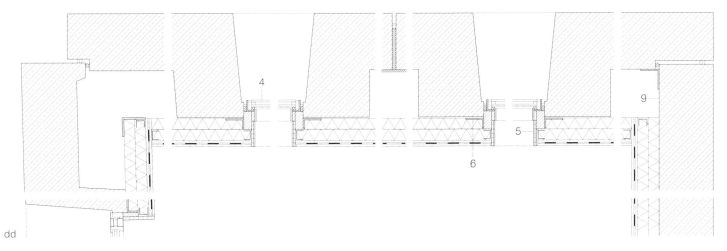

4

9

5

6

dd

Volksbank in Salzburg

Architects: BKK-3 with Johann Winter, Vienna

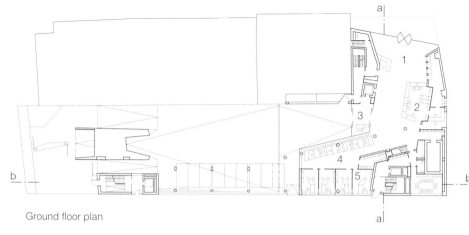

Ground floor plan

The structure is sculptural from within and without and provides a range of meeting opportunities for employees and clients.

The new head office of the Volksbank Salzburg is only a short walk from the main station on one of Salzburg's most important transport hubs. The company's management consciously decided not to move to the periphery of the city, but rather to consolidate its narrow site in the historical Gründerzeit quarter. In 2003 the Volksbank held an invited competition. The idea was to extend the existing head office to the south and east with a new building. The winning project, by BKK-3, reacts to the neighbourhood with a sculptured L-shaped building. The structure, painted in beige, follows the building lines of the site, continues them along the boundaries of three further buildings and opens on to an inner courtyard with narrower and wider points. The differentiated roof landscape culminates in a high projecting volume at the end of the wing.

Fluid inner rooms

The entrance into the generous, double volume banking hall, which also has a direct connection to the inner courtyard, is marked by a deep recess in the structure. The optical continuity between exterior and interior is ensured by red terrazzo flooring peppered with Murano glass shards that continue on to red mastic asphalt with light-coloured sprinklings in the external area. The banking hall has a large information counter and self-service area that remains accessible from the

outside overnight. The rear section contains consultation spaces, and more client rooms are located along an open gallery. Curved light strips set into the ceiling continue the hall up to the first storey.

The offices are located in the upper storey and are designed as cellular offices for one or two employees. Continuous window strips in the facade enable the rooms to be divided freely and their height is orientated towards the work spaces (75 cm parapet) and human dimensions (226 cm lintol). The offices are visually linked by "pilot windows" in the dividing walls between them. These both enable visual contact with one's neighbour whilst also creating the necessary private space by virtue of their trapezoid structure. The interior sections of the floor plans, 20 m-deep in parts, are occupied by service functions such as archive, photocopying area or toilet etc. The transit zones link not only the individual offices, but also provide the opportunity for brief conversations. This widens the corridors and makes them into reception zones for clients; floor and wall give rise to island-like seating areas for the bistro, or a lounge landscape in the quiet zone. In the first storey the "blue salon" offers a panoramic view of the city and provides for a relaxed atmosphere for the employees.

Materials and colour

The colour white dominates the interior, both in terms of the office walls and furniture. This blurs the boundaries between architecture and furniture. The floors are covered with dark red carpet. Only the bistro was fitted with deep-brown stained parquet to create a different ambience.

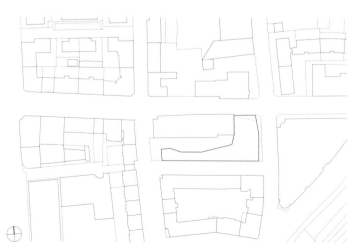

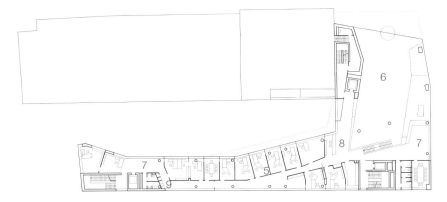

Intermediate level

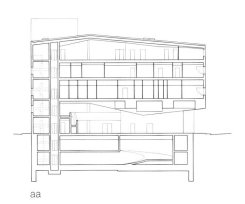

aa

Second floor plan

Project data:

Function:	Office
Structure:	Reinforced concrete
Dimensions:	75 × 32 m
Clear room height:	2.6 – 4.0m
Gross volume:	16,500 m³
Gross floor area:	5,303 m²
Floor area of communal areas:	560 m²
Office floor area:	2,800 m²
Floor area of meeting rooms:	560 m²
Construction costs:	€ 10 million (gross)
Year of construction:	2007
Construction period:	24 months

Siteplan
Scale 1:3000
Floor plans · Sections
Scale 1:800

1 Banking hall
2 Main counter
3 Information
4 Consultation zone
5 Cellular office
6 Banking hall void
7 Waiting area
8 Reception
9 Kitchenette
10 Foyer
11 Archive
12 Seminar room
13 Storage
14 Cafeteria
15 Kitchen

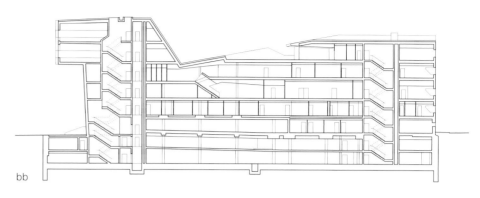

bb

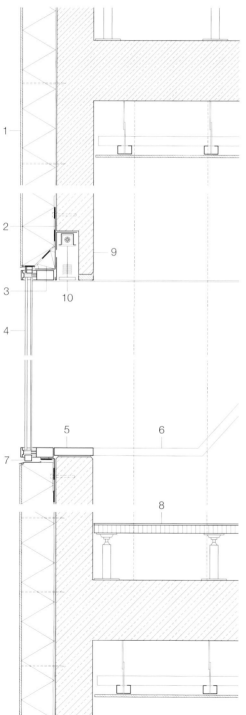

Cross section   Scale 1:800
Vertical section   Scale 1:20

1 Wall structure:
   Finishing plaster, 2 mm, glass fibre mesh
   Base coat render, 8 mm
   Thermal insulation, 180 mm
   Adhesive mortar, 5 mm
   Reinforced concrete, 200 mm
2 Galvanised mounting brackets
3 Insulation wedge
4 Aluminium framed window
   with sun-protection glass
5 Aluminium window sill

6 Fixed glazing between the offices
   laminated safety glass, 2× 5 mm
7 Silicon joints with incorporated compriband
8 Floor structure:
   Carpet tiles on
   dispersion adhesive, 10 mm
   False floor slab, 20 mm
   False floor support, 250 mm
   Reinforced concrete slab, 320 mm
   Dry lining, 300 mm
   Suspended ceiling gypsum plasterboard,
   12,5 mm
9 Precast reinforced concrete unit, 80 mm
10 Sun blinds

AachenMünchener head office in Aachen

Architects: kadawittfeldarchitektur, Aachen

Old building and new building create a unity via their central circulation route and are integrated into the expanding city.

The AachenMünchener insurance company wanted to consolidate its business divisions, which were previously spread across various sites in the city, into a contiguous building. The challenge was to integrate an office complex of 30,000 m² into an existing urban structure, taking into account the existing building stock, without shielding the area from public view.

The architects succeeded both in complying with the developer's requirements for a representative, central head office as well as satisfying the needs of the city and its citizens. Thus the site which is private, was made publicly traversable at key points, which established the pedestrian link between the main station and the city centre. Four buildings that house the offices of the insurance company were erected, and a fifth is sublet to retailers, for example to post office, shops and restaurants.

Walkway

The folded volumes are linked by a glazed connecting pier. The inner walkway connects the various parts of the buildings on the site and can be used as an area for informal communication. All common areas are located here, such as the employee restaurant, cafeteria, conference, training and seminar rooms. The passage widens at some points and narrows at others, which breaks it down and creates space for ad hoc meetings. At the newly-built "Aachen-Münchener Platz" the walkway is connected to street level by a projecting staircase and opens onto the urban space with a prestigious foyer. Concrete slabs in the foyer and anthracite-coloured terrazzo as floor finish for the walkway serve to create an urban atmosphere. All necessary technical installations, such as sprinklers and smoke detectors, are concealed behind a suspended ceiling made of painted expanded metal. The floor-to-ceiling glazing that merges into the ceiling plane allows for generous views of the urban environment.

All upper storeys accommodate the offices for one or two employees in a cellular structure optimised for space. An axis dimension of 1.35 m and moveable dividing walls provide various office types, such as combi-offices. Cupboards integrated into the dividing walls provide adequate storage area.

Facades

Floor-to-ceiling transparent window elements that alternate with opaque, gold-anodised aluminium panels give a rhythm to the facades of the office levels. The basement level, in which storage areas, parts of the garage, maintenance depot and technical rooms are located, is characterised by primarily closed horizontal aluminium strips with the golden coating, contrasted with the generous, double-storey foyer with a fully-glazed facade. Thus the facade illustrates the different internal functions.

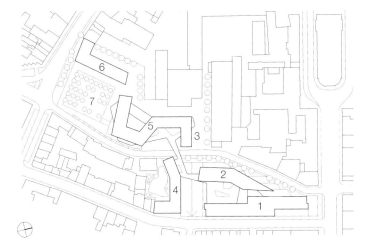

Siteplan
Scale 1:4000

1 House A: existing
  building
2 House B:
  new building
3 AachenMünchener
  square
4 House C:
  new building
5 House D:
  new building
6 House at the
  Pocketpark
7 Pocketpark

Project data:

Function:	Office
Structure:	Reinforced concrete
Clear room height:	2.75 m (Office)
	2.90 m (Boulevard)
Gross volume:	122,100 m³
Gross floor area:	34,900 m²
Office floor area:	16,850 m²
Year of construction:	2010
Construction period:	35 months

Section   Scale 1:750
Floor plans   Scale 1:1250

1 Walkway
2 Meeting room
3 Conference room
4 Seminar room
5 Inner courtyard
6 Void to the main entrance
   at the AachenMünchener
   square
7 Cafeteria
8 Staff restaurant
9 Kitchen
10 Cellular office
   in the old building
11 Cellular office
   in the new-build
12 Kitchenette

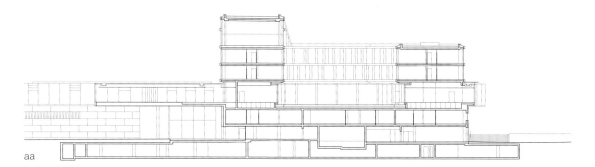

aa

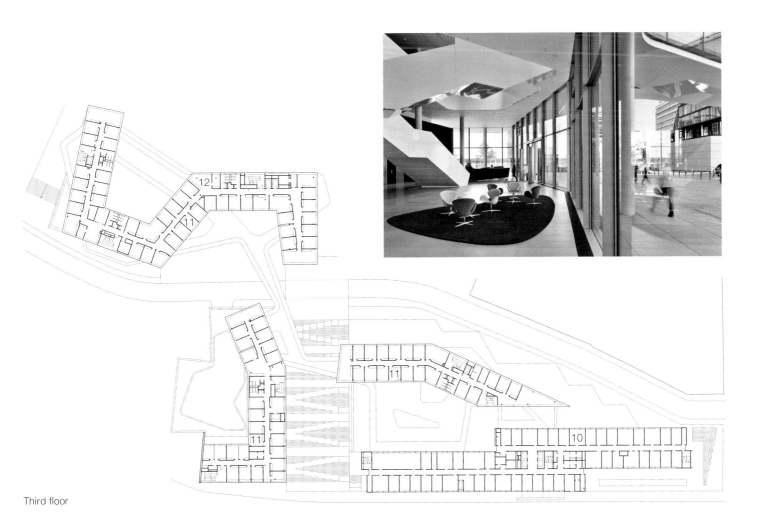

Third floor

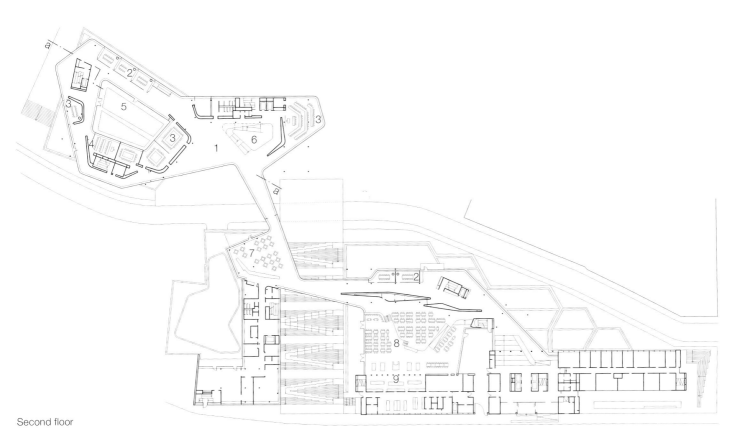

Second floor

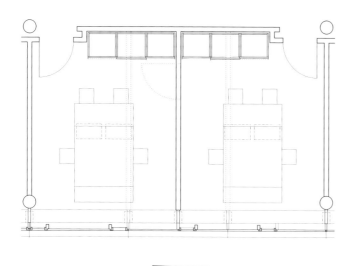

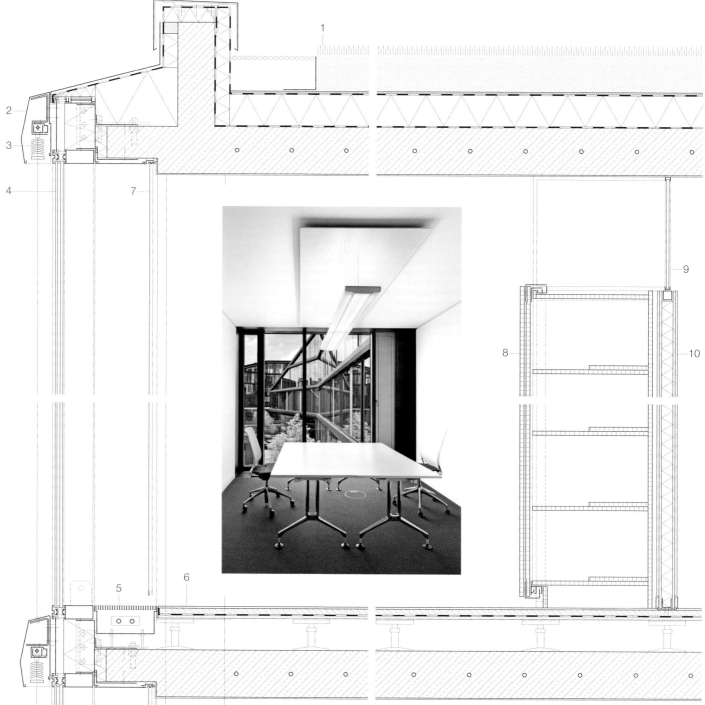

Office floor plan with moveable dividing walls   Scale 1:100
Vertical section office   Scale 1:20
Vertical section boulevard
Scale 1:20

1 Roof structure:
   Extensive roof greenery, 180 mm
   Drainage mat, 8 mm
   Sealing sheet, 2 mm
   Thermal insulation, 160 mm
   Vapour barrier
   Reinforced concrete roof with
   activated concrete core, 250 mm,
   plaster, 6 mm
2 Cover plate:

anodised aluminium, 2 mm
3 Sunshading blinds
4 Double glazing:
   toughened glass 10 mm +
   16 mm gap between panes +
   laminated 15 mm
5 Ground convector
6 Floor structure:
   Loop-pile carpet, 10 mm
   Anhydrite flowing screed, 35 mm
   Separation layer
   Gypsum mounting plate, 18 mm
   Hollow floors, 180 mm
   Reinforced concrete roof
   with activated concrete core,
   250 mm, plaster, 6 mm
7 Anti-glare screen

8 Office cupboard MDF
   sliding door, 22 mm
9 Skylight laminated, 13 mm
10 Partition:
   Gypsum plasterboard,
   2× 12.5 mm,
   sub-construction steel profile
   ⌷ 60/60/3 mm between
   Mineral-fibre insulation, 75 mm
   gypsum plasterboard,
   2× 12.5 mm
11 Sheet-steel guttering with
   liquid-plastic seal,
   Fleece inlay, 2 mm
   Insulation, 60 mm
   Supporting sheet-steel tray, 5 mm
12 Steel profile, T 200/70/20 mm

13 Sun-protection insulating glass:
   toughened glass 10 mm +
   12 mm gap between panes +
   laminated 15 mm
14 Rod: brushed stainless steel,
   Ø 57 mm
15 Floor structure:
   Terrazzo, 50 mm
   Cement-bound plate, 20 mm
   Hollow floor, 36 mm
   Reinforced concrete floor, 160 mm
   Mineral wool insulation,
   2-ply, 120 mm
   suspended ceiling,
   gypsum plasterboard, 12.5 mm
   Plaster, 2 mm
16 HEM steel profile, 400 mm

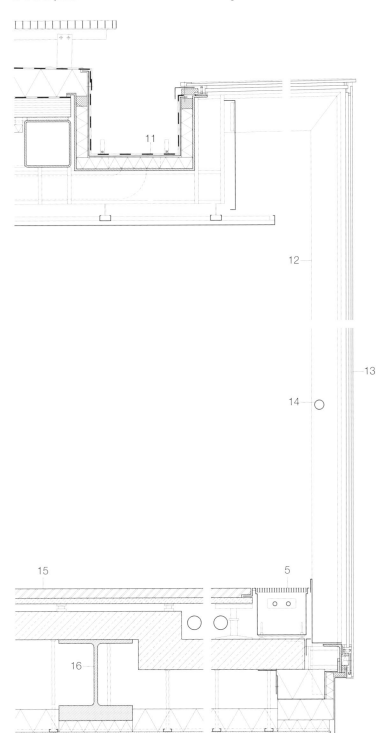

Smart working concept
for Credit Suisse in Zurich

Architects: Camenzind Evolution, Zurich

Rather than permanently-assigned workstations, different non-territorial working concepts provide space for creative ideas.

The Swiss company, Credit Suisse, has for many years endeavoured to provide its employees attractive, diverse and motivational working environments. For example, in 2005 a multi-space concept was introduced in which mostly open workspaces are grouped around a "market place" that unites all common functions. After the concept had been successfully implemented at several locations, the idea of developing and implementing non-territorial workstations matured. Following an ideas competition, the "smart working" pilot project was implemented on one floor of a Zurich office.

Organisation and technology
The concept of "smart working" envisages that the overwhelming majority of the 200 employees – depending on their responsibilities – move flexibly within various scenarios with approximately 160 workstations.
A technical framework has to be in place to ensure that it is possible to work anywhere at any time without limitations. For this reason all employees are given laptops that can be connected to standardised docking stations, monitors and keyboards. Furthermore, each employee can log on to any workstation with his or her own telephone number. All communication zones are fitted with power points and data connections or WLAN.

Varied working environments
Various themed concepts provide the framework for task-specific activity and communication requirements. On entering the building, the different colours, materials, lamps and furnishing elements that are not usually found in offices are immediately apparent. The office areas are accessed via two differently designed lounges. Whilst the "club lounge" has more of a formal character and is decorated in dark colours, the "city lounge" has a relaxed, easy-going atmosphere. In both lounges there is an espresso bar, sofas, small tables and bistro tables with presentation capability that enables employees to exchange ideas with colleagues over a drink. Between the two lounges, special zones provide space for different ways of working. A "project area" in the style of a

workshop can be flexibly fitted out and also reserved for longer, extended projects.
The "business garden", with its dense greenery, provides a stark contrast to the standard office spaces. Materials and colours underpin the extrovert character of this area in which both working and discussion spaces are available. The "business garden" gives way to the "reading room". This houses both the specialist library and also private books and photo collections. The "reading room" is flanked by small working niches that accommodate highly focused work.

Home-base
Despite non-territorial workstations, permanently defined team- or group-based spaces are part of the concept. In each of the four "home-bases", decorated in violet, green, blue and yellow, which each extend towards the building's corners, 50 employees share 22 standard workstations. Along the building cores each employee has a small personal locker and further storage space is available in the team repositories. Three small, individual rooms, reserved not only for management, but which can be used by all employees, are available for concentrated work and also small meetings. Between the workstations and the building core is the "comline". This zone provides a range of additional functions alongside the standard workstations: a standing meeting area for spontaneous meetings, a "think-tank" as a retreat for work phases that require high levels of concentration as well as confidential meetings, a cloakroom and a "document centre" that accommodates the technical infrastructure such as copiers, printers and fax machine. What is known as the "touchdown" groups three small workplaces that are used for periods of up to one hour.
The most concentrated work can be done in the "quiet areas"; thanks to their location at the ends of the buildings there is only minimal through traffic. Screened individual workstations, also optionally in small cabins, only open on one side, support concentrated working via their seclusion and subdued colouring. A strict ban on telephones and conversation is enforced.
The pilot project has shown, after just a short time, that the variety of options and high quality of the facilities has a positive effect on the satisfaction and productivity of the employees.

Ground plan   Scale 1:750

Project data:

Function:	Office
Dimensions:	103.20 × 27.6 m
Clear room height:	2.75 m
Gross volume:	6160 m³
Gross floor area:	2240 m²
Year of construction:	2010
Construction period:	5 months

1 Home-base
2 Comline
3 City lounge
4 Club lounge
5 Project area
6 Business garden
7 Reading room
8 Meeting room
9 Quiet area

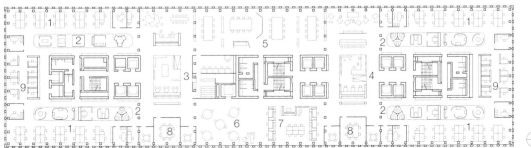

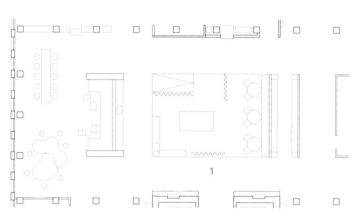

1

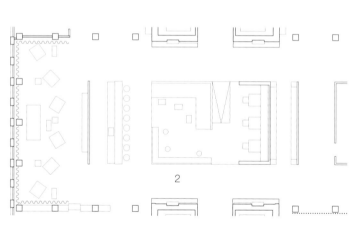

2

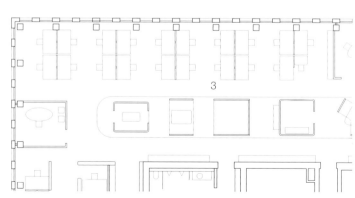

3

Floor plans
Scale 1:250

1 City lounge: friendly, light, fresh, open, communicative, informal
 • Bistro tables for 10–20 people
 • Coffee tables with seating
 • Sofa alcove
 • Espresso bar
 • Billard table
 • TV
 • Storage
2 Club lounge: cosy, high-class, representative

 • Sofa lounge for meetings
 • Espresso bar
 • Coffee tables with seating
 • TV
 • Storage
 • Book shelves
3 Home-base: neutral atmosphere, open
 • Open-plan office
 • Central zone with lounge, standing meeting area, think tank, touchdown workstations, cloakroom and document centre
 • Personal lockers
4 Reading room: silent, library-like

 • 6 secluded individual workstations
 • 6 workstations at a large desk
 • Armchairs with options to read and withdraw
5 Business garden: fresh, green, natural, communicative
 • 10 double workstations, extendible for meetings of up to four people
 • Small lounges for 1–4 people
6 Quiet area: secluded atmosphere, quiet, concentrated
 • Individual workstations, in part highly sound-proofed
 • Team repository

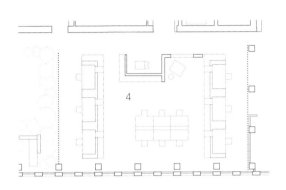

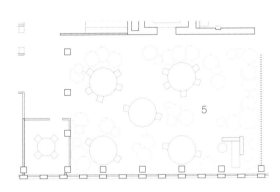

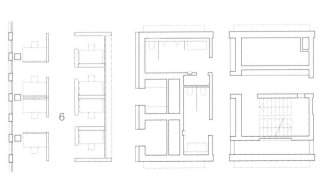

Factory building in Rehau

Architects: WEBERWÜRSCHINGER, Berlin / Weiden

aa

The flexible office layout promotes productivity, creativity and flexibility and enhances the staff's well-being and motivation.

At the beginning of the 1990s a globally operative plastics processing company purchased a former porcelain factory in the German town of Rehau. At the beginning of the new millennium it was decided to concentrate one of the company's three divisions here and to install modern offices at the old factory premises for a staff of 150 from the Sales, Application Technology and Design departments. The industrial character of the three buildings, dating in part from the beginning of the 20th century and in part the 1950s, was to be retained while realising an open-plan interior.

Working in the cockpit

To avoid impinging on the open and spacious character of the lofts, the closed meeting rooms and departmental managers' offices are located on the periphery. Extensive office premises which lend themselves to flexible use are accomodated in the remainder of the floor space. A range of different workplaces is available, from which the staff are able to choose the most suitable facility for any given task. In addition to the standardised open-plan work and discussion places there are also a number of smaller, sparsely furnished individual office units for work requiring a high degree of concentration. The architects refer to these rooms, which measure 8 m², as "cockpits". Open and closed meeting areas are available for brief, ad hoc get-togethers. In order to minimise the use of artificial light, the fixed workplaces are situated

close to the windows in the open-plan area. Installations in the centre of the room accommodate technical facilities or serve as exhibition areas, etc., zig-zagging their way through the new office layout. This space-defining, folding element also provides the spine for the engineering and technical facilities, with electrical installations, ventilation and lighting systems integrated in the ceiling of the installations. The white plastic surfaces of the furnishings are reminiscent of matt, cracked porcelain – an allusion to the site's history. Existing precast columns and sand-blasted and brushed concrete surfaces emphasize the ensemble's industrial character, the extensive concrete ceilings additionally serving as thermal storage volumes. Solid oak floor boards feature throughout the building. Felt coverings on partition walls, red and orange seating and walls featuring greenery add touches of colour to the interiors where calm whites and greys predominate.

Energy efficiency measures

The envelope of the buildings was brought into line with present-day energy efficiency standards by installing new windows, fitting an external wall insulation system to the facade and completely refurbishing the roof structure. The office lighting is controlled according to the incoming daylight, while all the window workplaces are fitted with automatic exterior sunshading and interior anti-glare facilities. Air flow simulations confirmed that the interior could be kept pleasantly cool in summer without full air conditioning, by means of a mechanical ventilation system with a low air change rate and low flow velocities combined with natural ventilation via the top-hung windows.

Section · Floor plans
Scale 1:1000

1 Entrance
2 Lounge
3 Exhibition
4 Cafeteria
5 Video conference room
6 Fixed workplace
7 Temporary workplace
8 »Cockpit«
9 Meeting room
10 Copy point
11 Tea point
12 Departmental manager's office
13 Wall with greenery
14 Storage

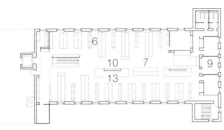

Third floor plan

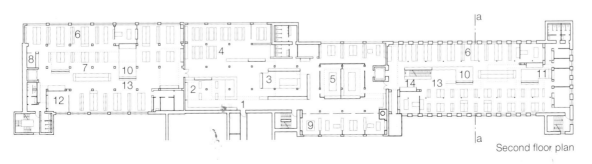

Second floor plan

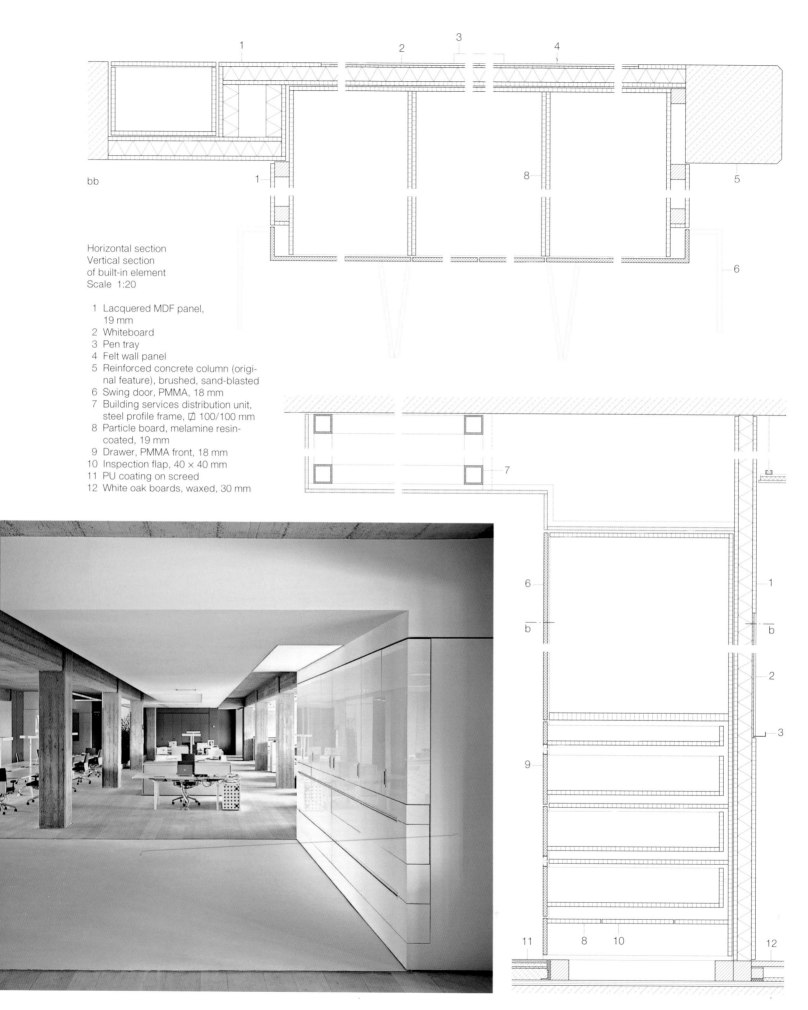

bb

Horizontal section
Vertical section
of built-in element
Scale 1:20

1 Lacquered MDF panel,
   19 mm
2 Whiteboard
3 Pen tray
4 Felt wall panel
5 Reinforced concrete column (original feature), brushed, sand-blasted
6 Swing door, PMMA, 18 mm
7 Building services distribution unit,
   steel profile frame, ⊘ 100/100 mm
8 Particle board, melamine resin-
   coated, 19 mm
9 Drawer, PMMA front, 18 mm
10 Inspection flap, 40 × 40 mm
11 PU coating on screed
12 White oak boards, waxed, 30 mm

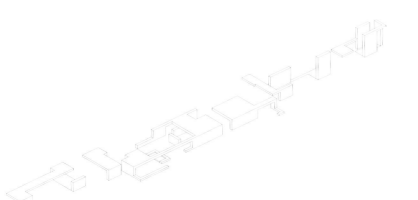

Axonometric
space-defining furnishings

Project data:

Function:	Office
Structure:	Steel
Dimensions:	Second floor 20.50 × 44.70 m
	Loft 17.20 m × 44.70 m
Clear room height:	3.17 m
Gross volume:	14,000 m³
Gross floor area:	3500 m²
Construction costs:	€ 6.15 million (gross)
Year of construction:	2004
Construction period:	15 months

group8 architects' office in Geneva

Architects: group8, Geneva

In a bright, open office setting, colourful stacked-up transport containers serve as rooms which perform various functions.

When architects set about designing an office for themselves, this obviously poses a special challenge. One of the key priorities for group8 was to lend expression to their firm's philosophy in a special manner. A former industrial building offered an ideal location with adequate space in which to create an informal, pleasant working environment for the benefit of the workforce as a whole. The layout of the work areas reveals no hint of hierarchy between the nine partners and their staff of around 70, as everyone works on one and the same level. The premises, which receive natural light through several shed roofs running in a north-south direction, are subdivided by pieces of white furniture whose stepped design allows the desired visual connections throughout the work environment. The members of the respective project teams sit together at separate groups of desks. A long bench running along the entire north side of the building offers an opportunity for a brief chat with colleagues at any time.

Space-defining containers

Sixteen stacked, colourful decommissioned transport containers occupy almost half of the premises and create the eye-catching accents in this predominately white office environment. In order to create larger spaces the containers are arranged in stacks of up to three. They serve diverse purposes for the staff – as a space in which to retreat, to work without any distractions, to construct models, enjoy lunch or a coffee, or as meeting rooms. The sanitary facilities are also accommodated in two containers on the ground floor level. On the side facing the open-plan office, the solid side walls of the containers are replaced by panes of glass, providing an additional influx of light into the rooms and enabling visual contact.

Two delicate steel stairways connect the two levels of the containers. An almost invisible tubular steel railing with a wire mesh filling provides the necessary protection to prevent people from falling, running both along the side facing onto the work room and along the access deck on the rear side of the containers. A long shelf for the library and for archiving purposes is situated at the rear wall of the building. The irregular layout creates spaces containing individual desks in front of the containers and open-top boxes in the work room which serve as informal meeting and relaxation facilities.

Project data:

Function:	Office
Dimensions:	20 × 33 m
Clear room height:	5.2–8.8 m
Gross volume:	5230 m³
Gross floor area:	790 m²
Year of construction:	2010
Construction period:	5 months

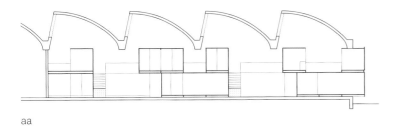

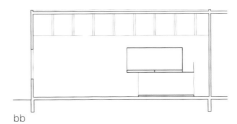

Sections
Floor plans
scale 1:400

1 Open-plan office
2 Model making
3 Meeting room
4 Informal meeting
5 Reception
6 Breakroom

aa

bb

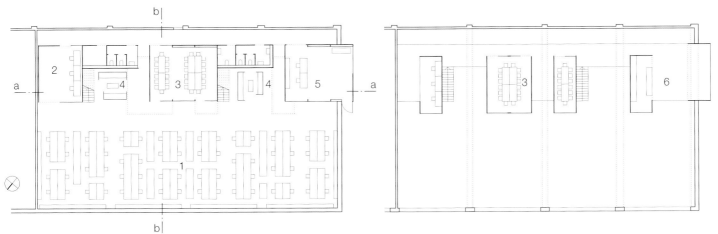

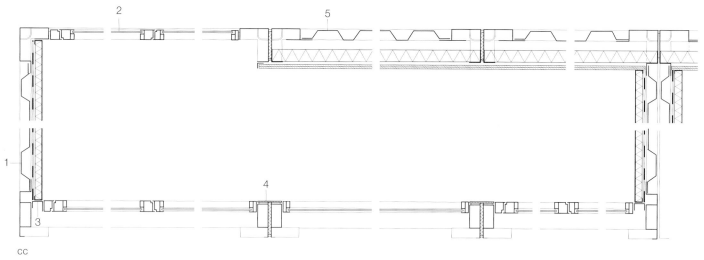

2   5

1

3   4   CC

Horizontal section
Vertical section
Scale 1:20

1 Profiled sheeting, 1.5 mm
   Heavy-duty sheeting, bitumen-elastomer
   compound sound-absorbing
   Mineral wool insulation, 40 mm
   Perforated aluminium sheeting, 1.5 mm
2 Glass door laminated glass,
   float, 2× 6 mm
3 Steel profile, 65 × 40 mm
4 Steel panelling, 130 × 6 mm
5 Profiled sheeting, 1.5 mm
   Mineral wool insulation, 60 mm
   Gypsum plasterboard, 2× 12.5 mm

6 Profiled sheeting, 2 mm
   Mineral wool insulation, 40 mm
   Perforated aluminium sheeting, 1.5 mm
7 Steel profile, 100 × 100 mm
8 Fixed glazing laminated glass,
   float, 2× 6 mm
9 Epoxy resin coating, 5 mm
   Screed, 45 mm
   Plywood, waterproofed and glued, 28 mm
   Steel profile, 120 × 40 mm,
   between longitudinal girders
10 Three-ply board, 27 mm
   Wood profile, 40 × 40 mm
   Steel profile, ⌀ 60 × 60 mm
11 Structural steel profile frame, ⌀ 50 × 20 mm
   Wire mesh infill

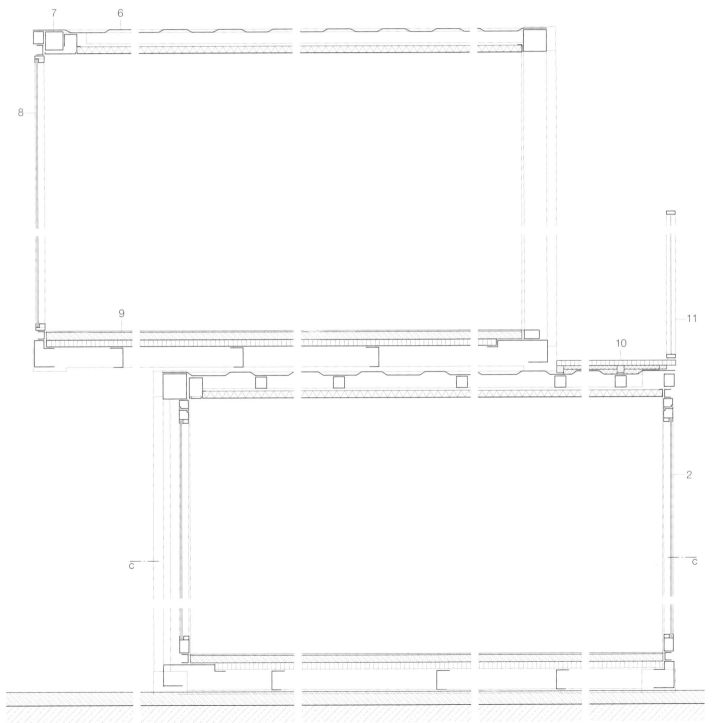

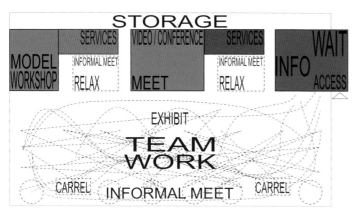

STORAGE

MODEL WORKSHOP

SERVICES

INFORMAL MEET

RELAX

VIDEO / CONFERENCE

MEET

SERVICES

INFORMAL MEET

RELAX

WAIT

INFO

ACCESS

EXHIBIT

TEAM WORK

CARREL

INFORMAL MEET

CARREL

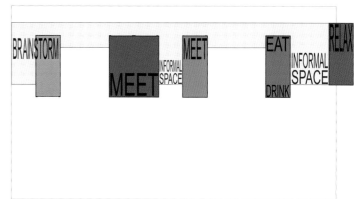

BRAINSTORM

MEET

INFORMAL SPACE

MEET

EAT

DRINK

INFORMAL SPACE

RELAX

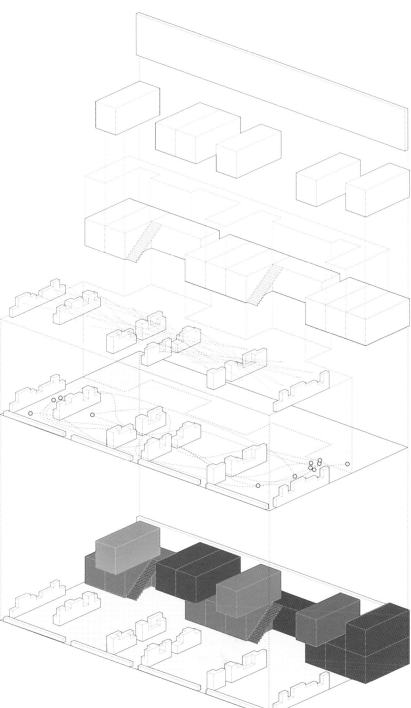

Storage for books
and archives

Container
Upper storey

Space

Container
Ground floor

Visual contact

Contact routes

Unilever headquarters in Hamburg

Architects: Behnisch Architekten, Stuttgart

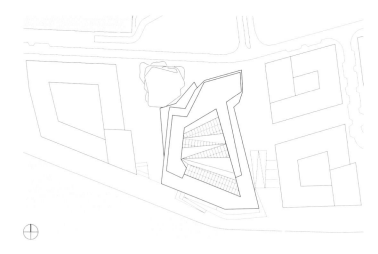

The building's architecture reflects the corporate philosophy by way of open floor plans and flexible structures.

The Unilever headquarters is situated directly on the River Elbe, at a prominent location in the HafenCity urban extension area to the south of Hamburg's city centre. Coming from the city centre, an axis leads over Grosser Grasbrook directly to the building, which invites the public to walk through the accessible ground floor. A spa, café and supermarket offering the company's products demonstrate the diverse scope of the different brands.

At the centre of the polygonal complex is an atrium extending over the entire height of the building. Various bridges, ramps and staircases offer unexpected glimpses into the offices on the upper storeys and views out of the building, towards the Elbe. The extensive glass areas inclined at varying angles in the roof supply adequate daylight to the atrium and the offices. In order to minimise the level of heat radiation entering the building, almost all glazed surfaces face northwards, while the south sides are opaque. A wide staircase leads up to the upper floors, which are only accessible to staff.

In the vicinity of the central access cores on the upper floors there are open spaces facing onto the atrium which serve as meeting points. These spaces afford access to the open-plan office zones which are located in the quieter area to the rear. Central functional facilities such as a copying and printing station, post office boxes and kitchenettes are also concentrated here. Large wooden tables, sofas and armchairs provide an informal setting in which staff can socialise. Lightweight wood-wool boarding and metal mesh on the interior facades reduce reverberation times to such an extent that peace and quiet largely prevail throughout the atrium, despite all the activity concentrated in this part of the building.

Lighting
The lighting throughout the entire building consists almost exclusively of LED light fittings. This inexpensive type of lighting enables energy savings of up to 70 %. Two large light rings measuring 9 and 7.5 m in diameter are the central eye-catching features in the atrium. These light objects are fitted with approximately 3000 LEDs. The offices are equipped with a total of 1400 LED workplace lights. The direct and indirect light from each of these standard lamps provides the required 500 lux of illuminance at the workplace. The meeting rooms, the corridors and the catering area also feature LED lighting.

Construction and facade
In the office areas two rows of columns arranged in a modular grid measuring 8.1 × 8.9 m support the joistfree, 35 cm thick flat reinforced concrete ceiling which protrudes by up to 3.5 m on either side. The lift shafts and stairwells provide the sole means of bracing for the building.

On the facade, a curtainwall-style foil construction protects the sunshading from strong winds and other weather influences. The outer facade layer consists of individual frames fitted with ETFE foil which are fixed to the shell of the building via two cantilever brackets. Thin compression struts and horizontal trussing cables between the edges of the frames push the foil outwards, providing the necessary curvature to withstand the strong winds which are prevalent in Hamburg.

The Unilever headquarters was one of the first buildings to receive the HafenCity eco label in gold. Introduced in 2007, the criteria pertaining to this award include low primary energy consumption (< 100 kWh/m²a) as well as the preservation of public space.

Siteplan
Scale 1:3000
Floor plans
Scale 1:1000

1 Main southern
  entrance
2 Café
3 Supermarket
4 Spa
5 Main northern
  entrance
6 Product develop-
  ment kitchens
7 Access to under-
  ground garage
8 Delivery point
9 Kitchen
10 Staff restaurant
11 Reception
12 Guest casino
13 Fitness area
14 Medical area
15 Open-plan office
16 Reproduction
17 Facility
   management
18 Conference
   centre

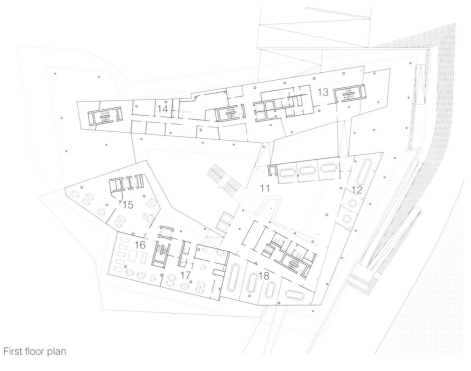

First floor plan

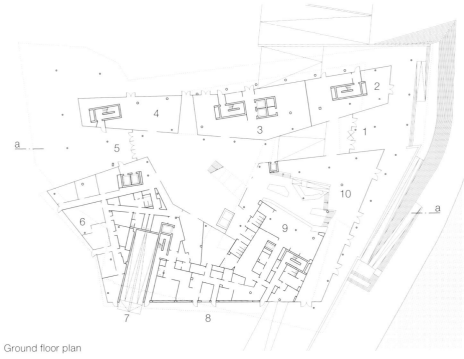

Ground floor plan

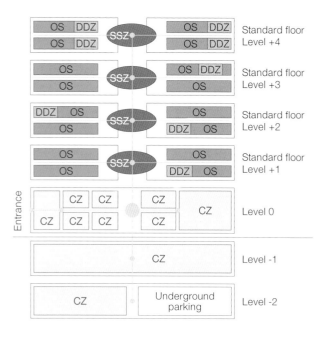

OS	DDZ	OS	DDZ
OS	DDZ	OS	DDZ

SSZ — Standard floor Level +4

OS	OS	DDZ
OS	OS	

SSZ — Standard floor Level +3

DDZ	OS	OS
OS	DDZ	OS

SSZ — Standard floor Level +2

OS	OS	
OS	DDZ	OS

SSZ — Standard floor Level +1

Entrance

CZ	CZ	CZ		
CZ	CZ	CZ	CZ	CZ

Level 0

CZ

Level -1

CZ	Underground parking

Level -2

Office concept

Openness, transparency and effective communications were key considerations in designing the Unilever headquarters. As the company's staff of around 1200 work in flat hierarchies and interfunctional teams, the responsible executives at the Unilever Group have adopted the open-plan office concept developed by the Quickborner team, to enable a flexible response to different team set-ups. The office levels have been designed according to sustainable principles and make effective use of the available space, offering the users a communicative and inspiring work environment.

Open communication zones

The areas for communication, concentration and relaxation need to be clearly defined in open-plan offices, in order to support the work processes in an effective manner. Well-conceived traffic routing reduces disturbances and distractions at the workplace. All office units are directly accessible from the access cores, without having to pass through other departments.

The so-called frames offer retreats within the respective departments. These acoustically screened-off "think-tanks" are integrated into the open-plan work areas.

Meeting points are linked to the office areas on all levels to enable working in interfunctional teams. These go by the names of Elbe, Strandkai, HafenCity and Marco Polo, according to the views on offer. The natural meeting points promote communication and provide a setting conducive to triggering inspired ideas which frequently provide crucial breakthroughs. Conference areas are additionally available for formal meetings.

Comprehensive technical service facilities and WLAN throughout the building enable staff to set up a temporary workplace or hold meetings almost anywhere, including the staff restaurant, which offers a view of the Elbe. Those in need of a break can freshen up in the bracing wind wafting over from the Elbe on the roof terrace, recharge their batteries in the relaxation room or tone up in the fitness centre.

Flexible office facilities

The communication zones are combined with private work areas conducive to concentration. On the standard storeys each workplace is allocated approx. 9–12 m² of floorspace including all special areas, plus 4 m of storage space. The workplaces are arranged for the most part in blocks of four and fitted out with a worktop measuring 160 × 80 cm, a roller container and a sideboard. The integration of workplaces by means of a desk-sharing system ensures particularly effective use of the available space. The so-called hot desks are available to around 160 employees who are out of the office for more than half of the week. Standardisation of the workplaces also ensures maximum flexibility for restructuring purposes. Individually controllable elements allow the users extensive scope for adaptation to their own requirements: each employee is able to influence their work environment by means of manually adjustable radiators, individually adjustable sun-shading and glare protection and opening windows – including windows facing onto the atrium. The brightly coloured pieces of furniture – from yellow through to orange and purple – can be combined according to a modular system. The office concept designed to promote communication and transparency is rounded off by a colour concept based on the company's corporate identity colours.

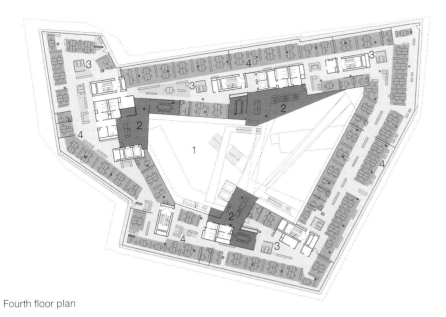

Fourth floor plan

Diagram of space allocation system
Floor plan   Scale 1:1000

1 Atrium
2 Meeting point
3 Frame
4 Open-plan office

Circulation zone (CRZ): space connecting different areas

Central zone (CZ): fixed areas available for general use which perform marketing, social and infrastructural functions

Storey-specific zone (SSZ): fixed areas available for general use offering a basic range of special facilities in the vicinity of offices

Departmental dedicated zone (DDZ): variable, department-specific areas which can be configured by the respective departments

Office spaces (OS): the space in which an employee is allocated a fixed/non-specific workplace

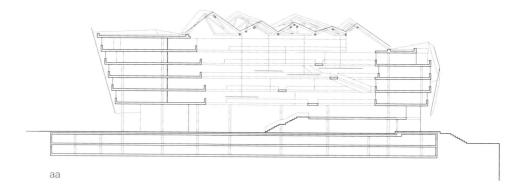

aa

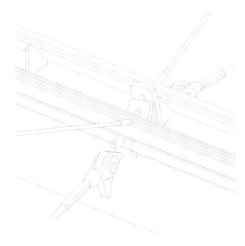

Section   Scale 1:1000
Axonometric projection –
panel frame with fixation of rear tensioning
Vertical section   Scale 1:20

1 Maintenance bridge, grating on steel angle
   L 100/50/6 mm
2 Hinged column, horizontal, tubular steel
   ⌷ 120/5 mm, fixed to reinforced concrete
   projection with thermal insulation
3 ETFE foil, 0.2–0.3 mm
4 Panel frame, tubular steel, Ø 140 mm
5 Compression strut, stainless steel, Ø 38 mm
   fitted diagonally behind frames
6 Sunshading blinds
   Box console with acrylic glass hood,
   sheathed stainless steel tensioning cables
7 Thermopane glazing: 8 mm tempered glass +
   16 mm gap between panes with
   argon filling + 10 mm laminated glazing
8 Aluminium panel on thermally insulated
   sub-structure, mineral wool insulation, 140 mm
   Reinforced concrete, 200 mm, plaster, 2 mm
9 Aluminium sheet, 3.5–5 mm
   Vehicle body plywood, 24 mm on
   aluminium profile, ⌴ 50/30/3 mm
   Diffusion-open film
   Mineral wool insulation, 140 mm
   Vapour barrier
   Reinforced concrete ceiling, 350 mm, plaster 2 mm

Project data:

Function:	Office, spa, café, supermarket
Structure:	Reinforced concrete
Dimensions:	128 × 85 m
Clear room height:	3.0 m (office storeys)
Gross volume:	165,000 m³
Gross floor area:	39,000 m²
Office floor area:	8000 m²
Meeting points floor area:	1240 m²
Year of construction:	2009
Construction period:	27 months
Office workspaces:	approx. 1140
Of which, hot desks:	approx. 90
Floor area, office storey:	9–12 m² per workspace
Storage area:	4 m² per workspace
Meeting facilities:	358 seats for up to 4 people
	546 seats for more than 4 people
Meeting points:	17 meeting points with seating for 135 and 5 smoking rooms
Casino/guest casino:	Seating capacity approx. 270

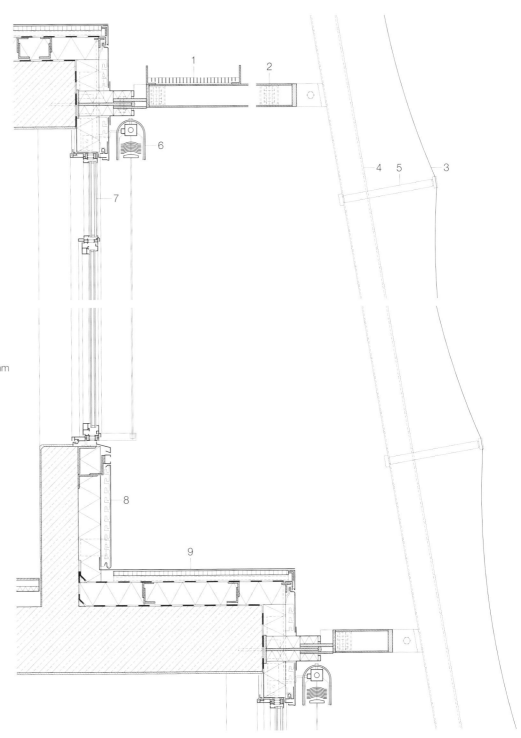

Office building on the Novartis campus in Basel

Architects: Vittorio Magnago Lampugnani with
Jens-Christian Bohm, Milan
Joos & Mathys Architekten, Zurich

Work cabinets divide the pleasant work areas into individual zones on all levels.

An imposing walnut staircase which beckons the visitor upwards is the core interior feature of the five-storey office building on the Novartis campus in Basel.
The same architect, Lampugnani, was also responsible for the master plan for the pharmaceutical company's entire site, which since 2001 has been undergoing a continual process of transformation from a former production location into a "campus of knowledge" with numerous new buildings designed by renowned architects. The light, sophisticated, character of Lampugnani's carefully proportioned, punctuated facade in white Carrara marble forms an interesting contrast to the warm, muted colours which conjure up an elegant, almost intimate atmosphere inside the building. The restaurant, on the ground floor, is characterised by wood panelling painted in ox-blood red, for example, while the entire 6-metre-high entrance hall is finished in walnut. Together with the floor covering of dark grey Italian marble, the mirrored and inverted veneer grain on the panelling creates a pronounced three-dimensional effect which emphasises the interior's materiality. The foyer provides the starting point for the long central staircase which extends throughout the entire height of the building and also functions as a light well. A high standard of craftsmanship is apparent here, too: the rift-cut veneer was obtained from one and the same tree for all the surfaces on each storey, in order to obtain a largely uniform grain pattern and colour. The walls on either side of the stairwell open up into posts and beams, allowing views throughout the entire depth of the building. Smoke barriers in the form of beams between the access zone and the staircase permit this open design while observing fire safety requirements. Despite the strict typological character of the floor plans and elevations, no two storeys are identical. The bridge-type landings of the single-flight staircase afford access to each storey at a different point. The storeys alternately incorporate a recreation room with kitchenette or a meeting room at this point. Smaller meeting rooms are generally situated in the corners of the building. Illumination is provided for the most part by natural lighting which enters the building through manually opening windows. Only the rooms situated further inside the building are provided with mechanical cooling and dehumidification.

Tailor-made furnishings

Work cabinets for up to three people feature as wooden furniture items on each storey, structuring the storeys into screened-off work areas of varying sizes which flow into one another. The open-plan office zones each contain groups of two to four height-adjustable desks with beige linoleum tops framed in walnut. Low, textured glass panels screen off the individual work areas, affording a degree of privacy. Filing cabinets with aluminium roll-up doors divide the work islands into zones. All furniture items and light fittings have been designed especially for this building in cooperation with the Michele de Lucchi studio, completing an all-embracing coherent design concept extending from the overall urban development scale down to the minutest details

Project data:

Function:	Office, restaurant
Structure:	Reinforced concrete
Dimensions:	55 × 18 m
Clear room height:	2.97 m
Gross volume:	32,343 m³
Gross floor area:	7412 m²
Office floor area:	4450 m²
Year of construction:	2008
Construction period:	21 months

Siteplan
Scale 1:10 000

1 Entrance:
  Marco Serra
2 Diener & Diener
3 SANAA
4 Peter Märkli
5 Yoshio Taniguchi
6 Rafael Moneo
7 Adolf Krischanitz
8 Frank Gehry
9 David Chipperfield
10 Tadao Ando
11 Fumihiko Maki

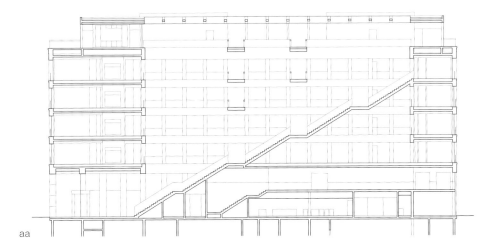

aa

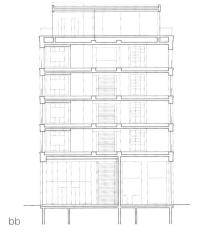

bb

Sections	12	Main entrance	14	Bar	17	Entrance hall	19	Kitchenette
Floor plans	13	Restaurant	15	Restaurant	18	Open-plan	20	Meeting room
Scale 1:500		entrance	16	Kitchen		office	21	Work cabinet

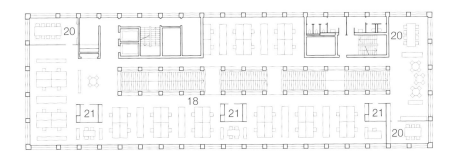

Fourth floor plan

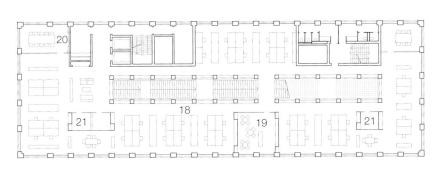

Second floor plan

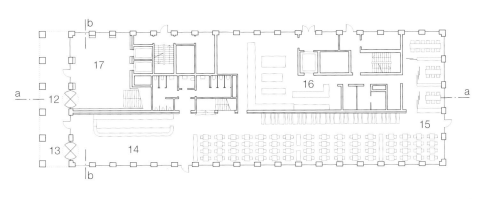

Ground floor plan

93

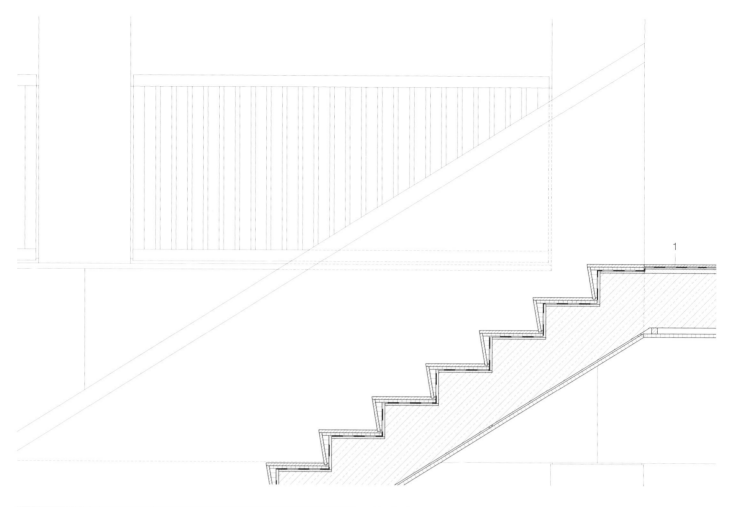

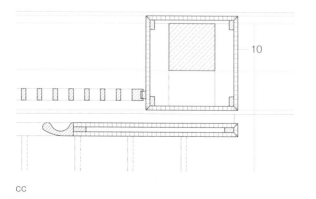

cc

Vertical sections · Horizontal section
Scale 1:20

1 Floor structure – landing:
   Parquet, European walnut, 11 mm
   Moisture barrier, 1 mm; smoothing layer, 5 mm
   Cement screed, 24 mm
   Reinforced concrete, 300 mm
   Lathing, 20 mm
   Particle board, 20 mm, surface:
   European walnut veneer
2 Tread: solid wood, 15 mm
   OSB board, grooved, 15 mm
   Moisture barrier, 1 mm, smoothing layer, 10 mm
   Stairway: reinforced steel
3 Riser: solid wood, 15 mm
   OSB board, wedge-shaped, grooved
   Moisture barrier, 1 mm, smoothing layer, 10 mm
   Stairway: reinforced steel
4 Wood core plywood, surface:
   European walnut veneer,
   sawn from one trunk per storey
5 Handrail, solid wood, European walnut
6 Banister: solid wood
7 Carpet, 10 mm,
   on false floor slab, 35 mm
   Supporting course, 355 mm
   Reinforced concrete roof, 220 mm
   Sub-construction steel profile
   Gypsum plaster board, 12.5 mm
   Mineral fibre board, 43 mm
   Capillary tube mat in microporous
   coating compound, 4 mm
8 Wood core plywood, veneer surface
9 Particle board, 20 mm, surface:
   European walnut veneer
10 Particle board, 20 mm, surface:
   European walnut veneer
   Support: pre-fabricated concrete unit, 250/250 mm

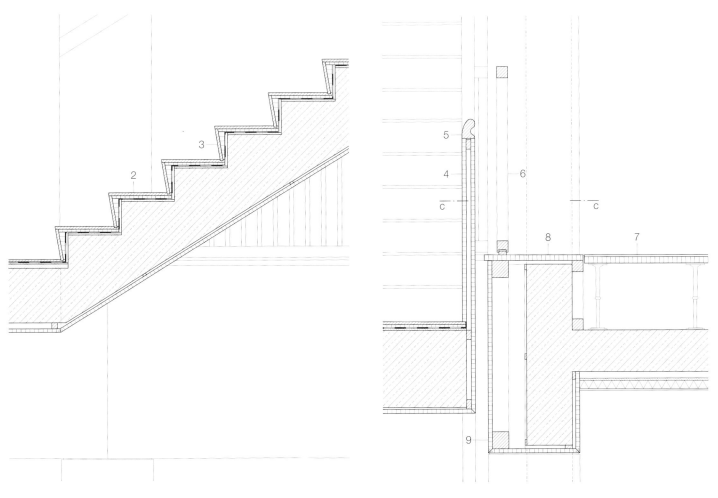

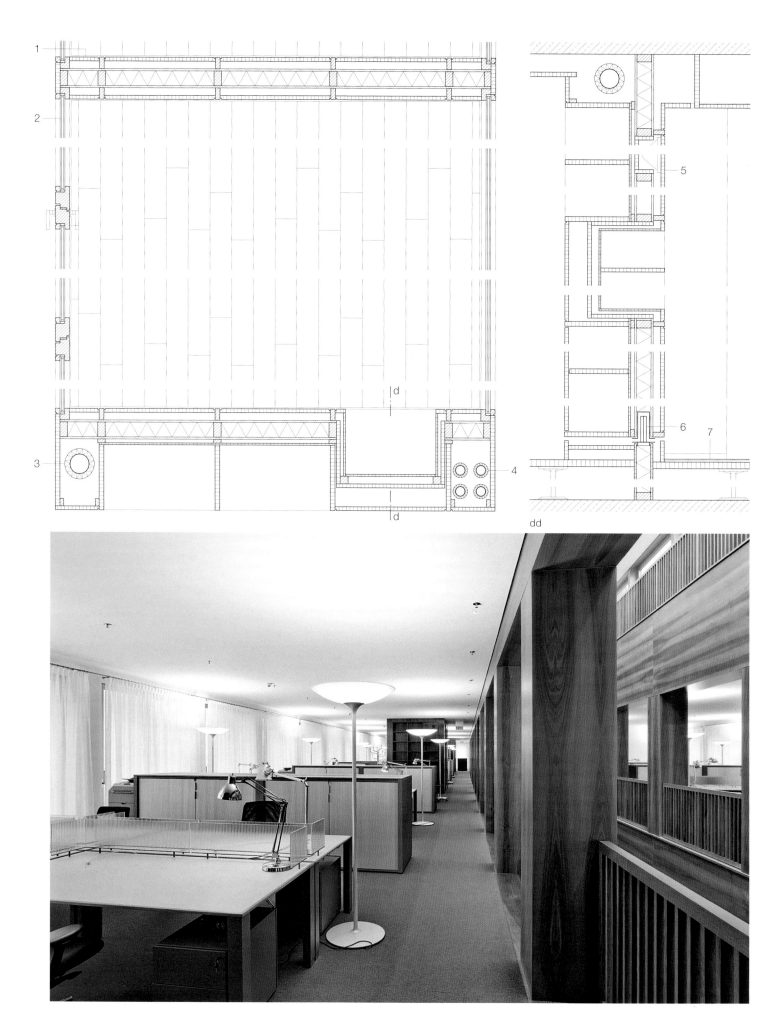

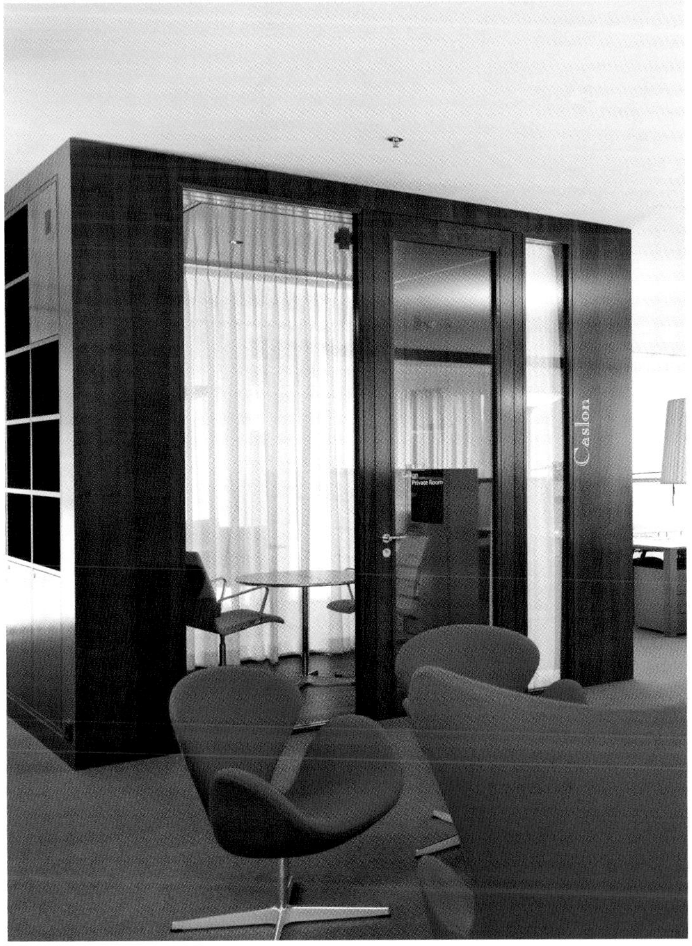
Caslon

Work cabinet
Horizontal section • Vertical section
Scale 1:20

1 Wall structure:
Particle board, 20 mm, surface:
European walnut veneer
Gypsum plasterboard, 10 mm
Timber post, 80/40 mm
Insulation between, 80 mm
Gypsum plasterboard, 10 mm
Particle board, 20 mm, surface:
European walnut veneer
2 Sound-insulating glass with film, 16 mm
3 Supply air
4 Heating/cooling lines
5 Inspection flap, particle board, 20 mm,
surface: European walnut veneer,
perforated around loudspeaker
6 Air overflow element, sound-damping
7 Floor structure:
2-layer bonded walnut parquet, 3.5 mm
Floor slab, 35 mm
Supporting course, 355 mm
Reinforced concrete floor, 220 mm

Desk
Axonometric projection
Detailed section Scale 1:2

8 Rough-cut textured glass, 8 mm
9 Stainless steel profile, ▭ 8/4 mm
10 Stainless steel, ◻ 8/8 mm
11 Linoleum, 2 mm
Timber board, 13 mm
12 Walnut timber, 15/15 mm
13 Hollow profile frame, ▭ 60/30 mm
14 Canted sheet steel table leg,
height-adjustable, 80/80 mm

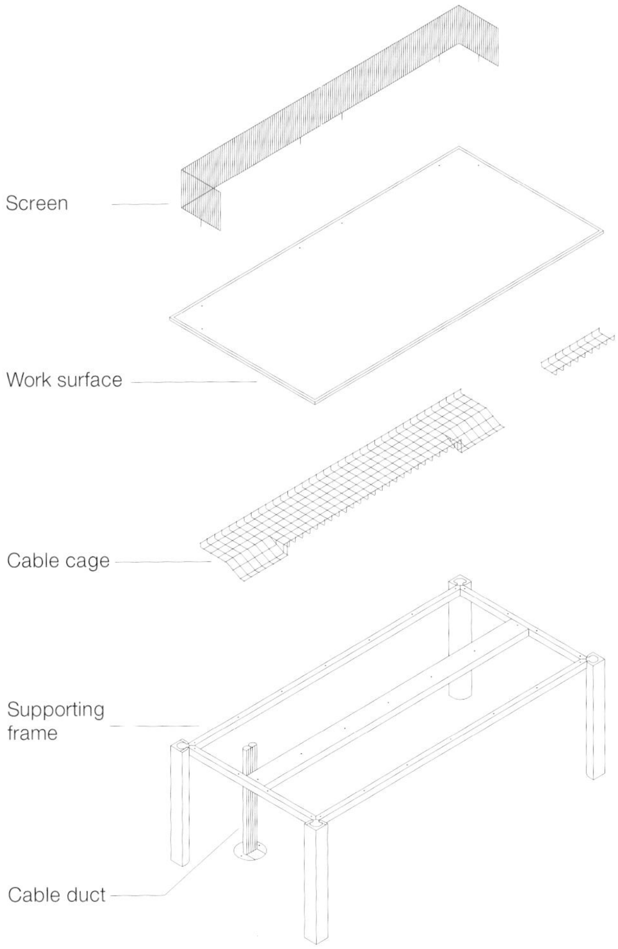
Screen
Work surface
Cable cage
Supporting frame
Cable duct

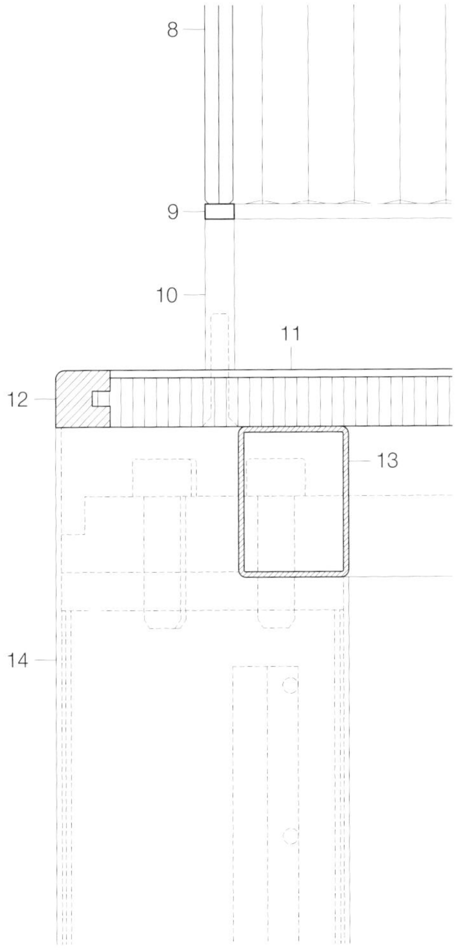
8
9
10
11
12
13
14

Rambøll head office in Copenhagen

Architects: DISSING + WEITLING architecture, Copenhagen

Project data:

Function:	Office
Structure:	Reinforced concrete
Dimensions:	105/125 m × 21,5–41,8 m
Clear room height:	2.6 m (ground floor)
Gross volume:	210,000 m³
Gross floor area:	6,400 m²
Office floor area:	19,000 m² (useful floor space)
Construction costs:	€ 134 million (gross)
Year of construction:	2010
Construction period:	30 months

Light, air and open spaces – concealed behind a glazed facade is a multi-space-concept conducive to communication.

Compared to the open-plan office, an office type favoured in the English-speaking world that promises high efficiency in terms of use of space – the multi-space-office combines the benefits of cellular and open-plan offices. This concept offers a combination of few individual work rooms and shared multi-function zones for communication – although it does require more floor space. The new head office of the Danish engineering company, Rambøll, is of a truly opulent size and dimensions. As one of the biggest multi-disciplinary and international engineering firms in Denmark, the company has made a visible statement with its head office in the new Copenhagen district of Ørestad on the island of Amager. At the beginning of the planning phase the employees were able to contribute their personal ideas for their future work place. The design was to be defined by "Nordic qualities" such as a high level of daylight and expansiveness. The architects' solution is a 40,000 m² reinforced concrete skeleton structure with a fully glazed 5,000 m² curtain wall to the north-west facade. The complex rises out of the new quarter like a solitaire and clouds appear to slide across its facade.

Open floor plan

The floor plan was largely predefined by the location, directly at the metro crossing, as well as road and rail links to the airport and the Øresund bridge that crosses to Sweden. The building is shaped like a boomerang. The rounded corner is where the main entrance is located, and around which all public areas, such as the canteen, fitness rooms and large conference areas, are arranged.

The eight office storeys vary in depth between 8 and 14 m. At the widest point they open centrally for the "La Rambla", a central, 80 m-long atrium that features continuous balconies and a cascading staircase. The walls that run perpendicular to the external facade and the "La Rambla" open up countless sight lines.

With the exception of the cores and individual office clusters, the floor plan is open. The different working areas are aligned towards the external facade. Several meeting rooms, lounge areas and kitchenettes separate noisier areas from the more privat quieter working areas (fig. B, p. 100).

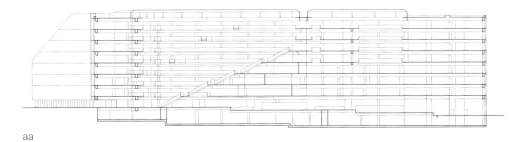

aa   bb

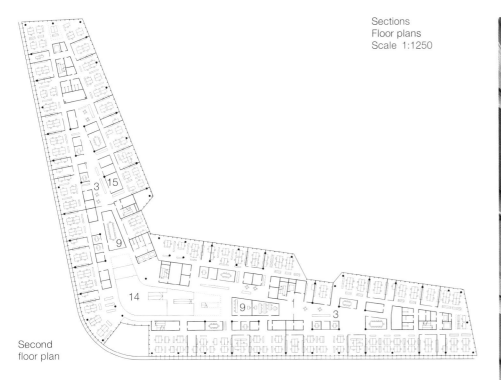

Sections
Floor plans
Scale 1:1250

Second
floor plan

1 Main entrance
2 Reception
3 Café
4 Canteen
5 Kitchen
6 Auditorium
7 Terrace
8 Exhibition
9 Conference room
10 Lounge
11 Fitness room
12 Training room
13 Office
14 Atrium
15 Meeting room

Ground
floor plan

Office concept

When developing the interior design concept for Rambøll's head office, it was particularly important for the office planners to involve the future users in all planning phases. To this end various groups made up of managers and employees met together to look at different, precisely defined topics and issues. These included, for example, the audio-visual equipment with flat-screens, projectors and speaker systems, IT systems, access control and, above all, the corporate identity and furnishings. In these meetings the participants compiled a series of concepts and values that were to play a key part in the design vocabulary and atmosphere of the new office building for users and visitors (fig. A).

Furnishings

The members of what was termed the "inventory group" initially defined the requirements for the function of the furnishing, visited suppliers to assess quality, and finally selected furniture on basis of the agreed concepts.

As a result of the large surface area that required furnishing, the office planners opted for several different designs to create a degree of variety. An outline plan in which the prescribed furnishings for each storey were entered served as an overview. In order to create vertical coherence and facili-

tate orientation, rooms with the same functions are always located above one another on the individual floors and fitted with the same furnishings.

Whilst the planners selected the interior design of the common areas in close consultation with the groups that had been set up, the design of the working areas was undertaken in dialogue with the individual departments. A manual was used to present various principles and ideas to the users. Each department was able to familiarise itself with the available options and express wishes for the respective working areas (fig. C).

Colour concept

In conjunction with an artist the groups also developed a colour concept that stipulated that only the walls in the common areas or the furnishings were to be brightly coloured. Whilst the working areas along the facade and the meeting rooms are decorated in subdued colours, the intensity of the colours gradually increases from the kitchenettes through the café and library up to the lounge areas. Translucent films on glass partition walls serve to shield working areas and meeting rooms and to give them privacy. In order to maintain the maximum possible transparency, however, films were applied initially only to a minimum of surfaces, later to be expanded or intensified as required.

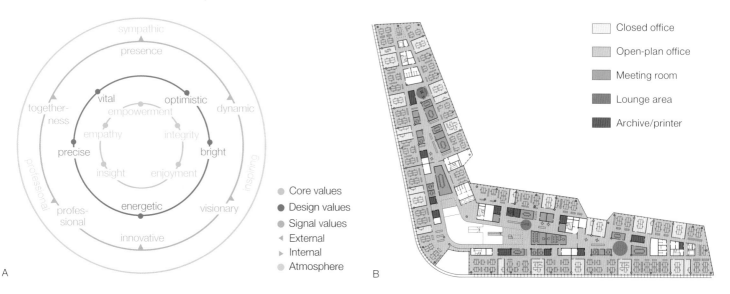

A

B

C

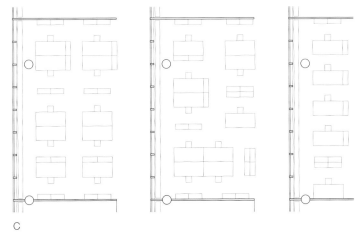

Floor plans
Scale 1:250

1 Open-plan office
2 Individual office
3 Multiple person office
4 Meeting room for 1–2 people
5 Meeting room for up to six people
6 Meeting room for up to eight people
7 Conference room
8 Kitchenette/café
9 Printer station/archives
10 Utilities

A Interplay of corporate values
B Ground plan layout: surface distribution
C Variants of workspace allocation

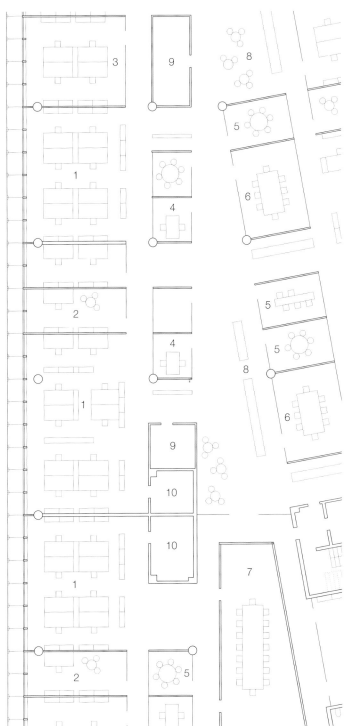

The Yellow building in London

Architects: Allford Hall Monaghan Morris, London

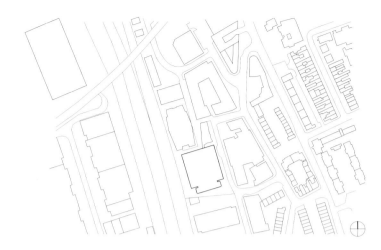

The headquarters of the fashion label is characterized by its open "factory floors", which are stabilised by a concrete diagonal structure.

An impressive atrium extending over the entire height of the building and featuring a striking concrete supporting structure characterises the "Yellow Building" in west London. The seven-storey headquarters of the British fashion label, Monsoon, houses the management offices, the design department and the company's art collection. Individual levels can be let to third parties, enabling a flexible response to growth or shrinkage of the company.

Loft atmosphere at the workplace

In response to the owner's wish for a loft atmosphere, the budgetary constraints dictated low floor area sizes with a simple, industrial aesthetic. In order to reinforce the stacked levels, architects and structural planners developed the ozenge-shaped concrete supporting construction which runs around the facade and the atrium. Its characteristic structure, which is also economically efficient, shapes the building's identity in the central atrium above all. This long space, from which a generously sized staircase leads upwards, not only connects and illuminates all the storeys and departments but also offers a location for informal meetings – and a stage for the art collection which is distributed throughout the building. In order to promote cooperation between the different departments, the office areas are open-plan on all levels and face

onto the central atrium. Smaller meeting rooms and individual offices are arranged along the facades. The minimalist approach to the use of the materials concrete and glass underscores the building's loft-like character. On the attic level the triangular construction is continued as a steel structure. A shed roof with circular skylights fittingly reinforces the workshop atmosphere. Cross girders along the sheds do away with the need for central supports in the design studios which are accommodated here. On the ground floor and the intermediate storey the atrium is cross-shaped to create space for events and larger objets d'art such as Carsten Höller's "Mirror Carousel". The access shaft with lifts, escape stairs and WCs is located to the south in front of the main volume of the building, thus also serving to shade the offices. A second, smaller core, which also incorporates the ventilation shafts, is incorporated on the north side of the atrium.

The supporting structure

The all-round lattice structure was optimised by means of parametric software with regard to material input and aesthetic appearance. The standard solution for an inclined, clearly complex geometry would have been prefabricated concrete elements. Instead, the architects chose an in-situ concrete structure which produces smooth, even surfaces. Wall shuttering elements were used for the inner and outer surfaces of the supports, between which v-shaped inserts were installed which are adjustable to different angles of inclination making them suitable for reuse.

Siteplan
Scale 1:5000
Sections · Floor plans
Scale 1:1000

Project data:

Function:	Office, design studio
Structure:	Reinforced concrete
Dimensions:	55 × 45 m
Clear room height:	3 m (office storeys)
	5 m (design studios)
Gross volume:	86,625 m³
Gross floor area:	15,288 m²
Construction costs:	£ 32.65 million (gross)
Year of construction:	2008
Construction period:	21 months

1 Reception
2 Atrium
3 Café
4 Restaurant
5 Training
6 Lobby with elevators
7 Open-plan office
8 Conference Room
9 Showroom
10 Design studio
11 Terrace

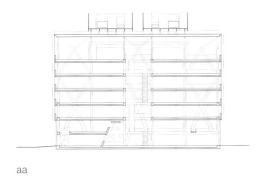

aa

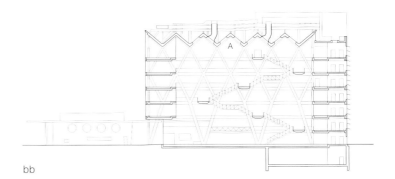

bb

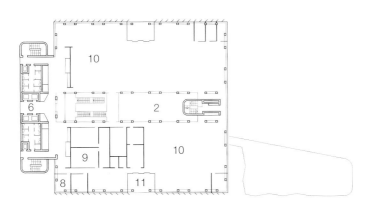

Top floor plan

Intermediate level

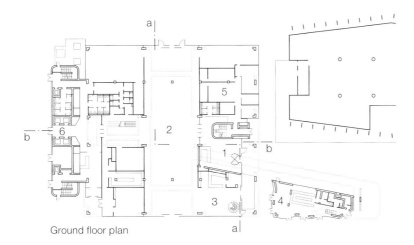

Ground floor plan

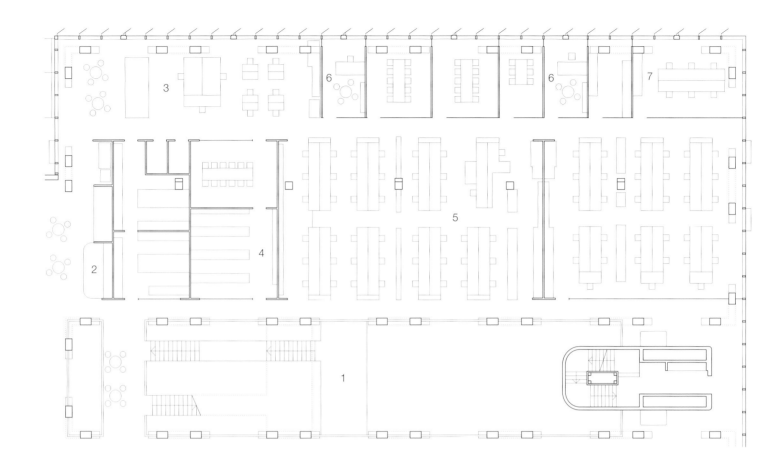

Floor plan
Scale 1:250

Storey-wise layout
of floor space

1 Atrium bridge
2 Kitchenette
3 Service station
4 Storage
5 Open-plan
   office
6 Cellular office
7 Meeting room

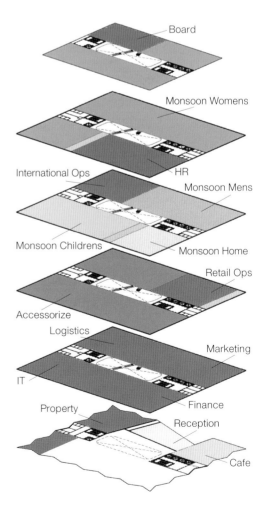

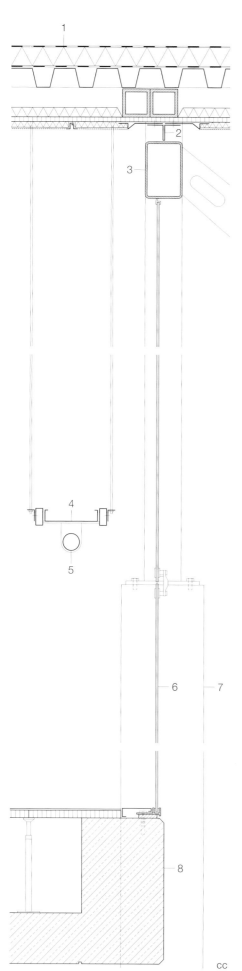

Vertical sections   Scale 1:20

1 Roof structure:
  Waterproof sheeting
  Thermal insulation, 100 mm, vapour barrier
  Trapezoidal sheeting, 100 mm
  Secondary supporting structure tubular steel,
  ⊡ 150/150 mm
  Acoustic insulation matting, 50 mm
  Birch plywood board, 24 mm
  Black laminated acoustic insulation matting,
  30 mm
  Perforated aluminium ceiling panel
2 glass fibre-reinforced
  plastic smoke seals
3 Steel profile ⊡ 200/200–400 mm
4 Cable run
5 Sprinkler system

6 Atrium glazing, smoke-proof:
  laminated glazing with dotted pattern
  up to 1100 mm over floor level
  (Ø 12 mm/44 % density)
7 In-situ support, 450/450 mm
8 Edge beam, reinforced concrete
9 Exhaust air pipe
10 Circular aluminium cover
11 Circular steel profile, ⊔ 125 mm
12 Accessible roof sealing course,
   slope insulation, vapour barrier,
   v-shaped steel sheet
13 Cover, canted aluminium sheet
14 End plate
15 Adjusting bolts, removable
16 Skylight, Ø 2400 mm, thermopane glazing
   with white dotted pattern with Low-E coating
17 Inspection opening bolts

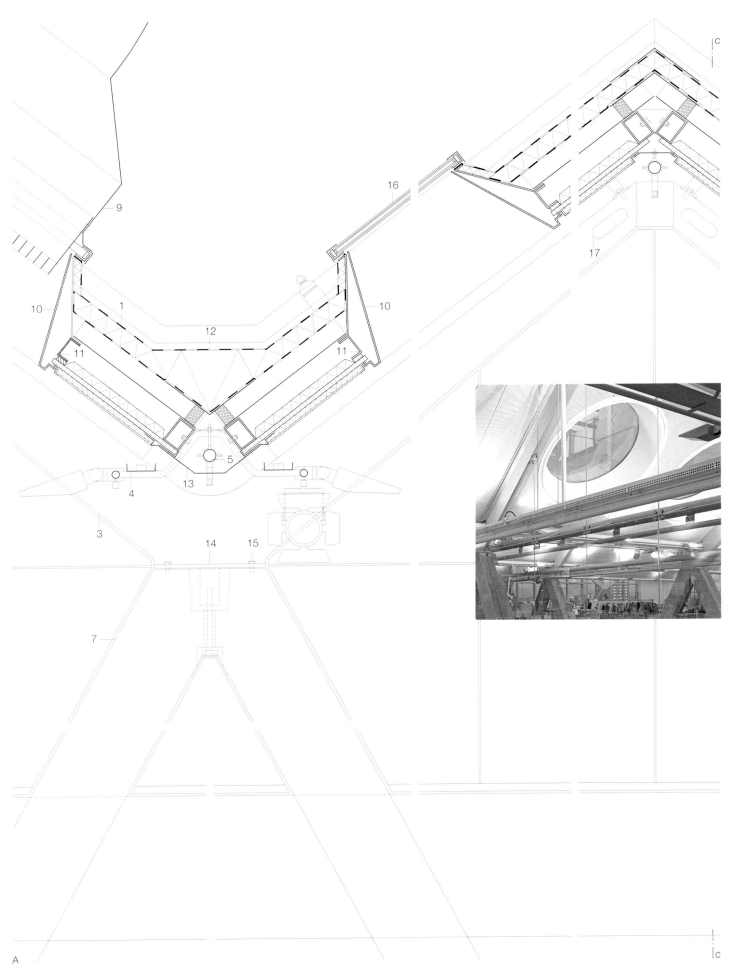

Rena Lange headquarters in Munich

Architects: David Chipperfield Architects, Berlin

The clear, sleek style of the fashion house is reflected in the building's exterior and interior architecture, underscoring the company's identity.

In 2004 the fashion company, Rena Lange, commissioned architect David Chipperfield to develop a design concept for a shop. Since 2005 the firm has created flagship stores in various cities, including London, Frankfurt and Munich. The vivid contrast of their black and white colour schemes projects the brand's high-quality corporate identity. At the company's home base in Munich, the store, administrative offices, showroom, warehouse and outlet were previously spread over four locations all over the city. The new company headquarters now unites the entire staff of 150 and all corporate functions under one roof. Located in an unalluring industrial zone in the north of Munich, the solitary building with its unconventional deep black colouring stands out from the prevalence of run-of-the-mill industrial buildings in the surrounding area. Large, horizontal windows protrude from the facade with wide, projecting dark frames.

Minimalist interior

Inside the three-storey building the floors, walls, ceilings and furniture are finished in light grey and white. The ground floor accommodates the foyer, the canteen, the storage and an outlet store which is accessible from the outside. An imposing single-flight exposed staircase, which is showcased by a skylight, leads to the upper storeys. On the first floor there are additional storage facilities and the offices for administrative staff, collection management and senior management.

The company's design activities are concentrated on the second floor, with the Design, Tailoring and Production departments. The focal point on this level is the showroom, where the latest collections are presented to selected customers. The interior's neutral and muted colour scheme ensures that attention remains focused solely on the fashion garments. All creative and representative areas are arranged around a green inner courtyard which provides natural lighting from both sides. The intense contrast between the light rooms and the dark facade is particularly apparent in the clearly laid-out work rooms where the clothing is designed and produced. The large vertical sliding windows, which do not open into the room, further reinforce the studio character. Interior anti-glare screening provides for uniform, glare-free natural lighting in fine weather.

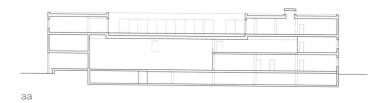

aa

Sections · Floor plan
Scale 1:750
Siteplan
Scale 1:10000

1 Foyer
2 Canteen
3 Storage
4 Delivery point
5 Access to underground garage
6 Outlet store

Project data:

Function:	Office, design, production, sales, storage
Structure:	Reinforced concrete
Dimensions:	57 × 80 m
Clear room height:	3.3 m (offices)
	6.2 m (storage)
Gross floor area:	7500 m²
Office floor area:	2500 m²
Storage floor area:	3300 m²
Construction costs:	€ 12 million (net)
Year of construction:	2007
Construction period:	13 months

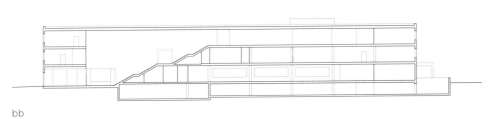

bb

Floor plans
Scale 1:750

1 Office
2 Sewing studio
3 Storage
4 Void
5 Inner courtyard
6 Showroom
7 Studio

Vertical section
Scale 1:20

8 Roof structure, skylight:
 Zinc plate roof covering, vertical joint
 Polypropylene backing sheet
 Fibre mat with nap structure
 2-layer bitumen sealing
 Wooden roof boarding, 24 mm
 Mineral wool insulation, 160 mm
 Vapour barrier
 Bitumen precoating
 Reinforced concrete roof, 200 mm
9 Roof structure:
 Extensive roof greenery
 Substrate, 70 mm
 Drainage course
 Filter fleece
 2-layer bitumen sealing course with
 root protection
 Polystyrene insulation, 160 mm
 Bitumen precoating
 Reinforced concrete roof, 300 mm
 Suspended gypsum plasterboards, 12.5 mm
10 Wall structure: plaster, 10 mm
 Mineral wool insulation, 100 mm
 2-layer bitumen sealing
 Reinforced concrete, 250 mm

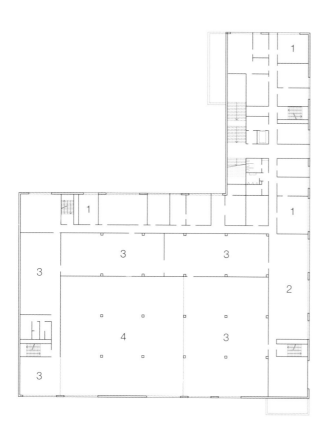

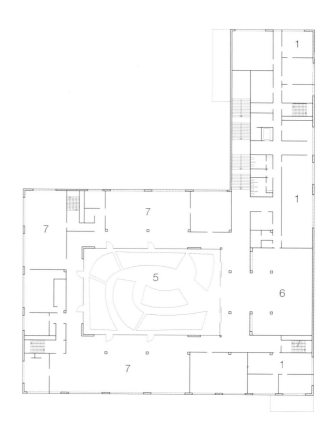

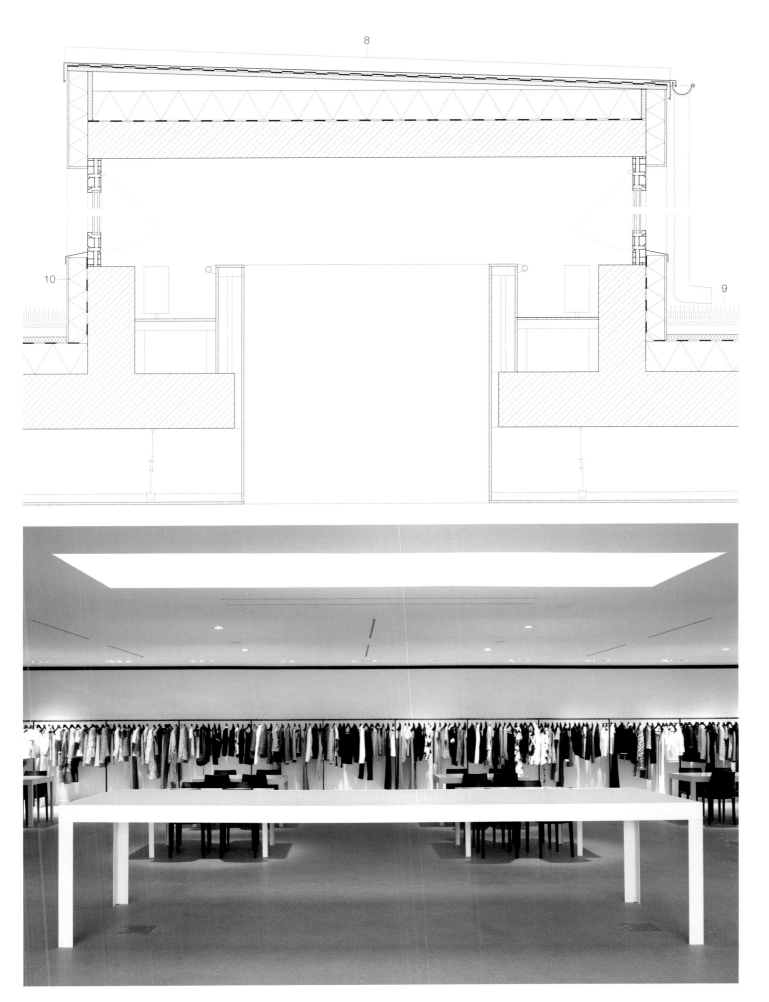

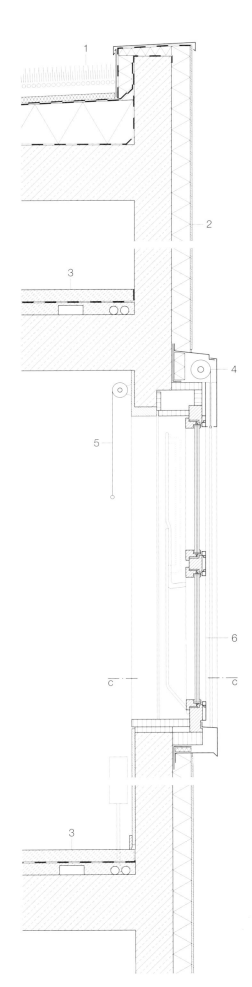

Vertical section
Horizontal section
Scale 1:20

1 Roof structure:
   Extensive roof greenery
   Substrate, 70 mm
   Drainage course
   Filter fleece
   2-layer bitumen sealing course with
   root protection
   Polystyrene insulation, 160 mm
   Vapour barrier
   Bitumen precoating
   Reinforced concrete roof, 300 mm
2 Wall structure:

Black finishing plaster,
self-coloured, 4 mm
Mineral reinforcing mortar with
glass fibre mesh, 5–7 mm
Mineral wool insulation, 80 mm
Reinforced concrete
in smoothed white finish, 200 mm
3 Floor structure:
   Ground cement screed, 60 mm
   Separation layer
   Screed with conduits, 60 mm
   Reinforced concrete ceiling, 300 mm
4 Sunshading
5 Interior anti-glare screening
6 Tilting/sliding window with aluminium/wood
   frame and thermopane glazing

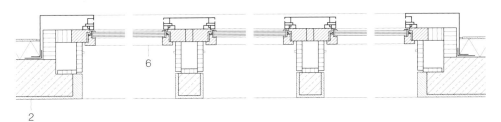

cc

Nya Nordiska headquarters in Dannenberg

Architects: Staab Architekten, Berlin

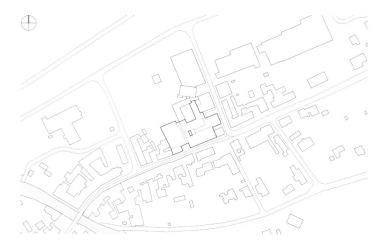

The extension to the existing half-timbered ensemble results in an interesting contrast between old and new.

In the small town of Dannenberg in northern Germany, Nya Nordiska designs and markets high-quality interior fabrics. The family-run company with a workforce of approx. 125 was established in Düsseldorf in 1964 and moved to Dannenberg in the mid-1970s. Two new buildings were added to the site in the historic old quarter in 1996, but the company's steady growth necessitated more space for production and administrative functions. A competition which was launched to resolve this situation was won by Staab Architekten, whose design combined functional clarity with harmonious integration into the townscape.

Patchwork arrangement of buildings

Six new buildings of varying sizes have been added to the existing ensemble of listed half-timbered buildings, a sample shop from the 1980s and the two administrative buildings dating from 1996. While the new buildings are clearly recognisable as such, their sizes, storey heights and roof typologies correspond to the surrounding buildings.

Approaching from the main road, a passage leads to the foyer, behind which the central courtyard is situated. The two main access ways, running in an east-west and north-south direction, intersect here, opening up onto the spacious entrance area and establishing visual links between the various buildings. The offices of the different departments and

the design studio are arranged around the common courtyard. They form the organisational heart of the complex and are quickly accessible from the production and storage areas. In the south, two listed half-timbered buildings which presently house the samples, make-up and accounting departments complete the ensemble.

Sculptural roofscape

The various roof designs on the new buildings tie in with the gable roofs of the surrounding buildings. At the same time, they also provide an indication of the activities within the buildings. The rooms of the design department, the work rooms and the store rooms are provided with a north-facing skylight strip which creates ideal light conditions in which to judge the colour effects of fabrics.

In contrast, the offices are covered with a gable roof which has an asymmetric slope. Daylight is supplied to the offices via long strips of large windows. Each room is thus endowed with an individual atmosphere conducive to the specific type of work involved. Even long corridors are showcased by means of rows of clerestory windows which follow the zig-zag course of the roof, while corner glazing affords a diagonal view through the building.

Use of colours and materials

The restriction to a reduced colour palette and carefully selected materials applies to both the interior and exterior. The interior walls and ceilings in neutral white contrast with the black, polyurethane-laminated floors.

On the exterior, a cladding of red anodised canted aluminium covers the entire extension like a fabric veil, alluding to the company's line of business. The different vertical lines of the canted edges – following a regular or alternating rhythm according to the facade segment concerned – enliven the facade. At the same time, this facade provides the new buildings with their own distinctive appearance and clearly sets them apart from the older buildings.

From the production shop through to the open-plan studio and to the small office unit; the site demonstrates a wealth of different work scenarios which reflects the similarly diverse spectrum of industry in the town. The new buildings demonstrate that a manufacturing location may also help to enhance the urban landscape in the context of town-centre urban development.

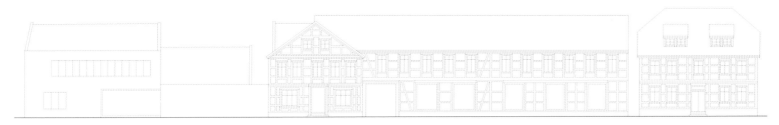

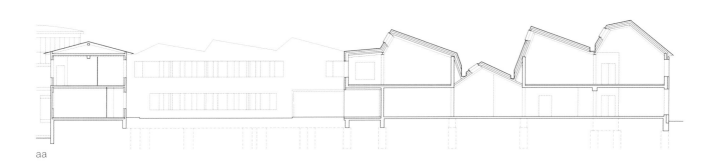

aa

Plan views
Scale 1:750

1 Storage
2 Accounts
3 Passage
4 Samples department
5 First-aid room
6 Staff entrance
7 Foyer
8 Delivery point
9 Storage
10 Office in new building
11 Office in existing
   building
12 Product development
13 Terrace
14 Recreation room
15 Design department
16 Training room

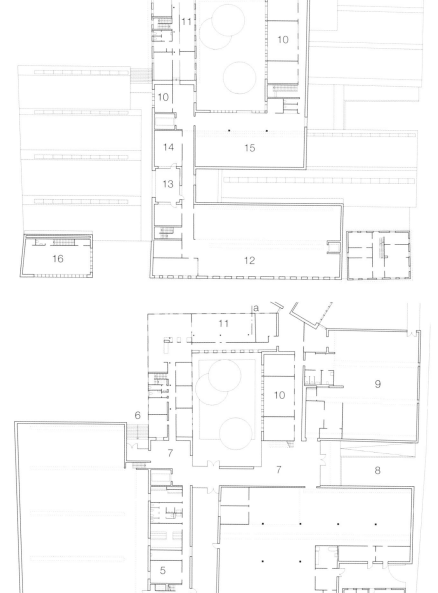

Project data:

Function:	Product development, office
Structure:	Steel, reinforced concrete
Dimensions:	78 × 60 m
	(new buildings only)
Clear room height:	2.85–5.30 m
Gross volume:	21,800 m³
Gross floor area:	4110 m²
Floor space, production:	2100 m²
Office floor area:	690 m²
Storage floor area:	120 m²
Construction costs:	€ 6.5 million (gross)
Year of construction:	2010
Construction period:	11 months

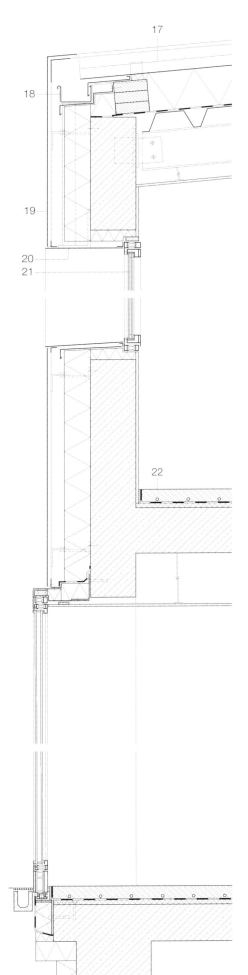

Vertical section, courtyard facade
Scale 1:20

17 Roof structure:
   Profiled aluminium sheeting, 50/429/1 mm
   Fixing piece
   Mineral wool insulation, 210 mm
   Vapour barrier
   Trapezoidal sheeting, 100/275/1 mm
   Steel girder HEA, 220 mm
   Suspended gypsum plasterboard ceiling,
   12,5 mm
18 Aluminium box gutter
   powder-coated, 90/150/100 mm

19 Wall structure:
   Profiled aluminium sheeting,
   anodised with coloured finish, 1 mm
   Substructure/ventilation, 30 mm
   Insulation, 140 mm
   Reinforced concrete, 240 mm, plaster, 3 mm
20 Aluminium reveal sheeting, anodised with
   coloured finish, 3 mm
21 Thermopane glazing, $U_g = 1.1$ Wm^2/K
   4 mm float 4 mm + 18 mm gap + 4 mm float
22 Floor structure:
   PU lamination in anthracite, 3 mm,
   floating anhydrite screed, heated, 70 mm
   Separation layer, insulation, 25 mm
   Reinforced concrete, 250 mm

Vertical section
Scale 1:20

1 Roof structure:
Profiled aluminium sheeting, 50/429/1 mm
Fixing piece
Mineral wool insulation, 210 mm
Vapour barrier
Trapezoidal sheeting, 100/275/1 mm
Steel girder HEA, 220 mm
2 Aluminium box gutter
powder-coated, 180/450/290 mm
3 Gutter sheet, 3 mm
4 Undersheet, 1.5 mm
5 Steel girder, HEA 220
6 Steel profile, 100/60/5 mm
7 Roof structure:
Roof tiles, lathing/counterlathing
Undersheeting
Mineral wool insulation, 210 mm
Vapour barrier
Trapezoidal sheet, 100/275/1 mm
8 Wooden eaves box
9 Wall structure, half-timbered facade:
Squared timber, in part from original
building, 100/150 mm,
whitewashed bricks in between, ventilation
Mineral wool insulation, 140 mm
Reinforced concrete, 240 mm
10 Contoured wooden boarding
11 Aluminium sheet, 2 mm
12 Thermopane glazing, U_g=1.1 W/m²K
8 mm tempered glass + 18 mm gap + 8 mm
tempered glass
13 Interior window sill
Painted wood, 30 mm
14 Floor structure, upper storey:
PU lamination in anthracite, 3 mm
Cement screed, 60 mm, separation layer
Insulation, 135 mm
Reinforced concrete floor, 250 mm
15 Floor structure, ground floor:
PU lamination in anthracite, 3 mm
Exposed ceiling, shot-blasted, 200 mm
Insulation, 100 mm
Waterproof membrane

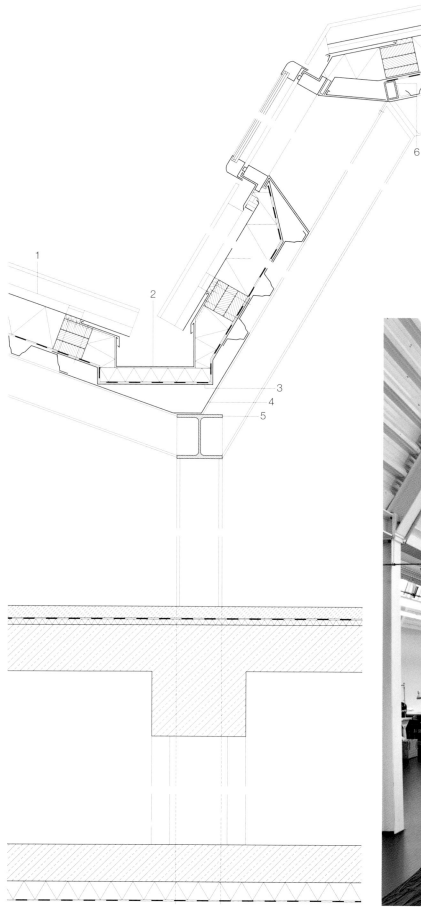

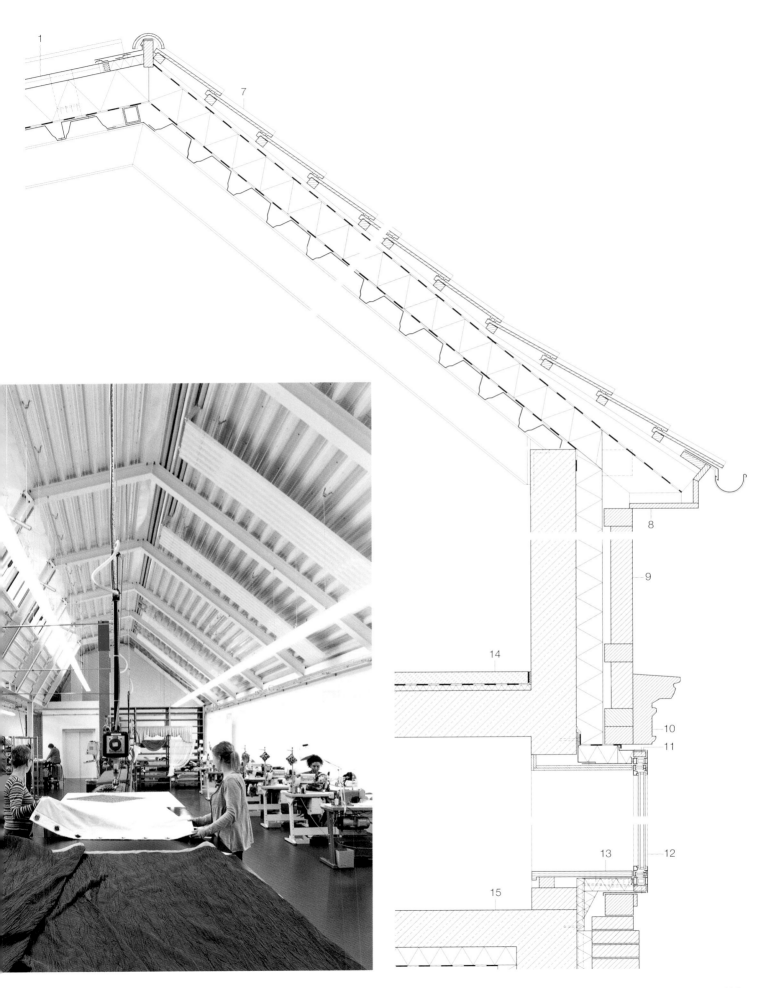

voestalpine Steel Service Center in Linz

Architects: x architekten, Linz/Vienna

aa

Production as representation – the industrial building is impressive with its clear lines, precise execution and logical production processes.

In the centre of an industrial area looking out on to the blast furnaces and gasometers of the voestalpine steel works we find the voestalpine Steel Service Center that specialises in high-precision made-to-measure steel slit strips and plates. For special requirements, a storage and production hall was added to the factory site on the opposite side of a busy traffic artery: directly at the interface between road, rail and water transport with its own ship-loading point at the port basin. Thanks to the regular structural grid, the building can be extended in a second phase without disrupting the functional relationships.

Two simple orthogonal structures which stand perpendicular to one another house the production hall and the raw material hall. Only the prominently-cantilevered canopy accentuates the main entrance. Several functions are located in this area at the front of the production hall: an office with two workplaces and changing and relaxation rooms for the employees. The generous openings in this area provide a clear view of the surroundings and, alongside the centrally-placed skylight strips, ensure that there is sufficient daylight in the interior.

Manufacturing process

The raw material is delivered directly into the raw material hall in the form of a steel coil by truck, ship or rail. A crane transports the coils along the crane track into the production hall, where it is put under tension and cut to size on 80 m longitudinal and transversal cutting lines. The finished pieces are then transported by truck.

Construction and materials

In line with principles of industrial architecture the new-build is designed as a steel structure. The design capabilities of steel are demonstrated using the company's own products. The steel structure – the supports and the truss girders – consists of welded, shaped tubes. Truss girders arranged at right angles to the main supporting structure, reinforced by shaped tubes, form the protruding apex. Prefabricated steel box panels with trapezoidal sheet casing were selected as the facade finish. The transparent parts of the production hall are constructed with a post and rail construction in steel and aluminium, whilst u-profile structural glass was used for the raw material hall.

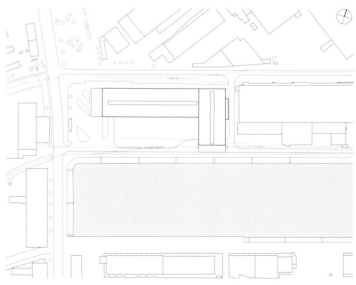

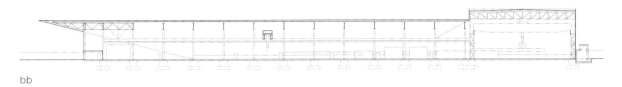
bb

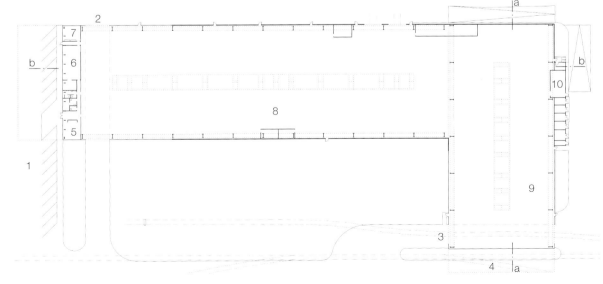

Siteplan
Scale 1:5000

Sections
Floor plan
Scale 1:1250

1 Car park
2 Truck access
3 Rail deliveries
4 Ship deliveries
5 Foyer/reception
6 Changing rooms
7 Social room
8 Production hall
9 Raw material hall
10 Transformer room

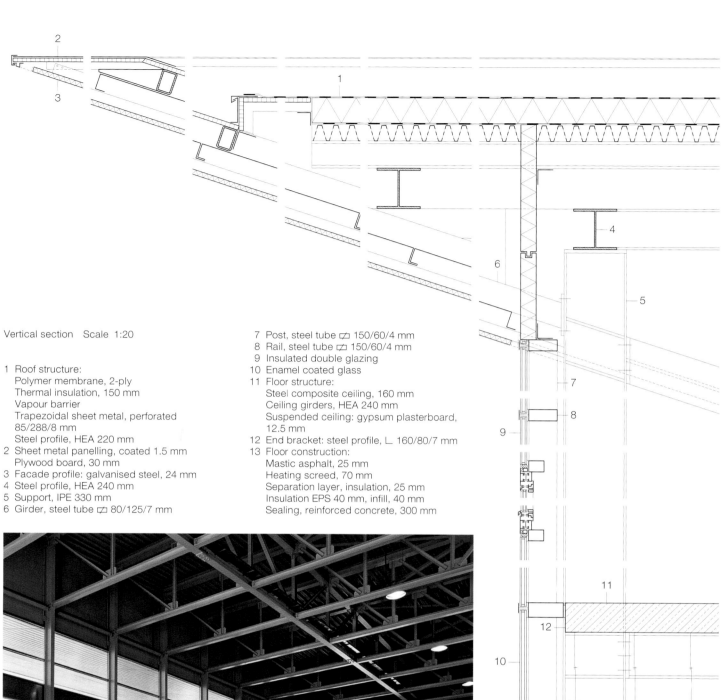

Vertical section   Scale 1:20

1 Roof structure:
   Polymer membrane, 2-ply
   Thermal insulation, 150 mm
   Vapour barrier
   Trapezoidal sheet metal, perforated
   85/288/8 mm
   Steel profile, HEA 220 mm
2 Sheet metal panelling, coated 1.5 mm
   Plywood board, 30 mm
3 Facade profile: galvanised steel, 24 mm
4 Steel profile, HEA 240 mm
5 Support, IPE 330 mm
6 Girder, steel tube ⊏⊐ 80/125/7 mm

7 Post, steel tube ⊏⊐ 150/60/4 mm
8 Rail, steel tube ⊏⊐ 150/60/4 mm
9 Insulated double glazing
10 Enamel coated glass
11 Floor structure:
   Steel composite ceiling, 160 mm
   Ceiling girders, HEA 240 mm
   Suspended ceiling: gypsum plasterboard,
   12.5 mm
12 End bracket: steel profile, L 160/80/7 mm
13 Floor construction:
   Mastic asphalt, 25 mm
   Heating screed, 70 mm
   Separation layer, insulation, 25 mm
   Insulation EPS 40 mm, infill, 40 mm
   Sealing, reinforced concrete, 300 mm

Project data:

Function:	Production and storage hall
Structure:	Steel
Dimensions:	75 × 163 m
Clear room height:	12,80–16,30 m
Gross volume:	109,000 m³
Gross floor area:	7,670 m²
Floor area of raw material hall:	2,630 m²
Floor area of production hall:	4,603 m²
Office floor area:	210 m²
Construction costs:	€ 6.2 million (net)
Year of construction:	2008
Construction period:	6 months

Office and warehouse of the Sohm company in Alberschwende

Architects: Hermann Kaufmann, Schwarzach

Enclosed by a facade of vertical wooden slats, the building combines an open shed with a double-storey office area.

The Sohm timber construction company has been based in the Bregenzer Wald region of Vorarlberg in Austria since 1991. As the firm grew over the years, its premises were extended several times. When the neighbouring plot of land became available for purchase, the company was presented with an opportunity to add another new building to its head-quarters. The architects incorporated the plot's irregular shape into their design for the new multi-purpose shed with an adjoining double-storey office section. Acrylic glass held between vertical timber enclose the shed facing the road. The site's pronounced slope enabled storage space and a new heating system to be integrated in the basement storey. The all-wood office area rests on this solid base, supporting the roof of the open shed. The ground floor of the office sec-tion, incorporating an extensive presentation area, a meeting room and two individual offices, is accessed via the large shed. A semi-circular staircase leads up to the open-plan

workplaces on the first floor, which are only separated by half-height walls. The u-shaped arrangement of the desks offers the staff adequate space for their computers and large-format plans. The north side is illuminated by natural light direct from the facade openings, while the desks orien-tated towards the roofed shed on the south side are supplied with light through slots between the ceiling elements.

Wood predominates throughout
All ceilings and walls are aptly produced from the pallet elements which the company manufactures itself. As such, the building demonstrates the design scope offered by this method of construction. In keeping with the building's exterior character, wood also shapes the appearance of the interior. The solid wood elements do not require steel connections or glued joints, and the individual timber elements are joined by means of diagonally inserted beechwood dowels. The wood has been left untreated, resulting in a healthy, contaminant-free interior climate throughout the building. Apart from such practical considerations, the designers also sought to project the company's philosophy.

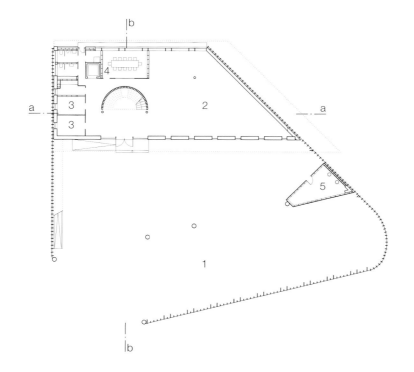

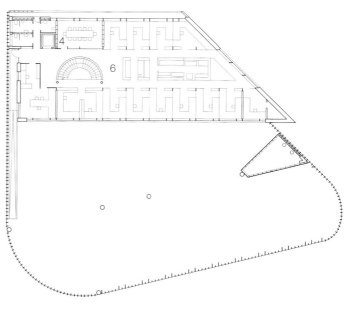

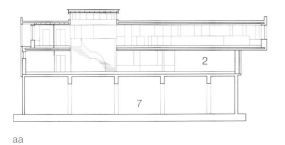

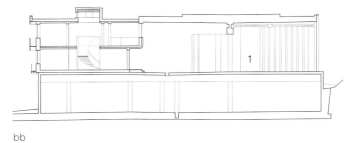

aa   bb

Floor plans
Sections
Scale 1:500

1 Loading zone
 with crane
 access
2 Exhibition room
3 Individual office
4 Meeting room
5 Dust collector
6 Open-plan
 office
7 Storage

Vertical sections
Scale 1:20

1 Two-layer bitumen sealing sheet
  Mineral wool insulation, 2× 120 mm
  Bituminous vapour barrier
  Boarding, 18 mm
  Installation level with 1.5 % slope
  Three-ply board, 16 mm
  Fir diagonal pallet, 120 mm,
  fair-faced underside
2 Spruce shingles, 30 mm
  Boarding, 30 mm
  Ventilated cavity and lathing, 40 mm
  Timber board, diffusion-open, 16 mm
  Cellulose insulation, 240 mm
  Three-layered board, 15 mm
  Fir diagonal pallet, 80 mm,
  fair-faced inside

3 Floor covering carpet, 10 mm
  Gypsum fibreboard with floor heating, 15 mm
  Particle board, 2× 19 mm
  Installation level for ventilation system, 132 mm
  Thermal insulation, 100 mm
  Anti-trickle matting, 15 mm
  Fir diagonal pallet, 240 mm
  Wood fibre insulation, 60 mm
  Timber board, diffusion-open, 16 mm
  Ventilated cavity and lathing, 40 mm
  Boarding, untreated, 30 mm
  Spruce shingles, 30 mm
4 Spruce facade,
  upright rough-sawn slats, 50 mm
  Three-layered board, 19 mm
  Cellulose insulation, 240 mm
  Three-layered board, 15 mm
  Fir diagonal pallet, 80 mm,
  fair-faced inside

Project data:

Usage: Office, warehouse and
                        multi-purpose shed
Structure: Wood
Dimensions: 44,50 × 38,50 m
Clear room height: 2,70 m
Gross volume: 2670 m³
Gross floor area: 815 m²
Year of construction: 2009
Construction period: 10 months

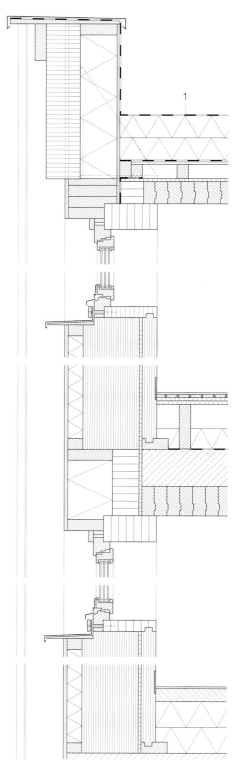

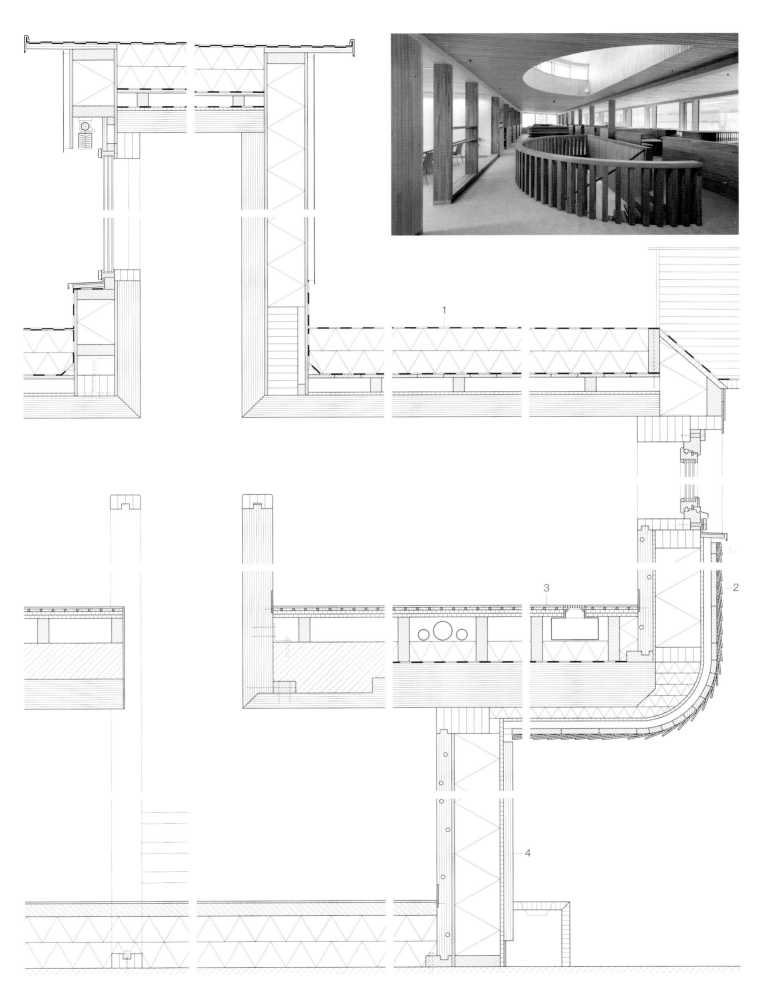

Depot of the Municipality Poing

Architects: Allmann Sattler Wappner Architekten, Munich

A shimmering, translucent facade clad in polycarbonate multi-wall sheet surrounds the workshops and administration rooms.

The increasing technical and infrastructure-related requirements of the expanding community of Poing, east of Munich, required a new building depot. The formerly constricted accommodation of the workshops, storage areas, social rooms and administration, extended across several sites, no longer satisfied the requirements of a modern and efficiently operating depot. In 2005 the municipal council announced a limited competition that was won by the practice of Allmann Sattler Wappner Architekten.
The new depot unifies all functions on one site in order to permit operations to be conducted economically and offers the employees a suitable, state-of-the-art and modern workplace.

Constellation of the buildings
Both buildings, which are positioned parallel to one another and are each around 51 m long but of different width, have different building heights dependent on the function. The ground floor of the narrower building that faces on to the street houses the workshop areas, such as transport engineering, the electrical workshop, the joiner's shop and horticulture. All rooms on the ground floor, which is constructed with a reinforced concrete skeleton, can be accessed from the outside and vehicle access is provided via the large doors. The solidly-constructed upper storey is divided into

two zones: on the one side of the stairwell are the administration rooms with secretary's office, office workplaces, meeting room, archive and photocopying room. On the other side are the employees' social rooms with changing rooms, sanitary areas and a large recreation room with a kitchenette.
The broad rear building contains a vehicular hall, 860 m², a vehicle repair workshop with servicing pit and crane track, a metalworking shop, a washing bay and associated technical rooms.
The upper storey houses the foreman's office for the vehicle repair shop with its gallery, from where the entire workshop can be overseen. Alongside one is lead into the daylight-flooded storage hall, measuring 700 m². Windows in the separating wall between the vehicle hall and the vehicle repair workshop, installed for fire-safety reasons, link the areas optically and allow visual communication.

Shimmering facade
The reinforced-concrete construction of the two buildings is shrouded in a transparent, heat-insulating facade made of polycarbonate multi-skin sheets. Depending on weather and lighting conditions, it remains visible in silhouette behind the facade with varying degrees of transparency. The polycarbonate facade in the ground-storey workshop areas serves as a thermal barrier to the outside, meaning that no additional heat insulation is required. The workshops are flooded with floor-to-ceiling glazing across the entire surface of the facade. The high levels of daylight produces a pleasant working atmosphere.

Siteplan
Scale 1:5000
Sections · Floor plans
Scale 1:1000

1 Entrance
2 Mains supply
3 Technical services
4 Horticulture
5 Transport engineering / signs
6 Storage
7 Electrical engineering
8 Painting room
9 Joiner's shop
10 Office
11 Metalworking shop
12 Vehicle repair shop
13 Washing bay
14 Power equipment room

15 Low vehicle bays
16 High vehicle bays
17 Boxes for bulk material
18 Area housing tank
19 Sweepings store
20 Boxes for chippings
21 Salt store
22 Area for housing mobile toilet / dish trolley
23 Salt silo / brine
24 Meeting room
25 Relaxation / training room
26 Terrace
27 Void

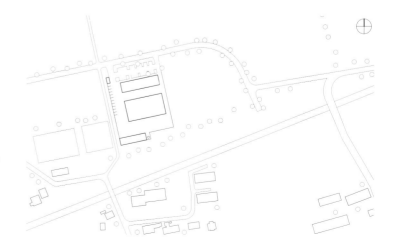

128

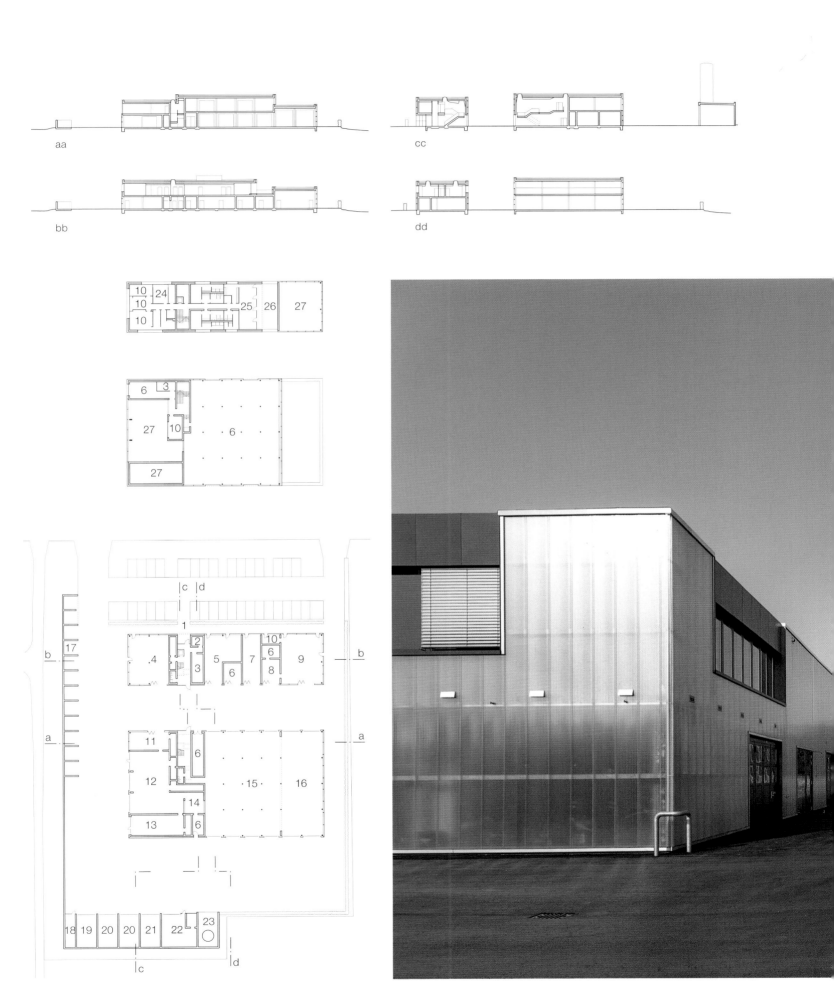

aa

bb

cc

dd

10	24						
10				25	26	27
10						

6	3			
27	10		6	
27				

c d

1

b | 17 | | 2 | | | | 10 | | b
| .4 | 3 | 5 | 7 | 6 | 9 |
| | | 6 | | 8 | |

a | 11 | 6 | | | a
12		15	16
14			
13	6		

| 18 | 19 | 20 | 20 | 21 | 22 | 23 |

c d

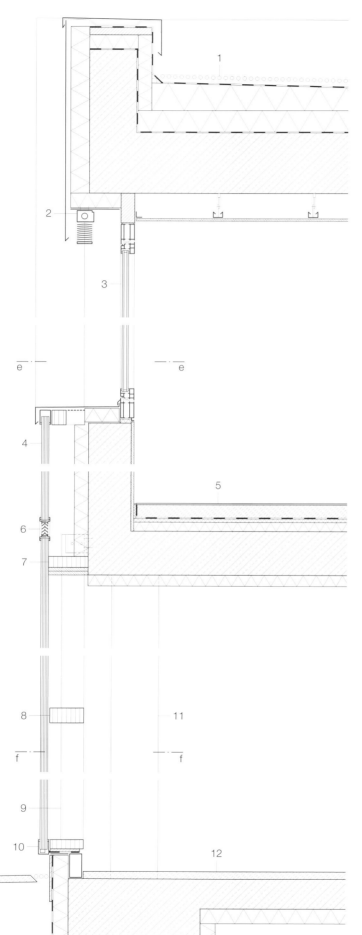

Project data:

Function:	Depot
Structure:	Reinforced concrete
Dimensions:	55 × 18 m
Clear room height:	3.90–6.45 m
Gross volume:	19,150 m³
Gross floor area:	3,840 m²
Construction costs:	€ 5,5 million (gross)
Year of construction:	2008
Construction period:	14 months

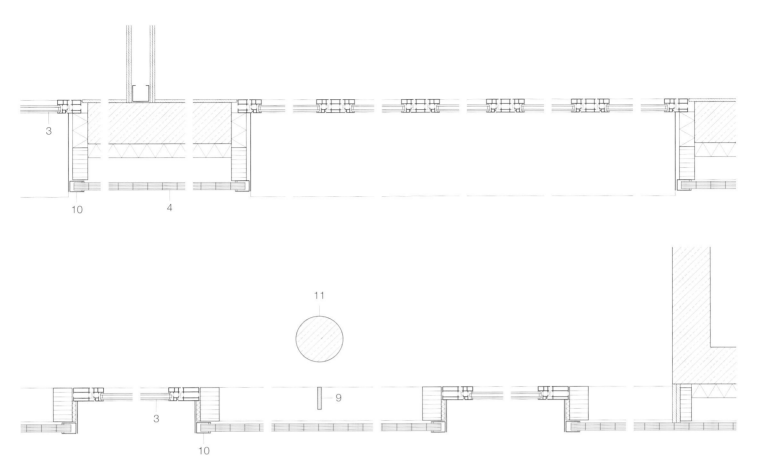

Vertical section · Horizontal sections   Scale 1:20

1 Roof structure:
   Gravel layer, 50 mm, protective felt, 3 mm
   Elastomeric bitumen seal, 5 mm
   Self-adhesive track elastomeric bitumen seal,
   EPS insulation to falls, 150 mm, EPS thermal insulation, 120 mm
   Asphalt sheeting vapour barrier, 4 mm, bituminous priming coat
   Reinforced concrete hollow core slab, 330 mm
   Suspendet gypsum plasterboards, 12.5 mm
2 Venetian blind sun protection
3 Insulating glazing: 8 mm float + 16 mm gap between panes +
   8 mm tempered safety glass
4 Wall structure:
   Polycarbonate multi-skin sheet, continuous, 40 mm,
   at least 1.2 W/m²K
   Thermal insulation wood wool multi-wall boards with
   polystyrene core, 75 mm
   Reinforced concrete, 225 mm, plaster, 2 mm
5 Floor structure:
   Linoleum floor covering, 5 mm
   Floating screed, 75 mm, separation layer
   Footfall sound insulation, 20 mm
   Insulation, 50 mm
   Reinforced concrete ceiling, 240 mm
   Thermal insulation wood wool multi-wall boards with polystyrene core,
   painted white, 60 mm
6 Ventilation element
7 Glued-laminated wood sub-construction, 60/180 mm with
   horizontal fire stops
8 Glued-laminated wood, 100/180 mm
9 Flat steel, 20/120 mm
10 Aluminium profile, bright-rolled ⌴ 80/60 mm
11 Reinforced concrete support, ∅ 250
12 Floor construction:
   Wearing course HZ 1
   Screed, 40 mm
   Reinforced concrete surface, shot-blasted, 160 mm
   Thermal insulation, 60 mm

Handicraft estate in Valbonne

Architects: Comte & Vollenweider, Nice

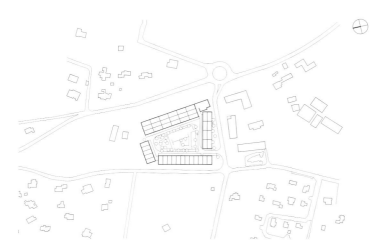

The Cité Artisanale is a handicraft estate combining workshops in various sizes and offering diverse views and routes through the ensemble.

The new handicraft estate in Valbonne, a small French town in the hinterland of the Côte d'Azur, is set between holm oaks and pines. It is thanks to the mayor's efforts that studios for artists and craftsmen have been built here, rather than a conventional industrial estate. He recognised the great importance of the handicrafts sector to Valbonne's economy as well as the need to counteract the overdevelopment of his town. In 2005 he launched a competition for a commercial zone of 4500 m² which was to be developed at a site near to the old quarter and subsequently sold off in small, reasonably priced plots. The French architectural practice, Comte & Vollenweider won the competition with their concept for an enclosed complex. They proposed an ensemble consisting of four elongated buildings, extending up to the site's boundaries and arranged around a green inner courtyard. The open corners of the trapezium offer views and routes in and

out of the ensemble. All the entrances to the studios and workshops face onto the interior green area with its car park which blends inconspicuously into the scenery.
The architects developed a 7 × 14 m basic module covered with a monopitch roof. These modules are joined together to produce units of varying sizes. The smallest module measures 50 m² and can be expanded up to a size of 900 m². The staggered arrangement of the modules creates a varied roofscape. Large wooden sliding doors and a generous room height of 6 to 8 m allow artists and craftsmen free reign in designing their objects. Various materials interact to lend the facades a distinctive character. Translucent polycarbonate panels, wooden sliding doors, metal gratings and corrugated aluminium sheeting fitted in alternating directions contrast with the outer wall of exposed concrete which encloses the ensemble. By using prefabricated wooden elements for the supporting structure and specifying simple materials, it proved possible to keep the construction costs down which, in turn enabled the studios to be sold at an affordable price.

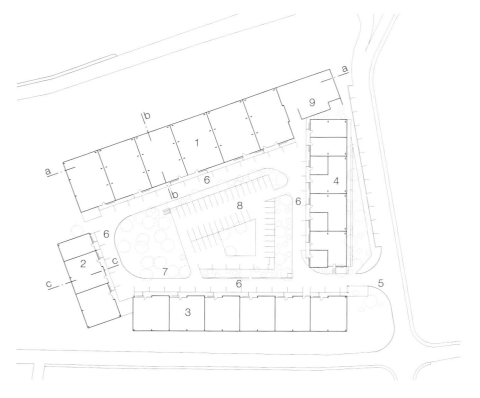

Siteplan   Scale 1:6000
Floor plan   Scale 1:1500
Section   Scale 1:500

1 300–900 m² module
2 100–200 m² module
3 100–200 m² module
4 50–200 m² module
5 Access
6 Delivery and parking
7 Integrated trees
8 Car park
9 Multifunctional area

Project data:

Function:	Studio, workshop
Structure:	Concrete, wood
Dimensions:	7 × 14 m (module)
Clear room height:	6–8 m
Gross volume:	26,660 m³
Gross floor area:	4500 m²
Construction costs:	€ 4.28 million (gross)
Year of construction:	2007
Construction period:	24 months

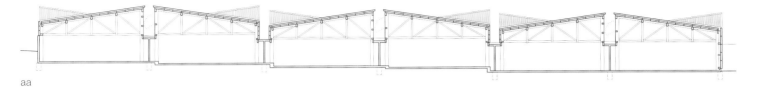

aa

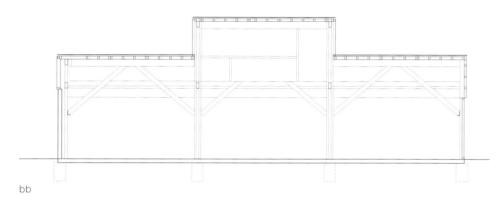

bb

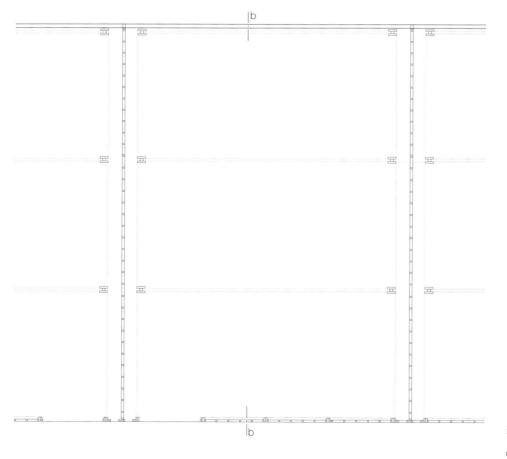

b

b

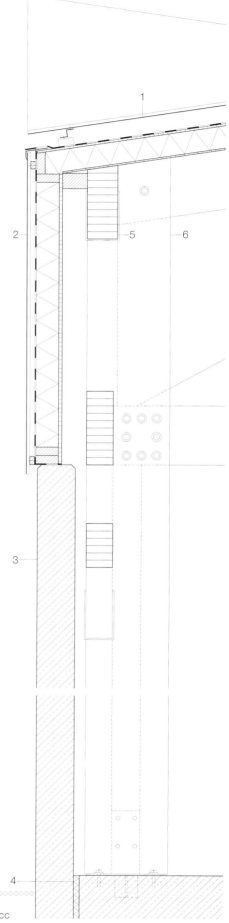

1

2

3

4

5

6

cc

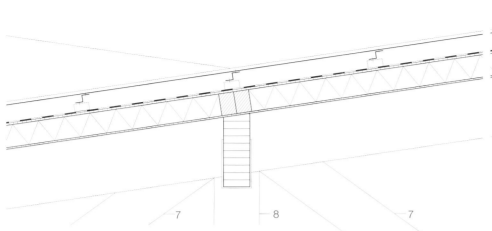

Section · Floor plan, 300–900 m² module
Scale 1:200
Vertical section   Scale 1:20

1 Roof structure:
   Galvanised corrugated sheeting, 1.8 mm,
   on galvanised steel profile, PVC sheet,
   OSB board, 12 mm,
   Rafters, 80/120 mm, with 120 mm of rock wool
   in between, OSB board, 9 mm
2 Wall structure:
   Galvanised corrugated sheeting, 1.8 mm
   Lathing, 40/25 mm, sealing
   Wooden rails, 45/120 mm,
   with 120 mm of rock wool in between,
   OSB board, 18 mm
3 Exposed concrete wall, 200 mm, shuttered
   with OSB boards

4 Building joint to ensure
   earthquake resistance
5 Laminated timber purlin, 160/400 mm
6 Laminated timber supports
   2× 100/440 mm, rigid-jointed
7 Laminated timber braces, 140/240 mm
8 Laminated timber posts, 100/240 mm
9 Laminated timber, 140/320 mm
10 Cover plate, galvanised
11 Aluminium profile
12 Polycarbonate, translucent, 40 mm,
   on galvanised steel profile
13 Solid wood rail, 100/160 mm
14 Solid wood rail, 160/300 mm

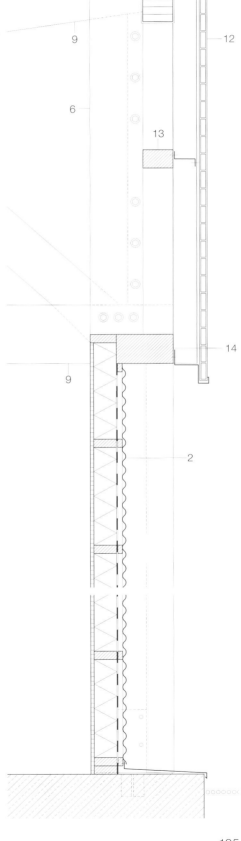

Sedus Stoll research and development centre in Dogern

Architects: ludloff + ludloff Architekten, Berlin

The architects' choice of materials on both the exterior and interior of this building showcases visual and sensory contrasts.

Shimmering white, translucent vertical strips of silicone-coated glass-fibre fabric enclose the new research and development centre of the Sedus furniture manufacturing company. When the sunshading (also made in the same material) is closed on all the windows, the building appears to be completely enshrouded. In the interests of smooth planning, all the departments involved in the development process are grouped together under one roof. The close proximity of design, development, production and adminis-tration departments gives rise to ease of communication with the aim of designing economically viable office furniture. The ground floor is entered via a foyer where nigged con-crete surfaces contrast with the light character of the facade. Woodworkers, upholsterers and varnishers craft the proto-type furniture items here, subsequently testing their practical suitability. Storage, service and sanitary rooms are accom-modated in the basement.

Open-plan communication
From the foyer a solid concrete stairway leads up to a light and airy reception area with a bar on the upper floor. This area serves as a presentation platform for new furniture items or a place for staff to meet or take time out. Three revolving doors which always move together provide access to the so-called project room, located in the fabric-enshrouded core in the centre of the 1000 m² area. This serves as an exhibition or meeting room.

Designers' workstations and administrative offices are arranged according to an open-plan concept around the central core. The depth of the offices and the tables varies according to the area of work concerned. A pitched sky-blue ceiling covers the diagonal floor plan. The folded design pro-duces zones offering varying degrees of privacy within the open-plan office structure. Although the room is as high as 7.5 m in some areas, a reduced reverberation time provides for muted acoustics and reduces the general noise level. A so-called think tank in the attic storey offers complete seclusion. This quiet, secluded room, illuminated solely by a skylight strip, is accessed via a spiral staircase in the core which interconnects all the storeys.

Structural design
The ground floor with its solid reinforced concrete construc-tion serves as a base for the building. In contrast, the upper storey and the roof are constructed with wood. This has made it possible to illuminate the office workplaces via an approx. 2 m high window strip running all around the build-ing. The pitched roof appears to hover over this window strip.

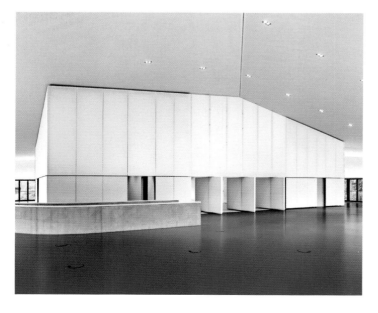

Project data:

Function:	Office, design, product development
Structure:	Reinforced concrete (ground floor), wood (upper storey)
Dimensions:	55 × 45 m
Clear room height:	4,00 m (ground floor)
	5.00–7.50 m (upper storey)
Gross volume:	14,900 m³
Gross floor area:	3200 m²
Office floor area:	875 m²
Floor area, production:	815 m²
Construction costs:	€ 5,92 million (gross)
Year of construction:	2009
Construction period:	12 months

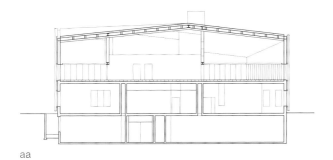

Siteplan
Scale 1:4000
Section
Floor plans
Scale 1:500

1 Foyer
2 Testing
3 Machine room
4 Welding
5 Paint shop

6 Break room
7 Upholstery shop
8 Metal workshop
9 Wood workshop
10 Wood machinery
11 Reception area/bar
12 Workplaces
13 Meeting room
14 Project room
15 Kitchenette
16 Printer

aa

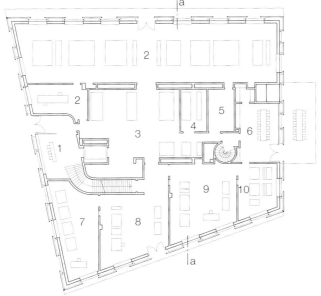

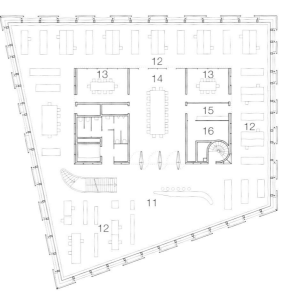

Vertical section
Scale 1:20

1 Roof structure:
   Polyurethane spray sealant
   Insulation, mineral fibre, 2× 100 mm
   Bituminous vapour barrier
   Timber board, 25 mm
   Glued laminated wood rafters, 120/350 mm
   Heating/cooling ceiling, gypsum plasterboard
2 Wall structure:
   Glass-fibre fabric, silicone-coated
   on aluminium tension spring
   Substructure steel tube ⌀ 100 mm
   Cross bracing steel tube ⬚ 80/80 mm in between
   Polyester-glass matting, polyacrylate-coated
   Timber board, 22 mm
   Cellulose insulation, 260 mm
   Vapour barrier
   Timber board, 22 mm
   Cellulose insulation, 40 mm
   Substructure, wooden lathing, 60/40 (air space 20 mm)
   Gypsum plasterboard, 9.5 mm
3 Sunshading roller blind
   Glass-fibre fabric, silicone-coated
4 Floor structure:
   Rubber floor covering, 2.5 mm
   Full-surface smoothing course, 2 mm
   Calcium sulphate flowing screed, 33–40 mm
   Mineral floor slab, 18 mm
   Dust-binding paint coating
   Reinforced concrete, 320 mm
5 Wall structure:
   Polyester-glass matting, polyacrylate-coated
   Mineral-fibre insulation, 100 mm
   Reinforced concrete, 200 mm
6 Floor construction:
   Mineral coating, 5 mm
   Composite screed, 45 mm
   Reinforced concrete surface, shot-blasted, 320 mm

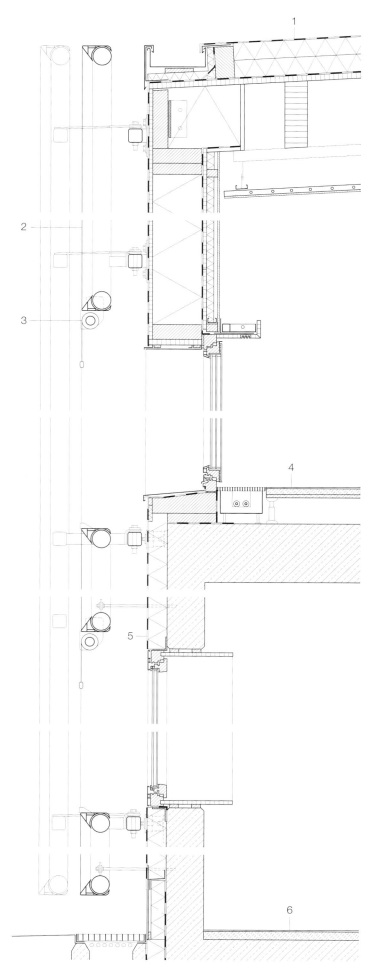

Trumpf development centre in Ditzingen

Architects: Barkow Leibinger Architekten, Berlin

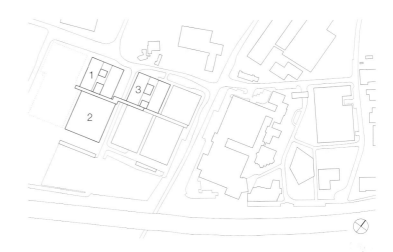

Close proximity between the directly adjoining production and office areas provide for effective communications between the various staff members.

Buildings for production, research, development, training, sales and administration have been completed in several construction phases since the middle of the 1990s at the headquarters of the Trumpf company, according to plans by Barkow Leibinger Architekten. The new development centre marks the completion of a further stage of the long-term master plan, offering over 880 workplaces on 34,500 m² of floor space in 3 modules. The laser technology centre and the development centre for machine tools are situated to the north of the central access route, while the testing facility for machine tools is situated to the south.

Spatial organisation

An unusual solution in industrial construction, which has proven effective in numerous instances at the company's site, is the location of production and office areas in direct proximity to one another. These two functions are also situated directly alongside one another at the new development centre, rather than physically separating them in different types of buildings. A new type of building has been developed for this purpose – an office building which ties in with the urban planning-style structures at the site while on an architectural level embodying an interpretation of factory architecture scaled down to office building proportions. In terms of external appearance, the different parts

of the building are barely distinguishable.
Open structures between production and office use are deliberately observed both in the laser technology centre and in the development centre. Single-storey connecting structures between machine shops and office buildings provide for the smoothest possible work flows between office area and workshop, while their green courtyards and roofs offer the staff additional recreation space.

Split-level solution in the open-plan office

The design specifications for the office areas required the principle of an open, split-level layout to be applied, following its successful introduction in the previous building phases. This arrangement of workplaces in open-plan offices on levels which are mutually offset by half a storey keeps distances short and promotes communication between the staff.

All office areas are organised along open-plan lines, with a tailor-made office furniture system ensuring efficient use of the available floor space as well as adequate privacy and noise control. Only the departmental managers are provided with a separate area at the ends of the respective elongated buildings, whereby glazing ensures sufficient openness here, too. On some levels the separated-off areas also serve as meeting rooms.

While the lower office levels have conventional ceilings, the folded roof structure rising to up to 5.5 metres in height defines the upper split levels. In these areas the clearly perceptible characteristic dynamic movement of the roofing is the predominant spatial impression.

Project data:

Function:	Production, laboratory, research office premises, customer centre
Structure:	Steel, reinforced concrete
Dimensions:	165.00 m × 157.75 m
Clear room height:	2.5–5.5 m (offices) 10–13 m (factory buildings)
Gross volume:	203,500 m³
Gross floor area:	34,500 m²
Floor area, offices:	22,000 m² (gross floor area) 12,900 m² (useful floor space)
Floor area, production:	10,500 m² (gross floor area) 6,800 m² (useful floor area)
Construction costs:	€ 56 million (gross)
Year of construction:	2009
Construction period:	26 months

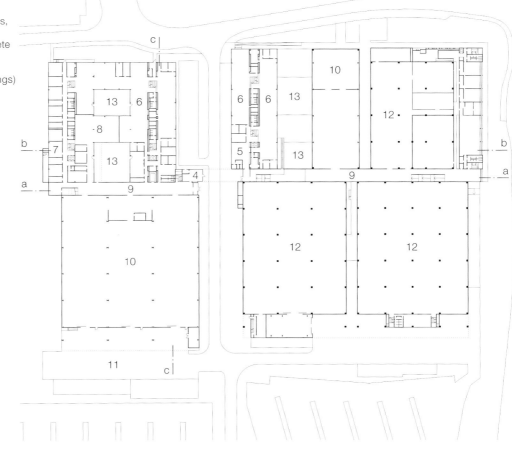

Siteplan
Scale 1:7500
Floor plan · Sections
Scale 1:2000

1 Machine tool development centre
2 Machine tool testing facility
3 Laser technology centre
4 Entrance
5 Lobby
6 Open-plan office
7 Laboratory
8 Workshop
9 Access unit
10 Machine shop
11 Delivery point
12 Existing building
13 Courtyard

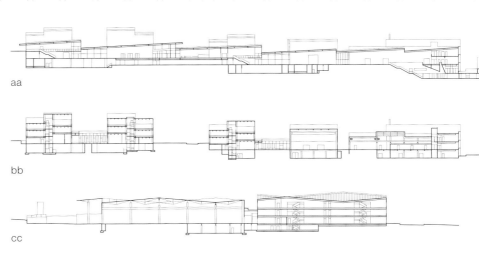

aa

bb

cc

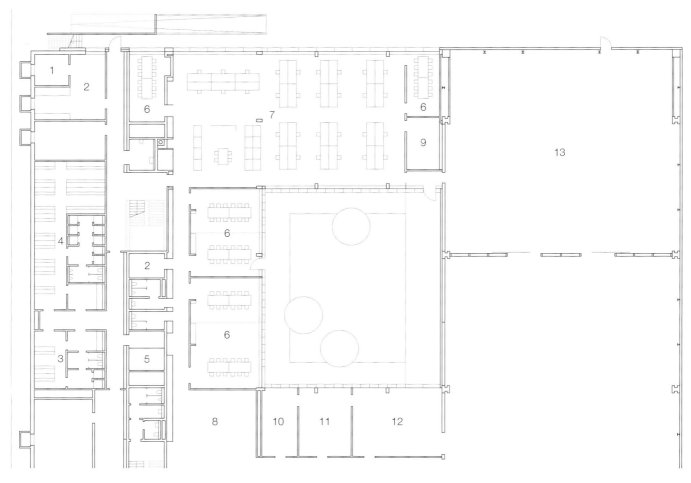

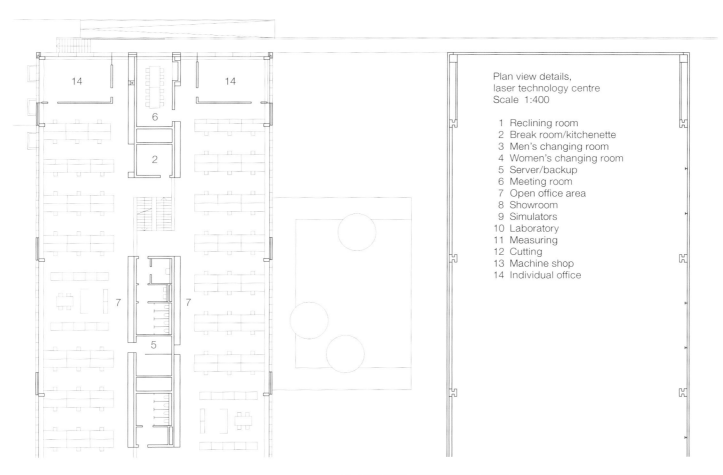

Plan view details,
laser technology centre
Scale 1:400

1 Reclining room
2 Break room/kitchenette
3 Men's changing room
4 Women's changing room
5 Server/backup
6 Meeting room
7 Open office area
8 Showroom
9 Simulators
10 Laboratory
11 Measuring
12 Cutting
13 Machine shop
14 Individual office

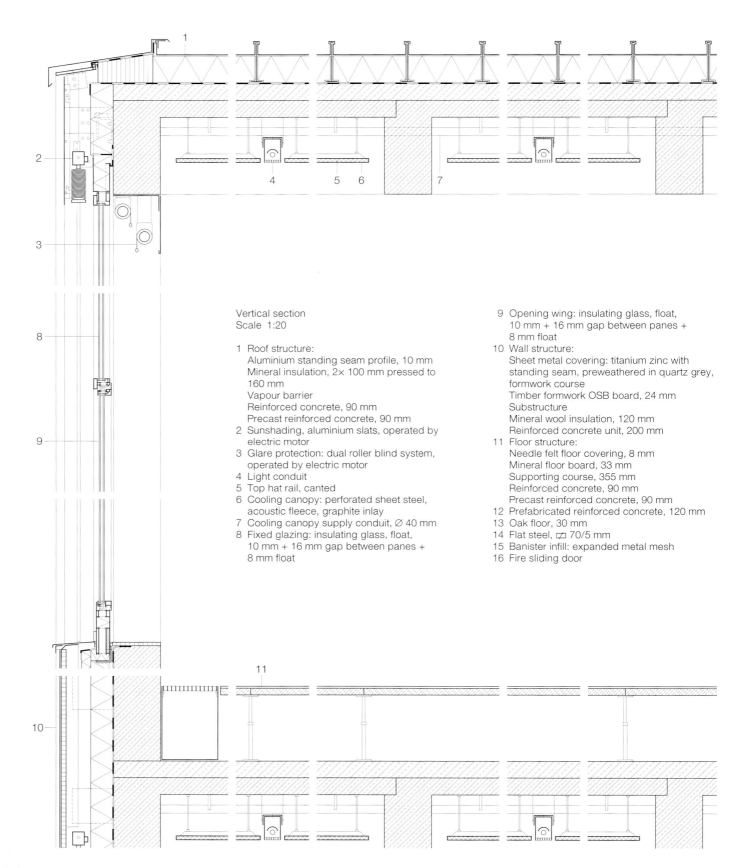

Vertical section
Scale 1:20

1 Roof structure:
   Aluminium standing seam profile, 10 mm
   Mineral insulation, 2× 100 mm pressed to
   160 mm
   Vapour barrier
   Reinforced concrete, 90 mm
   Precast reinforced concrete, 90 mm
2 Sunshading, aluminium slats, operated by
   electric motor
3 Glare protection: dual roller blind system,
   operated by electric motor
4 Light conduit
5 Top hat rail, canted
6 Cooling canopy: perforated sheet steel,
   acoustic fleece, graphite inlay
7 Cooling canopy supply conduit, ⌀ 40 mm
8 Fixed glazing: insulating glass, float,
   10 mm + 16 mm gap between panes +
   8 mm float

9 Opening wing: insulating glass, float,
   10 mm + 16 mm gap between panes +
   8 mm float
10 Wall structure:
   Sheet metal covering: titanium zinc with
   standing seam, preweathered in quartz grey,
   formwork course
   Timber formwork OSB board, 24 mm
   Substructure
   Mineral wool insulation, 120 mm
   Reinforced concrete unit, 200 mm
11 Floor structure:
   Needle felt floor covering, 8 mm
   Mineral floor board, 33 mm
   Supporting course, 355 mm
   Reinforced concrete, 90 mm
   Precast reinforced concrete, 90 mm
12 Prefabricated reinforced concrete, 120 mm
13 Oak floor, 30 mm
14 Flat steel, ⌑ 70/5 mm
15 Banister infill: expanded metal mesh
16 Fire sliding door

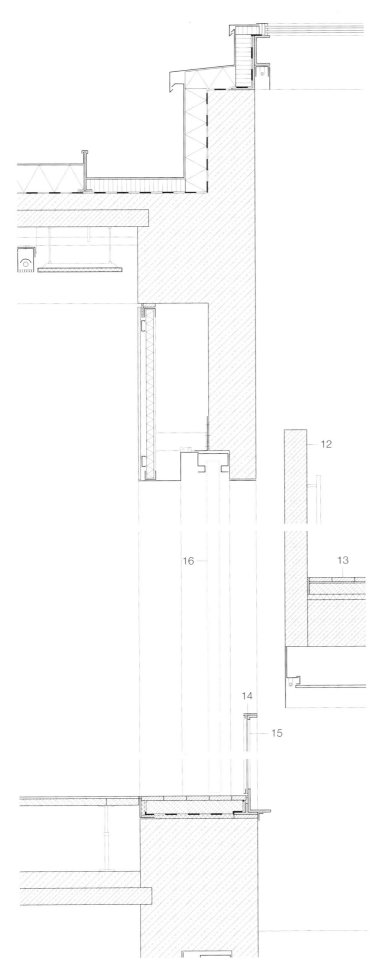

12

16

13

14

15

"Projekthaus" of the BMW Group in Munich

Architects: Henn Architekten, Munich

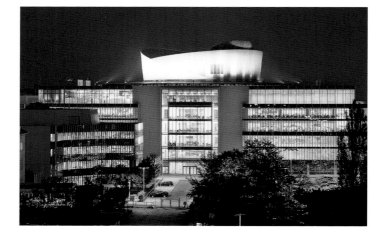

The "Projekthaus" at the BMW Group's Research and Innovations Centre facilitates a new form of collaboration by virtue of its spatial organisation.

Research and development is a key component of today's products and services. The substantive value-creation process is increasingly shifting from the manufacture of products to their development, which is having a profound knock on effect for working environments.
It is no longer enough merely to apply knowledge: it needs to be created. This is the natural territory of the group as knowledge is created through inter-personal communication. By speaking and listening a common context is constructed that changes in the course of the conversation. The context is virtual in the first instance, but can also be made real if examples are needed, such as via drawings on paper or a quickly-produced model.

Communication in the group

For many products and services, cooperative collaboration in a group of 10 to 15 employees is no longer enough. Complex products, difficult markets and different cultures require many different skills to come together for product development: it is not uncommon for 200, 1,000 or even more employees to collaborate in developing a product. The question, therefore, arises as to whether the cooperative model of communication in a small group can be transposed on to a collective of many. This is possible in principle, but pure scaling is not enough. The collective cannot communicate like a group. Not even interventions at organisational level will achieve the objective; instead they may disrupt cooperation. The small group as a successful mode of cooperation must be retained, even where there are many participants. This contradiction needs to be resolved.
For this reason it is not enough to facilitate ad hoc and informal encounters, but instead a special communication architecture is required. Collaboration in the collective does not arise as a result of everyone talking to everyone else. Temporary groups need to emerge from existing groups and then dissolve once again. This interconnection generates communication links between everyone, but only when it is necessary. Space handles the temporal management of this process.

Interdisciplinary product development

The "Projekthaus" in the Research and Innovation Centre of the BMW Group in the north of Munich is an ideal model of this type. Experts from the entire development division are "loaned out" there; 2,000 employees work on the development of the vehicles in around 200 groups of, on average, ten employees. In the most complex phase of product development that takes place in the "Projekthaus", the design specifications are implemented and other departments, such as bodywork, chassis and engine are integrated at this stage. At the same time, alongside the designers, the research engineers and the workshop come together here. The prototype is thus created in several steps.
The architecture has the task of creating a space for perception and movement in which the interconnections can unfold freely. A vertical and horizontal transparency of the office world enables the employees to be aware of one another. A prototype of the car being designed in the centre of the atrium, which is updated at regular intervals, creates a perceptible and real context for everyone and makes everyone's accomplishments visible. This is the collective's "short-term memory" that, so to speak, can watch itself at work.

Interconnecting architecture

The interconnecting architecture in the "Projekthaus" is comparable with the interconnectedness of the brain. Here, there are local connections that form centres or cortices – visual cortex, speech cortex etc. – as well as connections between the cortices. Its effectiveness is a product of the quality of the interplay of the connections and is not generated by a central instance. The core of the "Projekthaus" is not a decision-making centre that issues directions. The centre serves to facilitate the interconnection of the employees who themselves decide what they would like to contribute to the communication.

Project data:

Function:	Office, research, development
Structure:	Reinforced-concrete skeleton
Dimensions:	110 × 110 m
Gross volume:	500,000 m³
Gross floor area:	90,000 m²
Office floor area:	35,500 m²
Prototyping floor area:	4500 m²
Year of construction:	2004
Construction period:	23 months

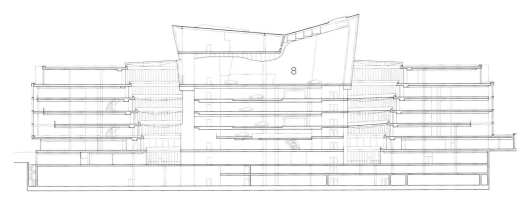

aa

Floor plan · Section   Scale 1:1000

1 Project area
2 Meeting rooms
3 Kitchenette
4 Prototyping
5 Atrium
6 Connecting pier
7 Vehicular lift
8 Studio

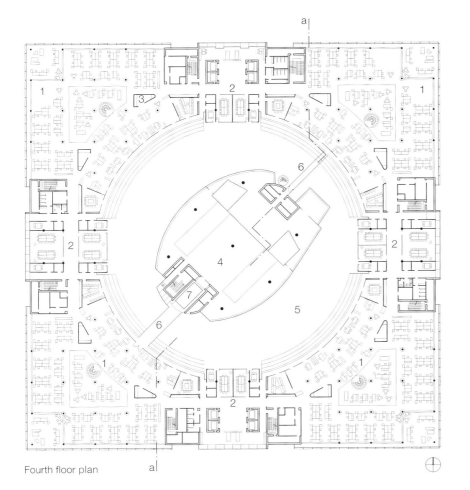

Fourth floor plan

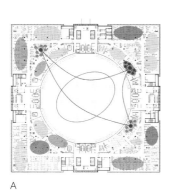

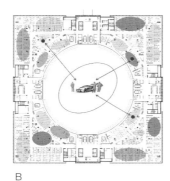

Floor-plan diagrams of communication channels

A   Direct and indirect communication between the project groups
B   Indirect communication via the convergence centre, which contains the prototype
C   Architecture of interconnectedness

A   B   C

Special laboratories at the University of Leipzig

Architects: schulz & schulz, Leipzig

Siteplan
Scale 1:5000
Sections
Scale 1:500

1 Institute for Bio-
   chemistry
2 Institute for Geo-
   physics and Geology
3 Old boiler house
4 Institute for Life
   Sciences, Pharmacy
   and Psychology
5 Laboratory building
6 University hospital

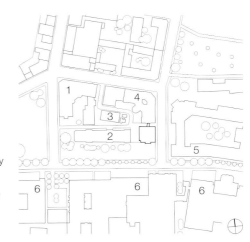

The clearly laid-out, highly specialised labora-tory building offers the research scientists ideal conditions in which to work at high levels of concentration.

The new building of the Faculty of Life Sciences, Pharmacy and Psychology has closed a vacant gap as a homogeneous cube adjoining the historical institute building, with sides measuring around 19 m. A bridge on the first floor is the only passageway connecting the detached new building to the old building. The facades, consisting of white pre-fabricated exposed concrete units, appear like a minimalist version of the adjoining stucco-decorated punctuated facades.

Special laboratories under one roof

The new building accommodates special laboratories such as acoustic, isotope, genetic engineering and molecular biology laboratories, which are not suitable for integration in the old building on account of their high safety and air-condi-tioning requirements. The old building houses all the offices, storage, recreation and teaching rooms. The floor plan typol-ogy of the new building has thus been designed specifically for laboratory use as a compact, triple-loaded complex. Modern box-type windows with integrated sunshading and generous dimensions of around 3 × 3 m establish strong links between the interior and the exterior environment and their configuration indicates the positions of the individual laboratory units on the facade.

The high safety standards for the bespoke laboratories require complete mechanical ventilation of the building and a sprinkler system throughout parts of the building. The new building is additionally provided with safety benches, acous-tic cabins, a special air management and filtering system, lock doors and readily decontaminable paint on the walls. Storey heights of 4 m and extensive engineering areas in the basement and attic storey enable integration of the nec-essary service installations, avoiding the need for roof-top installations which are typical of laboratories.

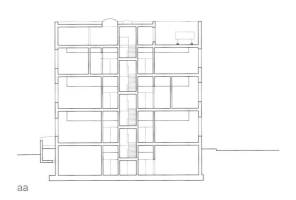

aa

Interior colour contrasts

The minimalist interior design of the laboratories, with light ceilings, walls and furniture combined with dark floors, is intended to promote undisturbed research work requiring high levels of concentration. In contrast, the circulation areas are designed as colourful communication zones with yellow flooring and reflective metal surfaces.

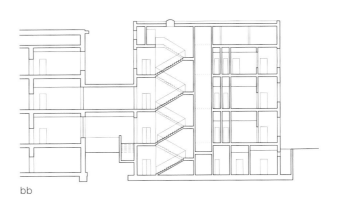

bb

149

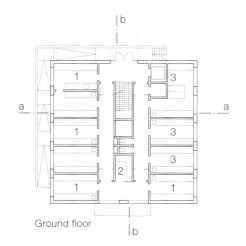

Ground floor

Second floor

Floor plans
Scale 1:500

1 Molecular biology laboratory
2 Scullery
3 Sequential analysis laboratory
4 Administrative room
5 Genetic engineering laboratory
6 Decontamination chamber
7 Mass spectroscopy laboratory
8 Service/engineering room
9 Experimentees' waiting room
10 Acoustic laboratory
11 Decay room
12 Isotope laboratory
13 Bridge to old building

Basement

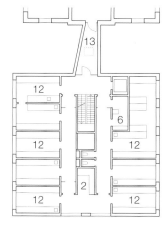

First floor

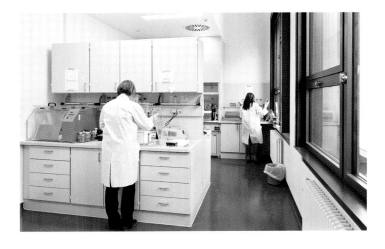

Floor plan detail, first floor
Scale 1:100

14 Isotope laboratory
15 Radionuclide outlet
16 Filter cabinet for radionuclide outlet
17 Equipment workplace
18 Wet workplace area
19 Workbench system with wall-mounted cupboards
20 Refrigerator/freezer
21 Space for equipment
22 Safety workbench

Project data:

Function:	Laboratory
Structure:	In-situ concrete, pre-fabricated facade
Dimensions:	19 × 19 m
Clear room height:	3 m
Gross volume:	7900 m³
Gross floor area:	1800 m²
Construction costs:	€ 6.5 million
Year of construction:	2009
Construction period:	20 months

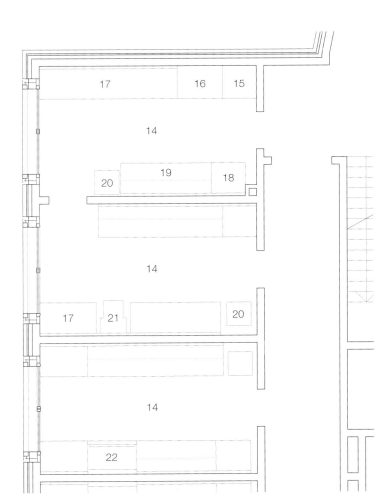

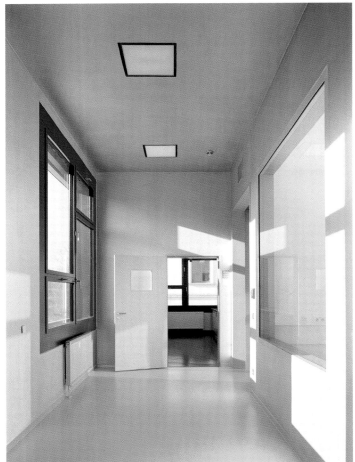

Fraunhofer Institute in Ilmenau

Architects: Staab Architekten, Berlin

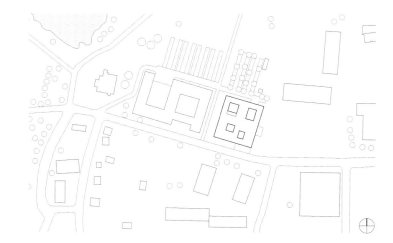

Modern offices, laboratories and special spaces provide ideal conditions for porductive research and work.

The aim of the institute's new building is not only to provide the scientists with premises tailored perfectly to the needs of effective, smoothly functioning experimental and development work, but also to present a distinctive face to the outside world. It is also important to offer researchers an attractive working environment, as such "soft" factors which undoubtedly play a role in the competition in head-hunting for the best staff.

Internal organisation

The Fraunhofer Institute for Digital Media Technology in the German town of Ilmenau was completed on a comparatively low budget as a building designed in keeping with its intended use which at the same time performs the necessary prestigious function. The compact, double-storey structure is defined by elegant restraint. Situated on the campus of the Technical University, it ties in with the scale of the existing buildings. Its translucent facade shimmers in varying guises according to the angle of the incoming light, adding a touch of stylish refinement. The interior is similarly unobtrusive, with a light colour palette prevailing throughout. The arrangement around four inner courtyards incorporating green areas provides the rooms with natural lighting, creating a pleasant working atmosphere. Two of these courtyards are accessible via an open connecting passage on the ground floor and lead to the

two entrances which, in turn, provide access to a joint public foyer from which the cafeteria and the seminar rooms lead off. The remainder of the building is not accessible to the public and is separated accordingly.

The access ways essentially follow the four courtyards to form a cross, at the intersection of which the corridors on both storeys widen into a recreation and communication area. The rooms for acoustic measurements are also located here, forming the core of the building in terms of both their key function and their central position. All the other functional rooms, such as offices and laboratories, are arranged around the courtyards in single- or double-level corridors. At the ends of the cross the main corridors lead into core functional areas, each incorporating a two-flight staircase, a copying room, toilets and a kitchenette. The openings onto the inner courtyard establish visual contact between the respective departments. The interior is finished in a restrained beige colour throughout. For reasons of costs, a cellar runs beneath only part of the building, accommodating the mechanical service and engineering rooms.

Translucent facade

The translucent facade elements cause the solid structure to shimmer in various guises according to the incident light angle, lending the envelope an impression of depth and a lightness of touch. For reasons of appearance, the glass fibre-reinforced facade panels have additionally been provided with a faint sepia hue.

Siteplan
Scale 1:5000
Sections · Floor plans
Scale 1:750

1 Office
2 Workshop
3 Laboratory/work room
4 Kitchenette
5 Storage
6 Special room for acoustics
7 Courtyard
8 Meeting room
9 Recreation area
10 Main entrance
11 Foyer
12 Dead room
13 Seminar room
14 Side entrance
15 Cafeteria
16 Air space
17 Library

Project data:

Function:	Research building
Structure:	Reinforced concrete
Dimensions:	50 m × 57 m
Clear room height:	3.53–2.80 m
Gross volume:	22,532 m³
Gross floor area:	5,945 m²
Laboratory floor area:	725 m²
Office floor area:	1,600 m²
Floor area,	
Seminar rooms:	150 m²
Construction costs:	€ 9.30 million (gross)
Year of construction:	2008
Construction period:	19 months

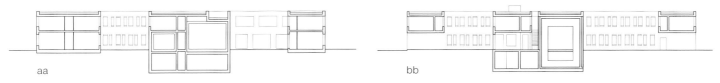

aa   bb

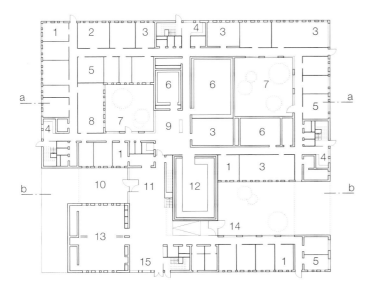

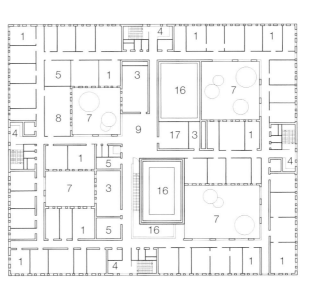

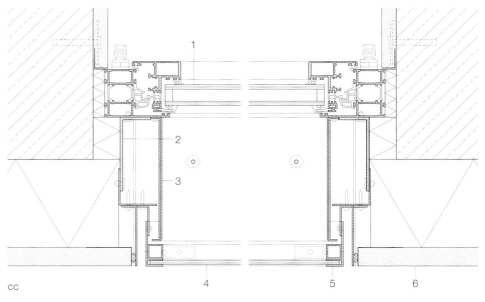

cc

Horizontal sections   Scale 1:5
Vertical section   Scale 1:20

1 Thermopane glazing U_g = 1.1 W/m²K,
  6 mm float + 16 mm gap between
  panes + 6 mm float
  Window frame in anodised aluminium
2 Steel angle, 40/100 mm
3 Facing, 2 mm anodised aluminium
4 Prestressed glass pane, 5 mm
5 Aluminium profile, extruded,
  as surrounding frame

6 Wall structure:
  Plaster featuring stone texture, 15 mm
  Insulation, 120 mm,
  Reinforced concrete, 200 mm
  Interior plaster, 15 mm
7 Sunshading with
  light-guiding slats, 80 mm
8 Floor structure:
  Carpet, 10 mm, cement screed, 60 mm
  PE film, two-ply
  Reinforced concrete floor, 250 mm,
  with activated concrete core, filling 5 mm

 9 Steel angle, 120/120 mm
10 Anodised aluminium sheeting, 3 mm
11 Glazed door in anodised aluminium frame
12 Floor structure:
   Cement-bound flowing screed, 5 mm
   Cement screed, 65 mm, PE film
   Footfall sound insulation, 30 mm
   Compensating insulation EPS, 35 mm
   Vapour barrier
   Reinforced concrete floor slab, 250 mm
13 Shadow joint with inserted
   insulating strip

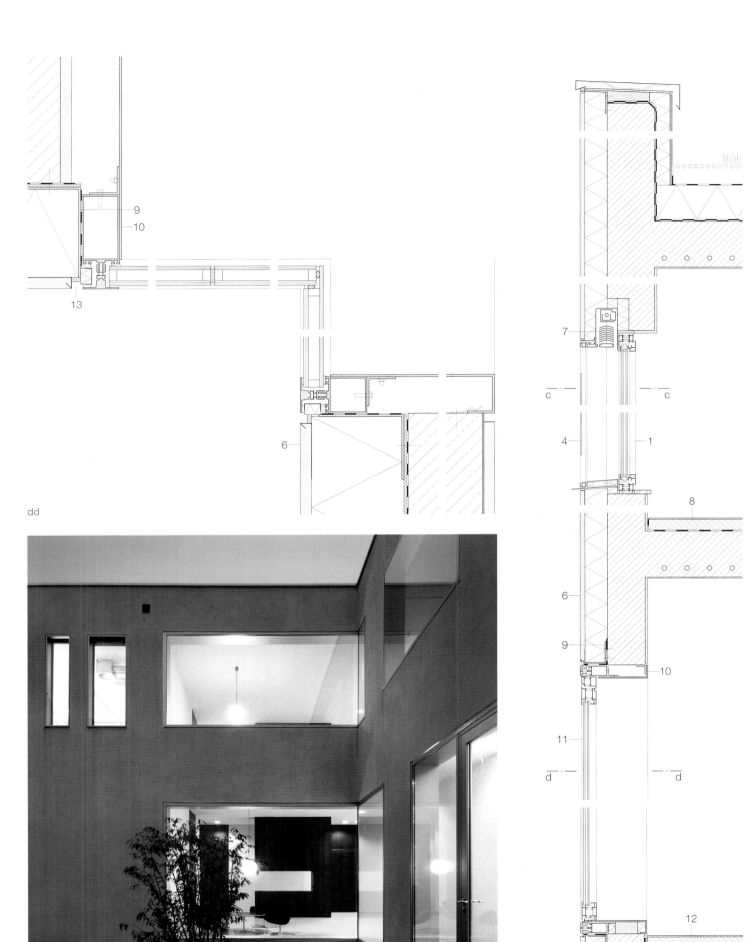

dd

c ——— c

d ——— d

9
10
13
6
7
4 — 1
8
6
9
10
11
12

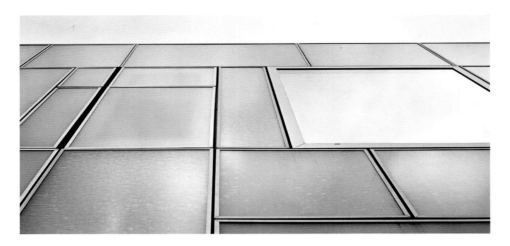

Vertical section
Scale 1:20
Horizontal section
Scale 1:5

1 Roof structure:
   Extensive green roof/gravel around edges
   Diffusion-open separating matting
   Thermal insulation XPS, 200 mm
   Waterproof course of bitumen sheeting,
   bituminous precoat
   Sloping lightweight concrete, 40–200 mm
   Reinforced concrete floor, 200 mm with
   activated concrete core, 5 mm filling
2 Sunshading with light-guiding slats, 80 mm
3 Prestressed glass pane, 5 mm
4 Aluminium profile, extruded,
   as surrounding frame
5 Thermopane glazing U_g = 1.1 W/m²K,
   6 mm float + 16 gap between panes +
   6 mm float

Window frame in anodised aluminium
6 Wall structure:
   Glass fibre-reinforced plastic panelling, 5 mm
   Ventilation, 40 mm
   Mesh infill
   Mineral wool insulation, 2× 60 mm
   Reinforced concrete, 200 mm, 250 mm in
   the staircase area
   Interior plaster, 15 mm
7 Aluminium emergency exit door with
   glass panel
8 Floor structure:
   Cement-bound screed, 5 mm
   Cement screed, 65 mm
   PE film, footfall sound insulation, 30 mm
   Compensating insulation EPS, 35 mm
   Vapour barrier
   Reinforced concrete floor slab, 250 mm
9 Sub-structure – steel angles with bracing
10 Anodised aluminium mounting construction
11 Anodised aluminium bearing frame
12 Anodised aluminium angle

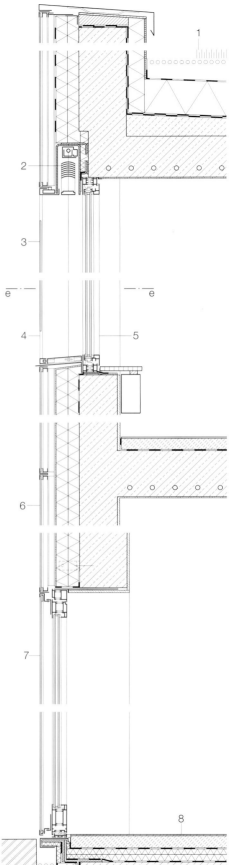

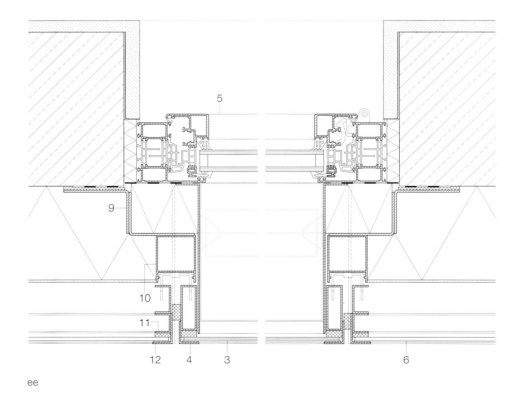

ee

Use, Research, Technology

The Fraunhofer Institute for Digital Media Technology (IDMT) conducts research in the area of audio-visual applications with a permanent staff, at present, of around 50 together with seven trainees, seven post-graduate students and around 60 students. The institute covers a broad spectrum of research fields. The Acoustics Unit is concerned with the development of solutions for public address systems, in particular for 3D sound and virtual acoustics. Other key fields of research are concerned with loudspeaker technologies and equipment acoustics.

Another key focus is the user-friendly management of multimedia data volumes and the exchange of data. Staff from the institute played a key role in the invention of the mp3 audio encoding standard, for example. The Fraunhofer IDMT also develops appropriate and reliable distribution models for digital content.

For the first time, the new institute building with 2,800 m² of effective floor space now offers the necessary capacity to provide a single base for all the post-graduates, trainees, scientific assistants and interns and allows for further growth of the institute. Concentrating all the personnel at the same premises results in improved conditions for effective communication and working, in particular with regard to cooperation on interdisciplinary topics. The new building, with its modernly appointed offices, laboratories and bespoke rooms and the inviting corner areas conducive to communication, creates ideal conditions for productive research and other work, as well as providing an effective basis for the strategic expansion of research activities.

Special rooms for acoustics

Special rooms are required for the above-described research activities. In the core of the building there is a so-called dead room, for example, in which precise acoustic measurements and audio tests can be conducted. Instead of being reflected by the walls as in conventional rooms, sound waves are absorbed by special wall panelling. In order to prevent any disturbing influences such as noises or vibrations, the room is also sound-proofed and isolated from the rest of the building. This makes it possible to acurately measure only those tones and sounds which are emitted from the sound source.

The dead room with shell dimensions of around 12 × 7.5 m and 9.5 m in height differs from other rooms of this type in particular by virtue of its extended frequency range (63 Hz to 20 kHz). This enables exact measurement of the entire range of human audibility in research and development work on loudspeakers and PA systems. A turning device has additionally been installed specifically for measuring the so-called balloon data of loudspeakers.

In addition to the dead room there is another room tailored to the requirements of acoustic research which is employed for development work on 3D audio-visual systems. This 3D presentation room is equipped with a mobile beam system which enables loudspeaker systems to be set up in the most diverse three-dimensional arrangements. A visual tracking system makes it possible to follow the viewer and/or listener and to adapt sound fields and visual playback to the current playback position.

Courtyard at the Czech Technical University of Prague

Architects: Vyšehrad Atelier, Prague

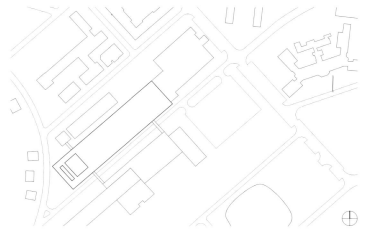

An inner courtyard which had been out of use for some years has been converted into a multifunctional "think-tank" for students.

The inner courtyard of the faculty of construction engineering had long fallen into disuse. Following a conversion project, the Czech Technical University of Prague now boasts a spacious multifunctional area which increases the available space while promoting interaction and communication between students and staff.

To begin with a new roof measuring 18 × 24 m was installed over the courtyard. A row of windows surrounding the newly enclosed space and the sawtooth glazing in the roof ensure a high level of natural light for the rooms. On the ground floor, mobile lockers demarcate the flexibly arranged work areas. The furniture is multifunctional in character, performing acoustic functions or serving as display areas for students presentations. It can be removed as necessary to enable the hall to be used for exhibitions, lectures and conferences. Two newly installed staircases and an access gallery running around the hall afford access to the teaching units which have green polycarbonate panelling suspended from the new roof structure on the upper floor. Rooms accessible via individual bridges enable teaching in separate units. The materials used, such as steel and concrete, have been left in their original state, foregoing the need for subsequent finishing treatment.

The result of the conversion and enclosure of the courtyard is a "think-tank" with an industrial charm which offers spaces for quiet contemplation as well as promoting communication.

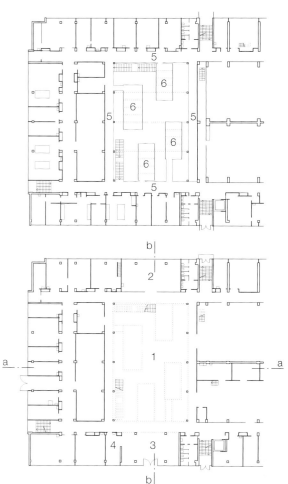

Project data:

Function:	Work area
Structure:	Steel
Dimensions:	17.20 m × 42.30 m
Clear room height:	2.40 m (teaching unit)
	6.80 – 8.95 m (atrium)
Gross volume:	6550 m³
Gross floor area:	1060 m²
Floor area of teaching units:	113.40 m²
Construction costs:	€ 1.8 million (gross)
Year of construction:	2008
Construction period:	7 months

Siteplan
Scale 1:5000
Floor plans · Sections
Scale 1:750

1 Multifunctional area
2 Workshop/ model making area
3 Relaxation room
4 Service/ engineering room
5 Gallery
6 Teaching unit

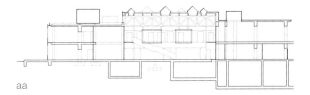

aa

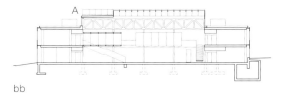

bb

Floor plans
Scale 1:250

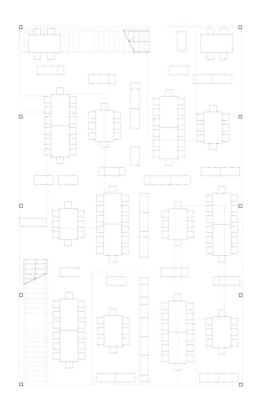

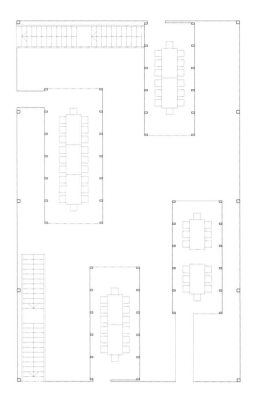

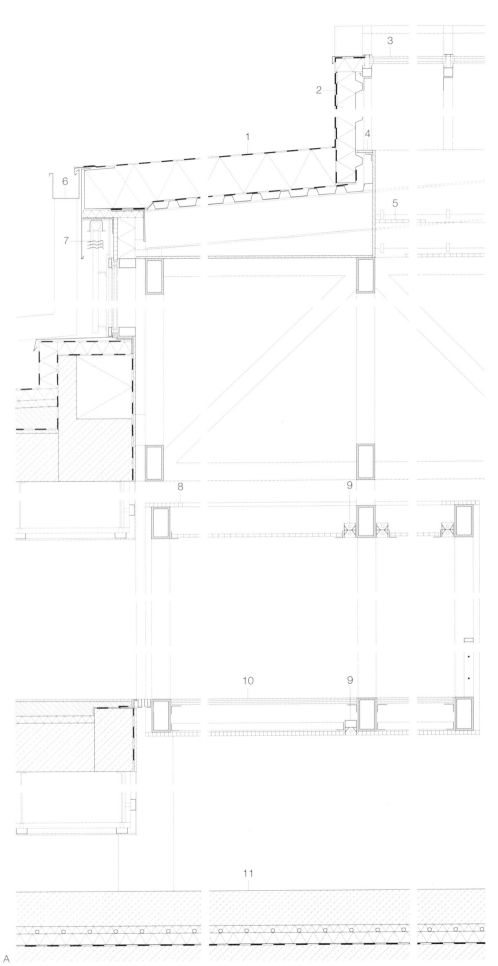

1 Roof structure:
  PVC seal sheeting
  Mineral wool insulation, 250 mm
  Vapour barrier
  Trapezoidal sheeting, 42 mm
  Steel girders, I 180 mm
2 Wall structure:
  PVC seal sheeting
  Sandwich panel with
  PUR insulation, 150 mm
  Steel profile, ▱ 75/50/5 mm
3 Sawtooth glazing:
  Laminated glazing comprising 10 mm
  tempered glass + 15 mm gap +
  10 mm tempered glass
4 Fibre cement slab, 12 mm
5 Polycarbonate web panel, white, 16 mm
6 Zinc plate guttering, 0.7 mm
7 Sunshading slats
8 Roof over teaching unit:
  Polycarbonate honeycomb panel, green, 21 mm
  Steel frame, ▱ 180/100/10 mm
  Polycarbonate web panel white, 16 mm
9 Recessed light fixture
10 Floor structure:
  Laminated glazing comprising 3× 10 mm
  tempered glass
  Steel angle bearings, 40/4 mm
  Steel profile, ▱ 180/100/10 mm
  Polycarbonate honeycomb panel, green, 21 mm
11 Floor structure:
  Steel-fibre concrete polished, 190 mm
  Profiled EPS system panelling with floor
  heating, 40 mm
  EPS insulation, 60 mm
  Separation layer
  Reinforced concrete, 100 mm

Rolex Learning Center in Lausanne

Architects: SANAA, Tokyo

The centrepiece at the university campus combines the most diverse functions on a single floor to promote interdisciplinary communication between the scientists.

The location of the École Polytechnique Fédérale de Lausanne (EPFL) on the north bank of Lake Geneva is as unique as the centrepiece at the campus: a rectangle measuring 166 × 121 m, undulating like the surrounding hills, from which 14 curvilinear courtyards of 7 to 50 m in diameter appear to have been punched out of the roof slab.
With its unconventional concept and organic shape, this example of sculptural architecture is a perfect embodiment of the university's values and aspirations such as transparency, networking and innovation. A further aim of the building is to offer an attractive setting which is likely to appeal to top international researchers.

Undulating interior
The Learning Center has the character of a micro-campus within the overall campus. Library, workplaces, offices, cafés, restaurant, bookshop, bank branch and multifunctional auditorium are all accommodated in a single room covering 17,000 m² of floor space – and all this virtually free of any partitions, doors and corridors. Views outside and throughout

the building, widening and narrowing areas and above all the undulations – with angles of up to 30° – accompanied for the most part by the curved roof, make walking through the 3.3 m high interior a unique experience. The curves in the floor and ceiling limit the view through the building to the next undulation. The manner in which the interior is organised only becomes apparent on an exploratory walk through the building. Specially developed inclined elevators and ramps ensure that all areas are readily accessible, despite the sometimes extreme sloping of the floor.
The courtyards establish contact with the outside environment even in the middle of the building and link up the outside areas beneath the concrete shell.

Different functional areas
Level platforms akin to viewing terraces enable seating to be installed even where the flooring is inclined. The installed curved areas vary according to requirements: open zones are used for individual and group work, while acoustically screened-off installations with transparent glass panels are provided for those who wish to remain undisturbed. The bookshop is surrounded by a shroud of white expanded metal, while the areas enclosed by gypsum plasterboard walls are used for teaching, administrative staff offices and various research facilities.

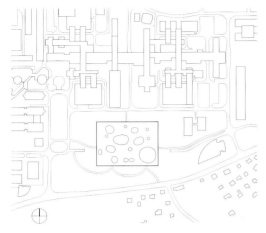

Siteplan Scale 1:10 000

Project data:

Function:	Office, library, work area
Structure:	Steel, wood, concrete
Dimensions:	166 × 121 m
Clear room height:	3.3 m
Gross floor area:	20,200 m²
Construction costs:	110 Mio. CHF
Year of construction:	2010
Construction period:	30 months

Floor plans · Sections   Scale 1:1000

1 Main entrance
2 Side entrance
3 Inclined elevator

4 Café, bar, canteen
5 Bank
6 Bookshop
7 Offices
8 Workplaces

9 Courtyard
10 Library reading area
11 Library
12 Restaurant
13 Multifunctional space

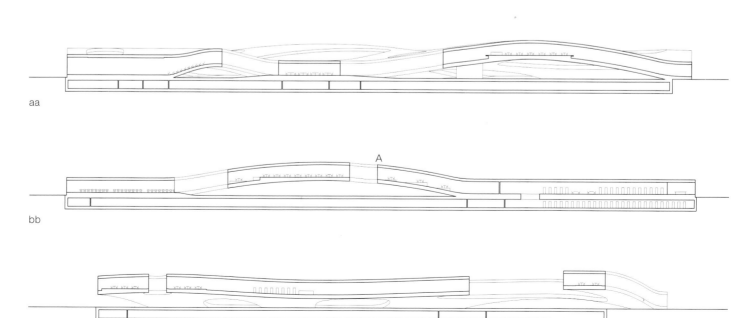

aa

bb

cc

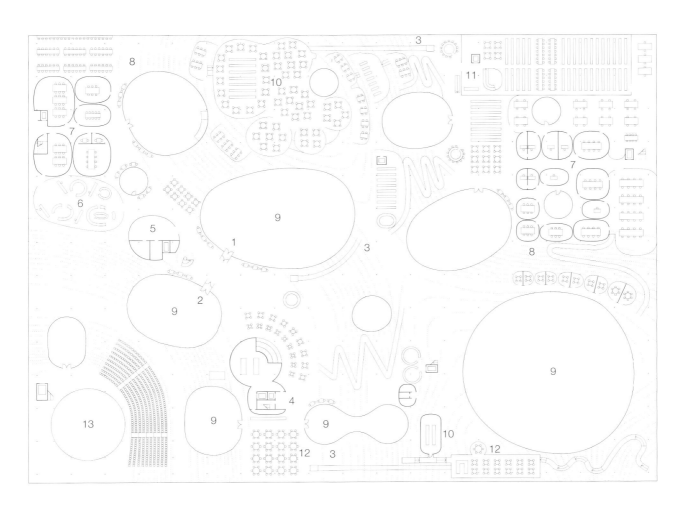

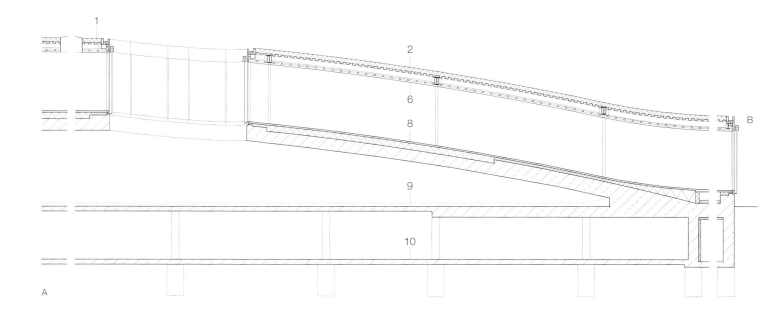

A

B

Section   Scale 1:200
Vertical section of facade   Scale 1:20

1 Light grey PVC sealing
   Mineral wool, 2× 110 mm, vapour barrier
   Supporting structure, level areas:
   Trapezoidal plating, 80 mm
   Main girders, IPE 400, spacing 9 m, l = 9 m,
   Secondary girders steel profile, IPE 300,
   spacing 3 m, l = 9 m

   Flat steel wind bracing
2 Light grey PVC sealing
   Mineral wool, 2× 110 mm, vapour barrier
   Supporting structure, curved areas:
   Trapezoidal plating, curved, 26 mm
   Main girders steel profile, IPE 400,
   polygonal folds, spacing 9 m, l = 9 m,
   segment length 3 m
   Secondary girders glue-laminated wood,
   curved, 360/200 mm, top and underside with

   inclined milled surfaces, spacing 1.50 m, l = 9 m
   Flat steel wind bracing
3 Sunshading blinds
4 Sunshading glazing (curved in patio area),
   10 mm tempered glass + 14 mm gap
   + 12 mm laminated glazing, U_g = 1.1 W/m²K,
   g = 58 %
5 Facade post, steel profile, T 70/90/10 mm
6 Coating, sound-absorbing, 8 mm
   Acoustic insulation, 25 mm

Gypsum plasterboard, curved, 12.5 mm
Aluminium rail substructure
7 Composite column, tubular steel, Ø 127 mm
8 Carpeting
Seamless reinforced screed, 80 mm,
with integrated component heating/cooling
Foil, thermal insulation 350 mm
Vapour barrier
Reinforced concrete C 50/60, fibre-reinforced,
seamless, curved, 600 mm

9 Limestone chippings, 150 mm
Sealing
Reinforced concrete, 280 mm/600 mm
at support point with integrated pretension-
ing device (tension cable of curves in shell
above)
10 Underground garage floor slab,
reinforced concrete, 250 mm
Bored piles, Ø 500, 600, 900 mm,
depth 14–20 m

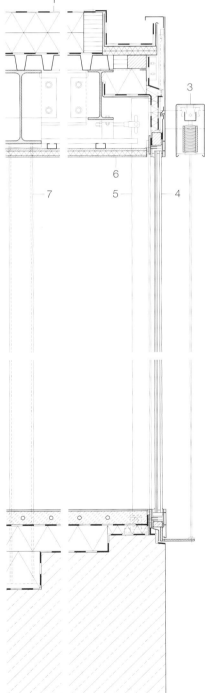

B

Project data – Architects

Office building of Claus en Kaan Architecten in Amsterdam

Owner: Zeeman Trust
Architects: Claus en Kaan Architecten
Project management: Felix Claus, Dick van Wageningen
Contributors: Marc van Broekhuijsen, Roland Rens, Joost Mulders, Jante Leupen, Romy Schneider, Surya Steijlen, James Webb
Construction: Adams Bouwadviesbureau, Druten
Contractor: Heijmerink Bouw Utrecht B.V., Bunnik
Building installations, electrical installations: Installatietechniek Thermos, Utrecht
Year of construction: 2007

www.clausenkaan.com
cka@cka.nl

Felix Claus
Born 1956 in Arnheim; graduated from Delft University of Technology in 1987; professor at ETH Zurich; teaching post at ETSA Madrid; guest lecturer at Berlage Institute of Delft University of Technology and Amsterdam Academy of Architecture.

Kees Kaan
Born 1961 in Breda; graduated from Delft University of Technology in 1987; visiting lecturer at various universities since 1993; professor at Delft University of Technology and visiting professor at RWTH Aachen University since 2006; visiting professor at the Syracuse University in Florence in 2007.

1987: formation of Claus en Kaan Architects.

Volksbank in Salzburg

Owner: Domus IC Leasing GesmbH
Architects: BKK-3 with Johann Winter, Vienna
Project management:
Dominik Hennecke, Corinna Eger
Contributors: Franz Sumnitsch, Johann Winter, Aljona Lissek, Tina Krischmann, Julia Teiwes, Christoph Eichler, Henning Schmidt, Christine Huber, Isabella Strauss, Tobias Hermesmeier, Mathias Bambuch
Project management: BKK-3 in conjunction with Johann Winter
Structural planning: Kraibacher structural engineers, Salzburg
Building physics: ZT-Kanzlei Bauphysik, Vienna
Landscaping: BKK-3, Vienna
Year of construction: 2007

www.bkk-3.com
mail@bkk-3.com

Franz Sumnitsch
Born 1961 in Klagenfurt; graduated from Graz University of Technology in 1990; 1987–1989: assistant to Günther Domenig; 1989: team BKK (Baukünstlerkollektiv – architects' collective); 1992: team BKK-2; 2000: formation of BKK-3; 2000–2006: BKK-3 in collaboration with Johann Winter; since 2006: direction BKK-3; since 2007: teaching post for Product design at Kärnten Technikon.

AachenMünchener head office in Aachen

Owner: Generali Deutschland Immobilien GmbH
Architects: kadawittfeldarchitektur GmbH, Aachen
Project management: Stefan Haass, Jascha Klusen
Contributors: Sebastian Potz, Michael Tremmel, Frank Berners, Gaby Inden, Roswitha van der Kooi, Susanne Lüschen, Christoph Schlaich, Julia Therstappen, Andrea Thörner, Sascha Thomas, Daniel Trappen, Eva Strotmeier
Structural design: Dr. Binnewies, Ingenieurgesellschaft mbH, Hamburg
Contractor: Alpine Deutschland GmbH with subcontractor in the construction phase: Nattler Architekten, Essen
Project management: Ernst & Young Real Estate GmbH, Troisdorf
Landscaping: Club L94 landscape architects, Cologne
Year of construction: 2010

www.kadawittfeldarchitektur.de
office@kadawittfeldarchitektur.de

Klaus Kada
Born 1940 in Leibnitz; graduated from Graz University of Technology in 1971; 1971–1985: partnership with Gernot Lauffer; practice in Graz since 1988; 1995–2006: professor at RWTH Aachen University; practice in Aachen since 1996.

Gerhard Wittfeld
Born 1968 in Moers; graduated from RWTH Aachen University in 1995; work with Klaus Kada, Graz, since 1994; 1997–2004: teaching post at RWTH Aachen University; partner at kadawittfeldarchitektur since 1999.

Smart working concept for Credit Suisse in Zurich

Owner: Credit Suisse AG
Architects: Camenzind Evolution, Zurich
Project management: Stefan Camenzind (Camenzind Evolution); Martin Kleibrink (Credit Suisse AG)
Contributors: Stefanie Wandiger
Office planning: congena GmbH, Munich, Christoph Kitterle
Supervision of works: Credit Suisse AG, Zurich, Silvan Schneider
Electrical planning: khp-ag engineering + management, Dietikon, Felix Hansmann
Year of construction: 2010

www.camenzindevolution.com
zurich@camenzindevolution.com

Stefan Camenzind
Born 1963 in Zurich; studied architecture at Technikum Winterthur; 1990–1995: architect at Nicholas Grimshaw & Partners; 1996–1998: architect at Renzo Piano Building Workshop; owner of Camenzind Evolution since 2004.

Stefanie Wandiger
Born 1981 in Wolfen; studied interior design at Darmstadt University of Technology; 2007: employment at Die Lichtplaner; 2008: employment at OAP Project Management; 2009: employment at CAPS architects, Zurich; employee of Camenzind Evolution since 2010.

Christoph Kitterle
Born 1960 in Bad Tölz; studied architecture in Munich and Berlin; consultant at congena in the field of organisational construction planning and user project management since 1996; partner at congena since 1998; managing partner at congena since 2002.

Factory building in Rehau

Owner: Rehau AG + Co.
Architects: WEBERWÜRSCHINGER, Berlin/Weiden; Michael Weber, Klaus Würschinger
Project partner: Haye Bakker, Berlin
Supervision of works: WEBER-WÜRSCHINGER, Berlin/Weiden; Rehau AG + Co., Rehau
Structural planning: Schneider + Partner Ingenieur Consult, Kronach
Building installations, electrical planning: Rehau AG + Co., Rehau
Acoustic design: Ingenieurbüro Leistner, Bayreuth
Year of construction: 2004

www.weberwuerschinger.com
info@weberwuerschinger.com

Michael Weber
Born 1968 in Neustadt a. d. Waldnaab; graduated from Augsburg University of Applied Sciences in 1993.

Klaus Würschinger
Born 1967 in Neustadt a. d. Waldnaab; graduated from Augsburg University of Applied Sciences in 1992.

Haye Bakker
Born 1966 in Waalre; 1992: Bachelor of Fine Arts, interior designer at Hogeschool West-Brabant; 2004–2009: freelancer for WEBER-WÜRSCHINGER; managing director since 2009.

1997: formation of WEBER-WÜRSCHINGER Gesellschaft von Architekten mbH, Berlin/Weiden.

group8 architects' office in Geneva

Owner: group8
Architects: group8, Geneva
Project team: Christophe Pidoux, Christian Giussoni, Richard Fulop, Marco Neri, Diana Alvarez
Furniture design: Dynamobel, Peralta
Structural planning: T-Ingénierie SA, Geneva
Acoustic design: D'Silence acoustique, La Tour-de-Peilz
Year of construction: 2010

www.group8.ch
info@group8.ch

Laurent Ammeter
1992: graduated from hepia in Geneva.

Adrien Besson
1991: graduated from hepia in Geneva; 1997: graduated from EPFL in Lausanne; 2009: PhD at EPFL.

Tarramo Broennimann
1997: graduated from University of Geneva (IAUG).

Oscar Frisk
1992: graduated from hepia in Geneva; 1998: graduated from EPFL.

François de Marignac
1995: graduated from EPFL.

Manuel Der Hagopian
1998: graduated from IAUG.

Grégoire Du Pasquier
1995: graduated from EPFL.

Christophe Pidoux
1995: graduated from EPFL.

Daniel Zamarbide
1999: graduated from IAUG.

2000: formation of group8;
2007: formation of group8asia.

Unilever headquarters in Hamburg

Owner: Strandkai 1 Projekt GmbH
Architects: Behnisch Architekten, Stuttgart; Stefan Behnisch, David Cook, Martin Haas
Project management: Peter Schlaier
Project architect: Stephan Zemmrich
Contributors: Andreas Leupold, Irina Martaler, Eckart Schwerdtfeger, Dennis Wirth, Andreas Peyker, Mandana Alimardani, Jens Berghaus
Office planning: Quickborner Team, Hamburg
Structural planning: Weber Poll Ingenieure für Bauwesen, Hamburg
Light planning: Licht 01 Lighting Design, Hamburg
Year of construction: 2009

www.behnisch.com
ba@behnisch.com

Stefan Behnisch
Born 1957 in Stuttgart; studied philosophy and economics in Munich; studied architecture at the Karlsruhe University of Technology; employment at Büro Behnisch & Partner; Behnisch Architekten since 2005.

David Cook
Born 1966 in Manchester; studied architecture at the Polytechnic in Manchester and the University of East London; employment at Behnisch Architekten since 1993; partner since 2006.

Martin Haas
Born 1967 in Waldshut-Tiengen; studied architecture at the Technical University of Stuttgart and at Southbank University London; employment at Behnisch Architekten since 1995; partner since 2006.

Office building on the Novartis campus in Basel

Owner: Novartis Pharma AG
Architects: Vittorio Magnago
Lampugnani, Milan
Project manager:
Jens-Christian Bohm
Contact architect in Basel: Joos &
Mathys Architekten, Zurich
Project manager: Patrik Walser
Contributors: Bea Maria Roth,
Claudio Tam
Structural planning: Walther Mory
Maier, Basel
Building installations: Waldhauser
Haustechnik AG, Basel
Electrical planning: Sytek AG, Basel
Light planning:
Licht Kunst Licht AG, Berlin
Year of construction: 2008

Vittorio Magnago Lampugnani
Born 1951 in Rome; studied
architecture in Rome and Stuttgart;
1977: PhD at University of Stuttgart;
1983: Dottore in Architettura at
University of Rom; 1984–1985:
professor at Harvard, 1990–1994:
professor at Frankfurt University;
professor of history of urban design
at ETH Zurich since 1994; guest
professor at Harvard, Pamplona
and Milan.

Rambøll head office in Copenhagen

Owner: SEB
Architects: DISSING+WEITLING
architecture, Copenhagen
Project management:
Stig Mikkelsen
Contributors: Niels Thorup, Renato
Skov, Birgitte Kullmann, Karsten
Brandt-Olsen, Jeanne Tofteng,
Jan Philip Holm, Anna Hallgren,
Michelle Regine Lange, Line
Krøjgaard Jacobsen, Rune Kirk
Møller, Sebastian Morten Soelberg,
Luise Lorenc, Signe Green
Minding, Richard Howis, Matteo
C.M. Barenghi, Frank Jørgensen,
Hans Rosenberg, Helge Skovbjerg,
Jesper Nielsen, Chris Foyd,
Reiko Nara
Office planning: mtre, Copenhagen;
DISSING+WEITLING architecture,
Copenhagen
Structural planning: Rambøll Group
A/S, Copenhagen
Year of construction: 2010

www.dw.dk
dw@dw.dk

Stig Mikkelsen
Born 1956 in Copenhagen; graduated from Royal Danish Academy
of Fine Arts, School of Architecture
in Copenhagen in 1985; member
of Danish Architects' Association
(MAA) and Danish Association of
Architectural Firms.

The Yellow Building in London

Owner: Nottingdale Ltd.,
Monsoon Accessorize
Architects: Allford Hall Monaghan
Morris, London
Project architect:
Sarah Hunneyball
Graphic design: Atelier Works,
London
Structural planning: Adams Kara
Taylor, London
Building installations, electrical
planning: Norman Disney & Young,
London
Year of construction: 2008

www.ahmm.co.uk
projects@ahmm.co.uk

Simon Allford
Born 1961 in London; 1980–1986:
studied architecture at the University of Sheffield and at The Bartlett,
University College London; joint
office with Jonathan Hall, Paul
Monaghan und Peter Morris since
1989; visiting professor at The
Bartlett, University College London
since 1987.

Sarah Hunneyball
Born 1977 in Birmingham; 2001:
degree in architecture from Cam-
bridge University; employment at
Allford Hall Monaghan Morris since
2001; associate at Allford Hall
Monaghan Morris since 2007.

Rena Lange headquarters in Munich

Owner: M. Lange & Co. GmbH
Architects: David Chipperfield
Architects, London/Berlin
Project management: Mark Randel
Project architect: Markus Mathias
Contributors: Katja Buchholz,
Dirk Gschwind
Structural planning: bwp Burggraf,
Weichinger + Partner GmbH,
Munich
General contractor: W. Markgraf
GmbH & Co. KG, Munich
Technical installations:
Climaplan GmbH, Munich
Landscaping: Burger Landschafts-
architekten, Munich
Year of construction: 2007

www.davidchipperfield.co.uk
info@davidchipperfield.co.uk

David Chipperfield
Born 1953 in London; graduated
from Architectural Association in
London in 1977; employment at
Douglas Stephen, Richard Rogers
and Norman Foster.

1984: formation of David Chipperfield Architects.

Nya Nordiska head office in Dannenberg

Owner: NYA Nordiska Verwaltungs GmbH
Architects: Staab Architekten, Berlin
Project management:
Alexander Böhme
Contributors: Madina von Arnim, Marion Rehn, Sabine Zoske, Marcus Ebener, Tobias Steib
Structural planning: ifb frohloff staffa kühl ecker, Berlin
Building installations: prg Ingenieurgesellschaft mbH, Berlin
Project management: Ralf Pohlmann Architekten, Waddeweitz
Light planning: Licht Kunst Licht AG, Berlin
Landscaping: Levin Monsigny Landschaftsarchitekten, Berlin
Year of construction: 2010

www.staab-architekten.com
info@staab-architekten.com

Volker Staab
Born 1957 in Heidelberg;
1977–1984: studied architecture at ETH Zurich; 1985–1990: freelancer at Bangert, Jansen, Scholz, Schultes; work as a freelance architect in Berlin since 1991; joint office and project-related collaboration with Alfred Nieuwenhuizen since 1996; 2005–2007: professor at Münster University of Applied Sciences; 2008–2009: teaching post at Stuttgart State Academy of Art and Design.

Alfred Nieuwenhuizen
Born 1953 in Bocholt; 1974–1984: studied architecture at RWTH Aachen University; freelance architect in Berlin since 1987; 1990–1991: freelancer for Bangert, Jansen, Scholz, Schultes; joint practice and project-related collaboration with Volker Staab since 1996.

voestalpine Steel Service Center in Linz

Owner: voestalpine Steel Service Center
Architects: x architekten
Project management:
Bettina Brunner
Structural planning: Hinterleitner Engineering GmbH, Linz; Praher und Schuster ZT GmbH, Linz
General planning: MCE Stahl- und Maschinenbau GmbH & Co KG, Linz
Year of construction: 2008

www.xarchitekten.com
linz@xarchitekten.at

Bettina Brunner
Born 1972 in Austria; studied architecture at the Graz University of Technology.

David Birgmann
Born 1973 in Austria; studied architecture at the University of Innsbruck.

Rainer Kasik
Born 1967 in Vienna; studied architecture at Vienna University of Technology, Graz University of Technology and at the E. T. S. Architectura in Barcelona.

Max Nirnberger
Born 1972 in Austria; studied architecture at the Graz University of Technology.

Lorenz Prommegger
Born 1969 in Schwarzach; studied architecture at the Graz University of Technology.

1996: formation of x architekten working group in Graz;
1999: x architekten office in Linz;
2003: x architekten office in Vienna.

Office and warehouse of the Sohm company, Alberschwende

Owner: Sohm Holzbautechnik GmbH
Architects: Hermann Kaufmann ZT GmbH, Schwarzach
Project management: Roland Wehinger
Contributors: Johannes Grissmann
Supervision of works: Christian Milz
Structural planning: Sohm Holzbautechnik GesmbH, Alberschwende
Year of construction: 2009

www.hermann-kaufmann.at
office@hermann-kaufmann.at

Hermann Kaufmann
Born 1955 in Reuthe; graduated from Vienna University of Technology in 1982; 1982–1983: assistant to Ernst Hiesmayr; 1983: formation of architects' firm with Christian Lenz in Schwarzach; 1998: visiting professor at Graz University of Technology; 2000: visiting professor at Ljubljana University of Technology; professor at Munich University of Technology since 2002.

Depot of the Municipality Poing

Owner: Municipality of Poing
Architects: Allmann Sattler Wappner Architekten, Munich
Competition team: Matthias Both, Sebastian Kordowich, Konstantin Lauber, Alex Wagner
Project management: Maren Kohaus
Contributors: Ulf Rössler, Martin Plock
Supervision of works: Thomas Hess
Structural planning: A. Hagl Ingenieurgesellschaft mbH, Munich
Year of construction: 2008

www.allmannsattlerwappner.de
info@allmannsattlerwappner.de

Markus Allmann
Born 1959 in Ludwigshafen; graduated from Munich University of Technology in 1986; 2005–2006: visiting professor at Peter Behrens School of Architecture in Düsseldorf; professor at the University of Stuttgart since 2006.

Amandus Sattler
Born 1957 in Marktredwitz; graduated from Munich University of Technology in 1985; teaching post at the Academy of Fine Arts in Munich since 2005; substitute professor at the Cologne University of Applied Sciences since 2009.

Ludwig Wappner
Born 1957 in Hösbach; graduated from Munich University of Technology in 1985; professor of building construction and design at the Karlsruhe Institute of Technology (KIT) since 2010.

1987: formation of the architects' firm Allmann Sattler in Munich; 1993: expansion to become Allmann Sattler Wappner Architekten.

Handicraft estate in Valbonne

Owner: City of Valbonne
Architects: Comte & Vollenweider
Architectes, Nice; Pierre André
Comte, Stéphane Vollenweider
Contributors: Fanny Combier,
Guillaume Fauguet
Structural planning: Ingénierie Bois,
Neuwiller-les-Saverne
Setor Ingénierie, Nice
Electrical planning: Cinfora, Nice
Landscaping: François Navarro
Landscape, Grasse
Year of construction: 2007

www.comtevollenweider.fr
pa.comte@wanadoo.fr
stef-vollenweider@wanadoo.fr

Pierre André Comte
Born 1970; 1996–1997: degree at
École Paris Belleville; 1997–2002:
employment with Marc Barani.

Stéphane Vollenweider
Born 1968; 1996–1997: degree at
École Paris Belleville; 1999–2001:
employment at B&V.

2002: formation of Comte &
Vollenweider Architectes, Nice.

Research and development centre in Dogern

Owner: Sedus Stoll AG
Architects: ludloff + ludloff
Architekten, Berlin
Project management: Dennis
Hawner, Sven Holzgreve
Contributors: Andrea Böhm,
Gabriella Looke
Supervision of works: SOE, Stinner
& Von der Oelsnitz, Weingarten
Structural planning:
Sobek engineers, Stuttgart
Building installations: Ziebell,
Willner und Partner, Berlin
Light planning: a·g Licht, Bonn
Year of construction: 2009

www.ludloffludloff.de
mail@ludloffludloff.de

Jens Ludloff
Born 1964 in Haan; studied in
Münster, Bremen and Krakau;
graduated from Polytechnic University of Krakau in 1994; 1995–1998:
project architect at Sauerbruch
Hutton architects; 1999–2007: partner at Sauerbruch Hutton architects; 2004–2007: managing director at Sauberbruch Hutton General-
planungsgesellschaft; 2010–2011:
teaching post for Master's course
msa/Münster school of architecture.

Laura Fogarasi-Ludloff
Born 1967 in Zurich; graduated
from Dortmund University of Technology in 1994; 1994–1995: project
architect at Josef P. Kleihues;
1995–1998: project architect at Ortner & Ortner; 2003–2004: project
architect at David Chipperfield
Architects; 2004–2007: project
architect at Anderhalten Architekten.

2007: formation of ludloff + ludloff
Architekten.

Trumpf development centre in Ditzingen

Owner: TRUMPF Immobilien
GmbH + Co. KG
Architects: Barkow Leibinger
Architekten, Berlin; Frank Barkow,
Regine Leibinger
Project management: Heiko Krech
Structural planning: Boll und Partner
Ingenieurgesellschaft mbH, Stuttgart
Building installations: Planungs-
gruppe M+M, Böblingen
Site supervision building installa-
tions: Ingenieurbüro Jürgensen und
Baumgartner, Pliezhausen
Electrical planning: Müller & Bleher,
Filderstadt
Facade consulting: Arup, Berlin
Landscaping: Stötzer & Neher,
Sindelfingen
Year of construction: 2009

www.barkowleibinger.com
info@barkowleibinger.com

Regine Leibinger
Born 1963 in Stuttgart; studied architecture in Berlin and at Harvard
University; teaching posts including
at the Architectural Association in
London and Harvard University,
professor of building construction
and design at Berlin University of
Technology since 2006.

Frank Barkow
Born 1957 in Kansas City/USA;
studied architecture at Montana
State University and Harvard Uni-
versity; teaching posts including
at the Architectural Association in
London, Cornell University, Harvard
University, State Academy of Art
and Design, Stuttgart, and EPFL
École Polytechnique Fédérale de
Lausanne.

1993: formation of Barkow Leibinger
Architekten, Berlin.

"Projekthaus" of the BMW Group in Munich

Owner: BMW AG
Architects: Henn Architekten,
Munich
Project management: Gunter Henn,
Jürgen Hartig, Christian Bechtle,
Wolfgang Wrba
Contributors: Ian Aitchison, Michael
Bauer, Ina-Maria Bernstein, Elke
Dafinger, Markus Ecker-Mießl,
Martin Erdinger, Erich Frey, Frank
Gebler, Heike Gradmann, Matthias
Hess, Johanna Niederdellmann,
Michael Mann, Georg Pichler,
Manfred Sauer, Andreas Schöler,
Monika Schönmoser, Tina Steffens,
Cord Wehrse
Supervision of works: Thomas Kiefel
Structural planning: Sailer Stepan
und Partner GmbH, Munich
Technical installations: ARGE
skm-Haustechnik GmbH, Munich;
NEK Energy Design GmbH, Munich
Technical infrastructure: Kuehn
Bauer Partner Beratende Ingenieure
GmbH, Hallbergmoos
Light planning: Kardorff Ingenieure
Lichtplanung, Berlin
Landscaping: Luz Landschafts-
architekten, Munich
Year of construction: 2004

www.henn.com
info@henn.com

Gunter Henn
Born 1947 in Dresden; studied
architecture and civil engineering
in Munich and Berlin; since 1979
head of Henn Architekten; visiting
professor at Massachusetts Institute of Technology (MIT) since
1994; professor of industrial construction at the Dresden University
of Technology since 2000.

Special laboratories at the University of Leipzig

Owner: Free State of Saxony, Saxon State Ministry of Finance, represented by SIB NL Leipzig II
Architects: Schulz & Schulz Architekten GmbH, Leipzig; Ansgar Schulz, Benedikt Schulz
Project management: Karsten Liebner
Supervision of works: Peter Gaffron
Contributors: Lutz Schilbach
Structural planning: Staupendahl und Partner, Leipzig
Building installations: IBG Ingenieurbüro GmbH, Leipzig
Laboratory planning: IFG Ingenieurbüro für Gesundheitswesen GmbH, Leipzig; Industrial Acoustics Company GmbH, Niederkrüchten
Year of construction: 2009

www.schulzarchitekten.de
schulz@schulzarchitekten.de

Ansgar Schulz
Born 1966 in Witten/Ruhr; 1985–1992: studied architecture at RWTH Aachen University and ETSA de Madrid; 2009: appointment to the convent of the German Federal Foundation for Building Culture; substitute professor of building construction at the Dortmund University of Technology since 2010.

Benedikt Schulz
Born 1968 in Witten/Ruhr; 1988–1994: studied architecture at the RWTH Aachen University and UC de Asunción/Paraguay; 2010: appointment to the Saxon Academy of the Arts; substitute professor for building construction at the Dortmund University of Technology since 2010.

1992: formation of schulz & schulz, Leipzig.

Fraunhofer Institute in Ilmenau

Owner: Fraunhofer Gesellschaft (FhG)
Architects: Staab Architekten, Berlin
Project management: Thomas Schmidt
Contributors: Florian Nusser, Tanja Klein, Kiri Westphal, Michael Schmid, Manuela Jochheim
Structural planning: office for structural design (osd), Frankfurt/M.
Supervision of works: Jens Helmich, Jan Weyh
Building installations: Planungsgruppe M+M AG, Naumburg
Electrical planning: Teamplan Ingenieure GmbH, Apolda
Acoustic design: Müller-BBM GmbH, Planegg
Landscaping: Levin Monsigny Landschaftsarchitekten, Berlin
Year of construction: 2008

www.staab-architekten.com
info@staab-architekten.com

Volker Staab
see p. 171

Alfred Nieuwenhuizen
see p. 171

Courtyard at the Czech Technical University of Prague

Owner: Czech Technical University, Prague; Faculty of Civil Engineering
Architects: Vyšehrad Atelier, Prague
Jiří Smolík, Zdeněk Rychtařík
Project management: Jiří Smolík
Contributors: Michal Tutter, Jiří Mašek, Štěpán Martinovský, Radka Machotková, Vojtěch Lstibůrek, Pavel Marek, Martin Šafránek
Supervision of works: Vyšehrad Atelier, Prague
Structural planning: Němec Polák spol. s.r.o., Prague; Ivan Němec, David Hamerský
Building installations: Jaroslav Sýkora, Dušan Záruba
Electrical planning: Propos MB s.r.o., Mladá Boleslav; Karel Červenka, Jiří Vacek
Acoustic design: Akustika Praha, Prague; Tomáš Rozsíval
Year of construction: 2008

www.vysehrad-atelier.cz
vysehrad@vysehrad-atelier.cz

Jiří Smolík
Born 1970 in Prague; 1989–1996: studied architecture at the Czech Technical University of Prague.

Zdeněk Rychtařík
Born 1971 in Prague; 1989-1996: studied architecture at the Czech Technical University of Prague teaching post at the CTU of Prague since 2005.

1996: formation of Vyšehrad atelier, Prague.

Rolex Learning Center in Lausanne

Owner: École Polytechnique Fédérale de Lausanne
Architects: SANAA, Tokyo; Kazuyo Sejima, Ryue Nishizawa
Contributors: Yumiko Yamada, Rikiya Yamamoto, Osamu Kato, Naoto Noguchi, Mizuko Kaji, Takayuki Hasegawa, Louis Antoine Grego, Tetsuo Kondo, Matthias Haertel, Catarina Canas
Structural planning: Matsuri Sasaki/SAPS, Tokyo; Bollinger Grohmann Ingenieure, Frankfurt/M.; Walther Mory Maier Bauingenieure AG, Münchenstein; BG Ingénieurs Conseils, Lausanne; Losinger Construction, Bussigny
Project management: Botta Management Group AG, Baar
Building installations: Enerconom AG, Baar
Year of construction: 2010

www.sanaa.co.jp
sanaa@sanaa.co.jp

Kazuyo Sejima
Born 1956 in the prefecture of Ibaraki, Japan; 1981: Master's at the Japan Women's University, Tokyo; professor at the Keio University in Tokyo since 2001.

Ryue Nishizawa
Born 1966 in the prefecture of Kanagawa, Japan; 1990: Master's at the Yokohama National University; 2001: assistant professor at the Yokohama National University.

1995: formation of SANAA.

Authors

Christian Schittich (editor)
Born 1956
Studied architecture at Munich University of Technology;
followed by seven years of practical experience, journalistic work;
since 1991: editorial staff of DETAIL, magazine for architecture and architectural details;
editor since 1992, editor-in-chief since 1998;
Author and publisher of numerous specialist publications and articles.

Martin Kleibrink
Born 1958
Studied architecture in Braunschweig, Karlsruhe and Rome;
PhD at University of Karlsruhe;
employed in several architectural firms;
consultant since 1994, managing partner of congena GmbH, Munich since 2000
since 2008: formation and management of the corporate architecture division of Credit Suisse. In this role responsible for the development and introduction of innovative office-usage concepts among other things.

Dieter Grömling
Born 1955
Studied architecture at the Darmstadt University of Technologie;
1991–2001: responsible for the institutional buildings of the Max Planck Society in the new German federal states; head of the construction division since 2001;
co-editor of "Research and Technology Buildings. A Design Manual" (Basel/Boston 2005).

Burkhard Remmers
Born 1960
Studied German studies and history in Augsburg;
1987: move to furniture industry;
1995: head of marketing and public relations at office-furniture manufacturer Wilkhahn; 2003: head of international marketing; head of international communication since 2006;
numerous international specialist publications on communication, space, ergonomics, design and sustainability.

Claudia Hamm Bastow
Born 1964
Studied business studies in Cologne, at the University of Texas and in Würzburg;
worked in a variety of American and British companies in the field of marketing, business development and public relations;
2007–2009: Head of marketing and communications at DEGW Deutschland GmbH; Managing Director since 2009; primary responsibility for corporate development, personal development planning, financial controlling and the development of marketing and media strategies.

Sylke Neumann
Born 1961
1981–1986: studied ergonomics at the Dresden University of Technology;
1986–1992: work at Pentacon Dresden;
since 1992: work at VBG in Hamburg in the area of prevention; consultancy to companies, manufacturers and planners; collaboration on state, employers' liability insurance and standardisation committees; lectures and publications on ergonomic design of office workplaces.

Andreas Wagner
Born 1959
Studied mechanical engineering at the University of Karlsruhe;
1987–1995: research assistant at the Fraunhofer Institute for Solar Energy Systems (ISE) in Freiburg;
professor of building physics and technical expansion in the faculty of architecture at the Karlsruhe Institute for Technology (KIT) since 1995, research interests: concepts and performance analysis for energy-efficient buildings and thermal/visual comfort and workplace quality;
1999: founding partner of the engineering partnership ip5, Karlsruhe;
2000–2004 dean of the faculty, research dean since 2005;
member of the steering committee and speaker for the area of "efficient energy utilisation" at the KIT Energy Centre; spokesman for the KIT competency field "Constructed Facilities and Urban Infrastructure".

Karin Schakib
Born 1960
Work as speech and language therapist and speech and language tutor; studied social behavioural sciences and educational sciences at the FernUniversität Hagen; collaboration on research projects, including the field of ageing (former Deutsches Zentrum für Alternsforschung/German centre for ageing research, Heidelberg);
various teaching posts;
since 2007: research assistant in building physics and technical expansion at the faculty of architecture at KIT, research interests: post-occupancy evaluation and sustainability; teaching post in the field of architectural psychology.

Katja Schölzig
Born 1981
Study of product design and architectural lighting design at the Wismar University of Technology, Business and Design;
2004–2008: transportation designer at BMW Designworks, Newbury Park, CA/USA: Design of motorised and non-motorised forms of transport;
since 2006: member of PLDA (Professional Lighting Designers' Association);
since 2008: employed in the firm of Peter Andres Lichtplanung, Hamburg; project work for private and public clients, design of daylight and artificial lighting systems; lectures and publications in Germany and abroad.

Rainer Machner
Born 1980
2001–2005 studied hearing technology and audiology at the Oldenburg University of Applied Sciences;
since 2006 concept designer at Saint-Gobain Ecophon GmbH in Lübeck;
member of the INQA working group of the Bundesanstalt für Arbeitsschutz und Arbeitsmedizin (Federal Institute for Occupational Safety and Health);
member of the working committee of the DIN and working group on noise protection and acoustic design in the office – VDI 2569.

Illustration credits

The authors and editor wish to extend their sincere thanks to all those who helped to realize this book by making illustrations available. All drawings contained in this volume have been specially prepared in-house. Photos without credits are form the architects' own archives or the archives of "DETAIL, Review of Architecture". Despite intense efforts, it was not possible to identify the copyright owners of certain photos and illustrations. Their rights remain unaffected, however, and we request them to contact us.

from photographers, photo archives and image agencies:

- p. 8:
  Chan, Benny, Los Angeles
- p. 10:
  Myrzik und Jarisch, Munich
- p. 12:
  McGrath, Shannon, Victoria (AUS)
- p. 15, 17:
  Thomson, Edward, Rotterdam
- p. 16, 73, 74, 75:
  Altenkirch, Dirk, Karlsruhe
- p. 19, 20, 60, 61, 108, 109, 110, 113, 139 bottom:
  Richters, Christian, Münster
- p. 21:
  Müller-Naumann, Stefan, Munich
- p. 24 top:
  Carpus + Partner AG, Aix-la-Chapelle
- p. 24 bottom:
  hammeskrause architekten, Stuttgart
- p. 25 top:
  Fritsch + Tschaidse Architekten GmbH, Munich
- pp. 26, 80–85, 169 3rd column:
  Golay, Régis, FEDERAL Studio, Geneva
- pp. 28 top und middle, 29 top, 30, 31 right, 32:
  Englich, Guido, Halle
- pp. 28 bottom, 29 middle left, middle right, bottom, 31 bottom left, 38:
  Wilkhahn, Bad Münder
- pp. 33 top:
  Rusch, Corinne, Zurich/Vienna
- pp. 33 middle left, 33 middle right:
  Foresee, Bad Münder

- pp. 33 bottom:
  Verhey, Arnoud, Rotterdam
- pp. 34, 58, 86–91, 98 bottom, 99, 100, 101 bottom:
  Mørk, Adam, Copenhagen
- p. 36:
  Gascoigne, Chris, London
- p. 37 top:
  Schmid, Andi, Munich
- p. 37 bottom:
  Browell, Anthony, Balmain (AUS)
- p. 41 bottom:
  LEUWICO GmbH & Co. KG
- p. 42 left:
  Perez, Eduardo/© Vitra, Birsfelden
- pp. 42 right, 54:
  Sedus Stoll AG, Waldshut
- p. 43 top:
  Steelcase, Rosenheim
- p. 43 bottom:
  licht.de
- pp. 44, 46 top, 48 top, 48 middle:
  Ecophon, Lübeck
- pp. 46 bottom, 47 top, 49 top left, 49 top right:
  HG Esch, Hennef-Stadt Blankenberg/Ecophon, Lübeck
- pp. 48 bottom, 49 bottom:
  Schilling, Stefan, Köln/Ecophon, Lübeck
- pp. 51 bottom left, 53 left:
  Frahm, Klaus/artur images
- p. 52:
  Hempel, Jörg/artur images
- p. 53 middle:
  Peter Andres Lichtplanung
- p. 53 right:
  Höhn, Martin/Hoffmeister Leuchten, Schalksmühle
- pp. 62, 63:
  Kramer, Luuk, Amsterdam
- pp. 64–66:
  Hurnaus, Hertha, Vienna
- pp. 68–71:
  Kirchner, Jens, Düsseldorf
- pp. 76–79:
  Weidlich, Markus, Weiden
- pp. 92, 93 top, bottom, 95, 96:
  Carrieri, Mario, Milan
- pp. 93 middle, 97:
  Leemann, Mathias, Basel
- p. 94:
  de Pietri, Paola
- pp. 98 top, 101 top, middle:
  Hansen, Thorbjørn, Copenhagen
- pp. 102, 103, 104 bottom, 106, 109:
  Schittich, Christian, Munich

- pp. 104 top, 105, 107:
  Soar, Timothy, London
- pp. 111, 112:
  Marinescou, Ioana London
- pp. 114–118:
  Ebener, Marcus, Berlin
- p. 119:
  Büldt, Rainer, Dannenberg
- pp. 120, 122, 123, 168 3rd column:
  Ott, Paul, Graz
- pp. 124–127:
  Klomfar, Bruno, Vienna
- pp. 128, 129, 130 top, 131:
  Holzherr, Florian, Munich
- pp. 133–135:
  Demailly, Serge, La Cadière-d'Azur
- pp. 136, 137, 138, 139 top:
  Bitter, Jan, Berlin
- pp. 140, 142, 143, 145 middle, bottom:
  Franck, David, Ostfildern
- p. 141:
  Arnold, Volker
- pp. 146–148:
  HG Esch, Hennef-Stadt Blankenberg
- p. 145 top:
  Pfisterer, Jens, Leinfelden-Echterdingen
- pp. 149, 150, 151 bottom:
  Huthmacher, Werner/artur images
- pp. 151 top left, 151 top right:
  Ouwerkerk, Erik-Jan, Berlin
- pp. 152–157:
  Huthmacher, Werner, Berlin
- pp. 158, 159, 160, 161:
  Šlapal, Filip, Prague
- p. 162:
  Kaltenbach, Frank, Munich
- p. 163:
  Halbe, Roland/artur images
- pp. 165, 166, 167 top, 167 middle:
  Mehl, Robert, Aix-la-Chapelle
- p. 167 bottom:
  Mayer, Thomas/artur images
- p. 169 4th column:
  Matthiessen, David, Stuttgart
- p. 170 2nd column:
  MEW
- p. 172 4th column:
  Rose, Corinne, Berlin
- p. 173 3rd column:
  von Heydenaber, Heinz, Baierbrunn
- p. 173 4th column:
  Okamoto, Takashi, Tokyo

from books and journals:

- p. 40 top:
  Neumann, Sylke: Arbeit & Gesundheit BASICS: Ergonomie. Herausgegeben von: Deutsche Gesetzliche Unfallversicherung (DGUV). Wiesbaden 2011
- pp. 40 bottom, 41 top:
  nach: BGI 5050 Office planning (June 2009)
- p. 55 top:
  Flade, Antje: Architektur – psychologisch betrachtet. Bern 2008
- p. 55 middle:
  Gossauer, Elke; Wagner, Andreas: Nutzerzufriedenheit und Komfort am Arbeitsplatz. Ergebnisse einer Feldstudie in Bürogebäuden. Bauphysik, 06/2008, S. 445–452
- pp. 56 bottom, 57:
  Wagner, Andreas; Schakib-Ekbatan, Karin: Nutzerzufriedenheit als ein Indikator für die Beschreibung und Beurteilung der sozialen Dimension der Nachhaltigkeit. Abschlussbericht. Stuttgart 2010

Articles and introductory b/w photos:

- p. 8:
  Advertising agency TBWA/ CHIAT/DAY, Los Angeles (USA) 1998, Clive Wilkinson Architects
- p. 10:
  Solon Headquarters, Berlin (D) 2008, Schulte-Frolinde Architekten
- p. 26:
  Communication space, architecture office in Geneva (CH) 2010, group8
- p. 38:
  Ergonomic office chair
- p. 58
  Rambøll head office, Copenhagen (DK) 2010, DISSING+ WEITLING architecture

Dust-jacket:

The Yellow Building, London
Allford Hall Monaghan Morris
Photograph: Timothy Soar, London

Project data are provided as is by the responsible architectural offices. The publisher is not responsible for correctness of provided data.